Innovationsmanagement und Entrepreneurship

Herausgegeben von
R. Gleich,
P. Spieth,
F. Täube,
Oestrich-Winkel, Deutschland

In unserer Schriftenreihe „Innovationsmanagement und Entrepreneurship" werden wichtige Ergebnisse der wissenschaftlichen und praxisorientierten Forschung des Strascheg Institute for Innovation and Entrepreneurship (SIIE) der EBS Business School veröffentlicht.

Our series includes excellent academic and practitioner oriented research in the area of innovation management and entrepreneurship which has been recently conducted at EBS Business School, Strascheg Institute for Innovation and Entrepreneurship (SIIE).

Herausgegeben von
Prof. Dr. Ronald Gleich,
Prof. Dr. Patrick Spieth,
Prof. Dr. Florian Täube,
EBS Business School, EBS Universität für Wirtschaft und Recht,
Strascheg Institut für Innovation und Entrepreneurship (SIIE),
Oestrich-Winkel, Deutschland

Jan Buchmann

Valuing the Innovation Potentials of Firms

What Theory Suggests, Practitioners do, and both Implies for Existing Theory

Foreword by Prof. Dr. Ronald Gleich,
Prof. Dr. Patrick Spieth and Prof. Dr. Florian Täube

Springer Gabler

Jan Buchmann
Oestrich-Winkel, Germany

Dissertation EBS Universität für Wirtschaft und Recht – EBS Business School, Oestrich-Winkel, 2013

Innovationsmanagement und Entrepreneurship
ISBN 978-3-658-09289-4 ISBN 978-3-658-09290-0 (eBook)
DOI 10.1007/978-3-658-09290-0

Library of Congress Control Number: 2015935065

Springer Gabler

Printed on acid-free paper

Springer Gabler is a brand of Springer Fachmedien Wiesbaden
Springer Fachmedien Wiesbaden is part of Springer Science+Business Media
(www.springer.com)

The concept of future prospects and particularly of continued growth in the future invites the application of formulas out of higher mathematics to establish the present value of the favored issue. But the combination of precise formulas with highly imprecise assumptions can be used to establish, or rather justify, practically any value one wishes, however high, for a really outstanding issue.

– Benjamin Graham, 2003, p. 564

Man kann Bewerten nicht methodisch abhaken. Es gibt kein Kochbuch dafür.

– Corporate finance professional

Diese Punkte sind schlichtweg nicht in Formeln zu packen. Das ist eher ein qualitatives auch beschreibendes Wesen. Das ist das Auseinanderfallen aus dem, was die Praxis macht, und der Wissenschaft. . . . Die Welt ist halt komplex und das ist das Spannende daran.

– Investment bank professional

Foreword

Firm valuation can be considered as an important but also ambiguous process of decision-making in economics and management science. Appraising the economic value that derives especially from innovation capabilities can be considered on the one hand as even more ambiguous because of the uncertainty associated with innovation efforts and on the other hand as highly relevant because of their impact on a firm's future development. Thus, the research at hand provides an excellent fit to our research agenda at the Strascheg Institute for Innovation and Entrepreneurship (SIIE) and we thank Jan Buchmann for enriching our series of publications with his dissertation.

Jan Buchmann does not take the approach to develop a new more detailed theoretical or mathematical model to guide practitioners. Instead, he investigates the approaches, methodologies, and information that practitioners use to appraise the value of a firm's innovation potential. By deploying a firm typology for valuation target firms he conducts his research in a highly structured manner. Thus, this investigation sheds light into practice and closes an important research gap by accompanying existing normative research with qualitative empirical insights.

The qualitative empirical research approach allows especially for identifying context factors influencing valuation decisions and description of root-cause relationships between valuation inputs, influencing variables, and outputs. It allows an investigation beyond the accuracy of mathematical valuation methodologies and, consequently, highlights differences between the current theory and practice of firm valuation. Thus, the investigation provides a starting point for future valuation research that is of increased relevance for the application in practice.

We hope you find this work of research an interesting and stimulating read!

Ronald Gleich
Patrick Spieth
Florian Täube

Acknowledgements

A dissertation is much more than this research paper. A dissertation project spans a time of excitement for the topic, some times of doubt, it leads you to a new work environment, new colleagues, new friends, and a lot of printed paper that is now ready for recycling.

First of all, I would like to thank Professor Ronald Gleich, Professor Rolf Tilmes, Professor Florian Täube, and Professor Meike Tilebein for not only supervising this dissertation. They also supported my decision of investigating the topic at hand, provided me with valuable advices, and suggested directions in the inevitable times of doubt.

This dissertation would have never been possible without the support of my family, friends, and colleagues.

During my time at EBS' Strascheg Institute and while writing my dissertation paper in Goethe university's library I also became good friends with Johannes Lux, Patricia Frey, Phillipp Hypko, and Oliver Strank. I thank them for lots of on- and off-topic discussions, all the shared parties and laughs, Patricia especially for her role as dissertation project controller and Hannes for the great times in the library. Likewise, I would like to thank my colleagues at the Institute and at our business partners; representatively, Stefanie Laquai for her insisting support and Professor Peter Russo for hiring me as well as Peter Schentler and Joachim Leicht for interesting discussions and the fun during our joint projects.

Last in this text but certainly first in my life I would like to thank my parents Margareta and Karl-Heinz, my sister Nina and my girlfriend Jana for their continuous support, guidance and love during that time, but also all of my life until today.

Jan Buchmann

Contents

Abbreviations

CAPM	capital asset pricing model
CEO	chief executive officer
CF	corporate finance
CFO	chief financial officer
DCF	discounted cash flow
DTA	decision tree analysis
EBIT	earnings before interest & tax
EBITDA	earnings before interest, tax, depreciation, and amortization
EV	enterprise value
FCFE	free cash flow to equity
FCFF	free cash flow to the firm
GDP	gross domestic product
IP	intellectual property
IPO	initial public offering
IRR	internal rate of return
KPI	key performance indicator
LBO	leveraged buyout
M&A	mergers & acquisitions
NPD	new product development
NPV	net present value
NSD	new service development
OECD	Organization for Economic Co-Operation and Development

PE	private equity
P&L	profit & loss (statement)
Q&A	questions & answers
R&D	research & development
RBV	resource-based view
ROA	return on assets
ROC	return on capital
ROE	return on equity
ROI	return on investment
USP	unique selling proposition
VC	venture capital
WACC	weighted average cost of capital

Figures

Tables

1 Introduction

1.1 Motivation

The initial question that motivates this research is a fairly simple one: What is the value of a firm for a potential acquirer and how does this value depend on this firm's capability to innovate?

If a firm's future economic success (or its survival depending on how one argues) depends on its revenue growth and profitability, these factors depend on the one hand on the firm's potential to develop new and enhanced products or services that better fulfill customers' needs or, on the other hand, on enhanced processes that increase its productivity, then the question arises: How is such a firm's 'innovation potential' considered in its valuation as basis for an investment decision? How is it considered in valuation theory and common valuation practices?

Why is it important to investigate how this innovation potential is valued in practice? Two reasons come to mind, which represent two sides of a coin: On the one side, a fundamental challenge of the resource-based view is the valuation of resources and resource bundles such as firms to aid in the decision whether to invest in the creation or acquisition of these resource bundles or not. On the other side, the question how innovation itself is created by allocating resources and financial means is a major research question since SCHUMPETER'S theory of economic development in the year 1911 (Schumpeter, 1997).

The *valuation of a resource* is an important process in strategic decision-making. To create value by creating or developing a resource, the created resource has to lead to more earnings than the creation of the resource generated costs. To create value by buying a resource, the buyer either has to identify more value in the resource itself than the current owner and other market participants that could also possibly acquire it, or he has to know a use for the resource that the owner or other market participants do not know (Lippman & Rumelt, 2003; Wernerfelt, 1984). Therefore, the valuation process aids in identifying a specific value of a resource for the acquirer that must differ from the value other market participants see in the resource.

Thus, valuing a firm's *innovation potential* can be understood as valuing the economic potential that might come from a firm's use of its resources, by developing and recombining them to create profitable growth (Drucker, 1985). Arguing from the perspective of the resource-based view and investigating the causes of *resource advantage* "a second approach to research on resource advantage is to concentrate directly on the process of deciding on the best 'use' of a resource." (Lippman & Rumelt, 2003, p. 1084) These decision-processes do not only include the evaluation of all the current and possible uses of the resources bound in a firm, but also the decision, whether and at which price to acquire a bundle of resources or a complete firm. Therefore, the valuation of such resources constitutes an important field of research within the resource-based view.

The *funding of innovation* is an important research field at the macroeconomics level as well as the investments in innovation from a single firm at a microeconomics level. How do strategic investors and their decision-making supporters value the innovation potential of the firms, they plan to invest in strategically? What information do they consider? How do they process this information? How do they take into consideration the risks that their projected future of the firm in focus does not realize the way it was planned during the valuation? How do they value the impacts of their investment or planned actions such as post-merger integration benefits and costs in the case of a merger or additional equity in the case of a venture capital investment?

So, what will be new with this investigation? Research on valuation has in large portions been conceptual. Corporate finance researchers developed and enhanced mathematical valuation models (Copeland, Koller, & Murrin, 2000; Damodaran, 2002; Myers, 1977; Rappaport, 1979). In some cases, researchers investigated the performances of valuation models and compared their accuracy empirically (Henschke, 2009; S. N. Kaplan & Ruback, 1995; Penman & Sougiannis, 1998; Schreiner, 2007). Other researchers investigated the use of valuation models by investment banks' analysts (Bradshaw, 2002; Demirakos, Strong, & Walker, 2004; Imam, Barker, & Clubb, 2008), by venture capitalists (MacMillan, Siegel, & Narasimha, 1985; Mason & Stark, 2004; Sanders & Boivie, 2004; Shepherd, Ettenson, & Crouch, 2000; Shepherd, 1999), or they investigated firm-internal corporate finance and capital budgeting techniques (J. R. Graham & Harvey, 2001; R. H. Pike, 1988; R. Pike, 1996; Sangster, 1993; Schall, Sundem, & Geijsbeek Jr., 1978).

Nevertheless, concentrating on mathematical models rather than on the factors that determine future prospects might be a misleading focus to enhance the valuation of firms and to enhance investment decision-making. As GRAHAM states: "The concept of future prospects and particularly of continued growth in the future invites the application of formulas out of higher mathematics to establish the present value of the favored issue. But the combination of precise formulas with highly imprecise assumptions can be used to establish, or rather justify, practically any value one wishes, however high, for a really outstanding issue." (B. Graham, 2003, p. 564)

Valuation theory seems to be missing in-depth research on practices and information inputs currently, even though the influence of data inputs and assumptions on the valuation output and quality is supposed to be larger than the (pseudo-)precision of a method's correct application as stated above.

1.2 Research Objective

The research objective of this dissertation is the investigation of the used practices and the considered information to determine the value of a firm's innovation potential. Innovation potential is, in a preliminary definition for this introduction, the value deriving from a firm's capability to develop new products or services, new processes, or whole new business models. To examine these practices, I investigate two sub-areas of these practices with a qualitative empirical investigation:

(1) The *methodologies* that valuators use to transform the data into proposed value
(2) The *information* that valuators use to determine the innovation potential's value

To support structuring the investigation, I defined a typology of firms (idea firms, growth firms, and mature firms) based on DAMODARAN'S (2009, p. 8) work and investigate differences in valuation practices between these idealized firm types. A typology allows deriving theoretical implications that are contingent on the contexts of the defined ideal types. These contexts contain for example different valuation purposes and decision processes surrounding the valuation practices. Additionally, as the typology is based on theoretical implications, a typology approach allows comparing what theory suggests for the defined firm types on the one hand and what the empirical investigation indicates on the other.

The purpose of this approach is to enhance existing theories dealing with the valuation of a firm's innovation potential. These are most notably the resource-based view, innovation theory, decision theory, and valuation theory.

A more detailed description of the research objective will follow in chapter 2.3 after a more detailed depiction of the research gap this dissertation tries to close.

1.3 Outline of the Dissertation

I structure the dissertation in seven chapters, according to suggestions for good qualitative research as proposed mainly by editors and authors of the *Academy of Management Journal* (Gephart, 2004; Morgan & Smircich, 1980; Pratt, 2009; Rynes, Bartunek, & Daft, 2001; Suddaby, 2006). Building on this suggested structure, I introduce the

(1) *research objectives* (chapter 2), the
(2) *underlying theory* (chapter 3), the
(3) *theoretical framework (typology)* and *implications from theory to embody the developed types* (chapter 4), and the
(4) *research methodology* for the empirical study (chapter 5), before I present the
(5) *empirical findings* and *discuss the findings* to complement existing theory (chapters 6 and 7).

There exist different ways of presenting theory enhancing qualitative research, but I will follow GEPHART'S suggestion to clearly separate goals, theoretical underlying, empirical findings and discussion to omit the problems he describes: "When methods are used but not described explicitly, or when findings are presented early in a study and prior to discussion of goals, theory, and methods, . . . problems arise." (Gephart, 2004, p. 458)

Chapter 2 contains a depiction of the *research gap* that I try to close with my research and *its significance*. The research gap is based on a literature review of more than 1,000 articles and books on the topics innovation, valuation, decision-making, and resource-based view. Derived from this gap, the *research objective* is stated. Thus, this chapter addresses two important prerequisites of good qualitative research:

(1) "A . . . problem is that the introductions to qualitative papers often lack adequate reviews of important literature relevant to the topics of the papers. A surprising number of qualitative papers provide literature reviews as part of their results, findings, or conclusions and only after results and findings have been stated." (Gephart, 2004, p. 460) SUDDABY (2006, p. 634) states for grounded theory research: "A common misassumption is that grounded theory requires a researcher to enter the field without any knowledge of prior research."
(2) "A . . . related problem is that qualitative submissions often fail to state explicit goals, objectives, or research questions that frame the papers and guide data analysis and research outcomes. It is important for qualitative research to have a clear focus and ba-

> ses on which to proceed. Also, the importance of the research questions posed is fundamental to the contribution made by a given paper. Through specification of research questions that reflect an important gap in the literature, a study can identify important lacunae in the scholarly domain." (Gephart, 2004, p. 460)

Chapters 3 and 4 depict basic *theoretical foundations* and deductions needed to understand the reasoning and discussion of the empirical results and structure the investigation by developing a *typology framework* from theory. These chapters address the challenge of building a common ground for researcher and readers of this dissertation. As GEPHART (2004, p. 460) states: "It is important for research papers—whether qualitative or quantitative—to define and explain key concepts in ways that allow the reader to anticipate how the concepts could be located in data or observations. Conceptual and empirical definition of key concepts is important even when a paper's authors seek to dispute or elaborate prior definitions. And the theoretical background to these concepts needs to be disclosed in ways that create consistency among theories, concepts, research questions, and methodologies." The foundation of my empirical research draws from five existing fields of research: theory of the firm, resource-based view, innovation theory, valuation theory, and aspects from decision theory.

"Although methodological issues are important to qualitative research, it is extremely common to find that the methodology is underspecified. . . . . It is important to describe the analytical method or approach used to address research questions: to *clearly describe the processes used to review data and to formulate themes and insights*. The reader needs to know how categories or themes were discerned in data and how key decisions were made in the research process. It is useful to refer to explicit and established research methods and literature to describe general methodological approaches and to indicate how such methods have been modified or adapted to address current research questions and data. But methodology should be explained and then used. It should not overwhelm the conceptual importance of a paper." (Gephart, 2004, p. 460) Therefore, the chapter 5 contains a description of the *research design* and a discussion why the chosen design fits the research objectives stated in chapter 2.

In chapter 6, I describe the study's *empirical findings* based on the typology developed in chapter 4. Finally, in chapter 7, I discuss the empirical findings in comparison to existing theory, and *complement the existing theory*.

The dissertation closes with a *conclusion* (chapter 8) that contains a summary and implications for managerial practice as well as limitations and an outlook on suggested further research.

2 Research Gap, Objective, and Strategy

As GEORGE & BENNETT (2005, p. 74) note, new research "should be embedded in a well-informed assessment that identifies gaps in the current state of knowledge, acknowledges contradictory theories, and notes inadequacies in the evidence of existing theories. In brief, the investigator needs to make the case that the proposed research will make a significant contribution to the field." In the following subchapters, I will first of all depict the significance of the topic, the gaps in the current state of knowledge, and the significance to close these gaps. Then, I will constitute particular research objectives, which I derive from the identified gaps.

2.1 Significance of Valuing Firms and Their Innovation Potential

Firm valuation is a critical step in the resource allocation process within an economy or for a firm's management. Within an economy, financial investors valuate firms as investment opportunities to determine which of them hold the best prospects of generating the highest rents for their financial investments. By this, the financial market allocate financial resources to firms with the best profitable growth prospects and advance economic growth (Block, 1999; Demirakos et al., 2004; Imam et al., 2008; Myers & Majluf, 1984; R. Pike, Meerjanssen, & Chadwick, 1993).

Within a firm, the firm's management (or the "entrepreneur" as COASE (1937) states) allocates scarce resources and capital to those initiatives with the highest prospects of supporting the firm's growth and its profitability (Barney, 1996, 1999; Myers, 1984; Wernerfelt, 1984). These initiatives also include the acquisitions of other firms to get access to technologies, resources, or capabilities, which would have been more expensive to build within the own firm (for example Angwin, 2007; Coase, 1937; Hagedoorn & Duysters, 2002; Wernerfelt, 1984, 2005). A prerequisite for the success of such initiatives is to assess whether or not the costs of such investments or acquisitions are lower than the value that is created for the acquiring company by the acquisition. A valuation determines the perceived value of firms that are acquisition candidates (Copeland et al., 2000; Damodaran, 2002; Penman, 2006a). This perceived value and its influence on the later agreed and paid price determines, if value is gained or lost for the acquiring firm by a firm acquisition or the investment in a firm.

Thus, the valuation of a resource is a critical process within the resource-based view: "The price paid for the acquired resource(s) greatly affects that resource's contribution to the firm's ability to create value, especially in terms of owner's wealth." (Sirmon, Hitt, & Ireland, 2007,

p. 278). WERNERFELT (1984, p. 172) further states: “An acquisition can be seen as a purchase of a bundle of resources in a highly imperfect market. By basing the purchase on a rare resource, one can ceteris paribus maximize this imperfection and one's chances of buying cheap and getting good returns.” This highlights the understanding that complex resource bundles and firms are traded in imperfect markets. LIPPMAN & RUMELT (2003) contribute an alternative description within the cooperative game theory. Within this theory, the value of various resource combinations must be determined. Value can only be created by trading resources as long as there are hitherto unexamined combinations available.

Thus, a resource becomes useful and valuable for an acquirer, if and only if, he alone recognizes more value in this resource for himself than the other market participants and the seller of this resource do (Barney, 1988). DENRELL ET AL. infer that strategic opportunities exist whenever a price fails to reflect the value of a resource’s best use.

Existing research about the success of firm acquisitions for the acquirer show mixed results. Acquisitions do not reliably yield desired financial returns for the acquirer (Agrawal, Jaffe, & Mandelker, 1992; Barney, 1988; Bradley, Desai, & Kim, 1988; Capron & Pistre, 2002; Healy, Palepu, & Ruback, 1992, 1997; King, Dalton, Daily, & Covin, 2004). It can be inferred that one reason of these empirical results might have been that the paid prices for the acquired firms were higher than the value the firm was able to contribute to the acquirer. Thinking one step further, this must be accredited to a “wrong” valuation of the target company (M. Hitt, Harrison, Ireland, & Best, 1998).

So, what are the influences on the value of a resource? “Every asset, financial as well as real has a value. The key to successfully investing in and managing these assets lies in understanding not only what value is, but the sources of the value.” (Damodaran, 2002, p. 1) But what determines in our case what value is and what the sources of this value are? KOLLER ET AL. state: “Companies create value by investing capital at rates of return that exceed their cost of capital.” (Koller, Goedhart, & Wessels, 2005, p. vii). This is a clear reference to “the concept of future prospects and particularly of continued growth in the future” (B. Graham, 2003, p. 564) that is widely used to value assets and firms (compare income approaches in chapter 3.3.2)

Having analyzed this relationship between value and future prospects, how can a valuator determine the future prospects of a firm or, if the firm will continually grow in the future? Innovation theory should provide an important input to answering this question. If innovation "is the act that endows resources with a new capacity to create wealth" (Drucker, 1985, p. 30), then analyzing this act of innovation should enable a valuator to draw conclusions on the "wealth generation" potential, the future prospects, and, in the end, the value of a resource such as a firm.

Summing up this theoretical deduction, as a firm's potential to innovate should have an influence on its value, this potential's appraisal should have an influence on a firm's valuation.

2.2 Existing Research and Research Gap

To legitimate new research projects, it is important to analyze existing scientific literature and depict new studies in the light of this existing research. Before starting with this study, I analyzed around 1,000 scientific articles and books about the topics innovation, corporate finance & valuation, mergers & acquisitions, intangibles, decision theory, resource-based view, and other views and theories of the firm.[1] Nevertheless, this dissertation has not the purpose to provide a literature review or aggregation. Therefore, and in respect to the chosen explorative empirical research design, which demands a certain openness in the perception of the collected empirical data, I will depict or reference only the existing literature relevant to depict the research gap (this chapter), relevant to build theoretical guidance for the empirical investigation (chapter 4), and the discussion of the empirical findings (chapter 6).

In this dissertation, I will focus on a context of valuation, in which investors are not able to diversify the risks associated with an individual investment by the means of the financial market, for example by managing a diversified portfolio of shares. This is the case when investors dedicate a significant share of their disposable resources to a single investment and therefore are supposed to conduct a thorough valuation of the resources they want to acquire or invest in. The firms or investors dealing with such investments and according valuations are in most cases strategic investors. Those are for example industrial firms with strategic intentions, venture capitalists[2], private equity investors or corporate finance professional service firms such as investment banks and auditors conducting valuation services for the afore mentioned entities. The reasoning behind this focus is that these entities are supposed to perform a much more thorough valuation than banks' investment analysts do when they regularly

---

[1] The sorted and categorized literature database is available from the author upon request (compare Appendix D).

[2] As will be presented in chapter 6, venture capitalists use diversification of their investments as instrument to minimize risk. Nevertheless, they conduct thorough valuations because they still invest critical shares of their investment capital in single investments.

analyze firms and industries to derive buy, hold, or sell recommendations for publically listed shares.

Existing research in the light of the focused research area can be summed up in the four following aspects that also point out the research gap:

(1) Focus on acquisitions and strategic investments rather than on valuation
(2) Focus on theoretical valuation models rather than on valuation practices
(3) Focus on financial analysts' valuation practices rather than on valuations for strategic investments
(4) Focus on a highly conceptual theoretical link between innovation and valuation rather than on empirical research

Focus on acquisitions and strategic investments rather than on valuation

The performance of M&A for acquiring firms has been widely investigated (Agrawal et al., 1992; Antoniou, Petmezas, & Zhao, 2007; Barney, 1988; Capron & Pistre, 2002; Capron & Shen, 2007; Harrison, Hitt, Hoskisson, & Ireland, 1991; Healy et al., 1992, 1997; Ingham, Kran, & Lovestam, 1992; Jensen & Ruback, 1983; S. N. Kaplan & Weisbach, 1992; King et al., 2004; Lubatkin, 1983; Straub, 2007; Weber, Reichel, & Tarba, 2006; Zollo & Meier, 2008). Researchers focused on the circumstances under which acquiring firms are able to receive short-term or long-term performance gains. Additionally, the market for corporate control and firm innovation (M. A. Hitt, Hoskisson, Johnson, & Moesel, 1996) and the innovation performance of acquiring firms (Ahuja & Katila, 2001) have been investigated by fellow researchers. All of the mentioned research focuses on the outcome of M&A transactions, but neither on the process of the whole transaction nor on the processes of M&A decision-making or valuation.

Focus on theoretical valuation models rather than on practices

A wide spectrum of publications on the topic of firm valuation methodology (Damodaran, 2002, 2009; Koller et al., 2005; Penman, 2006b; Rappaport & Mauboussin, 2002) exist, but empirical research in this area has rather been on their performance in the stock market (Henschke, 2009; S. N. Kaplan & Ruback, 1995; Penman & Sougiannis, 1998; Schreiner, 2007) than on practices in the strategic investment context.

Focus on financial analysts' valuation practices rather than on valuations for strategic investments

Little research exists on the topic which valuation models professional valuation practitioners use and why they use them. BRADSHAW (2004), DEMIRAKOS, STRONG, & WALKER (2004), SCHREINER (2007), and HENSCHKE (2009) investigated, which models financial analysts use. IMAM, BARKER, & CLUBB (2008) additionally investigated reasons, why investment analysts use certain methods, but also state that research on this topic is sparse, even for the context of financial analysts (Imam et al., 2008, p. 505). All of the previously mentioned investigations focus on financial analysts using valuation models to derive stock buy/hold/sell recommendations.

GRAHAM & HARVEY (2001) investigate the use of corporate finance techniques such as (net) present value, CAPM, and other investment decision-making techniques in CFOs' daily businesses. Similar investigations are conducted by researchers investigating strategic investment decisions (Alkaraan & Northcott, 2006; Arnold & Hatzopoulos, 2000; Farragher & Kleiman, 1999; R. H. Pike, 1988; R. Pike, 1996; Sangster, 1993).

This existing research completely leaves out firm valuations in M&A, venture capital, and private equity contexts, which are neither financial analysts' nor CFOs' daily business.

Focus on theoretical link between innovation and valuation rather than on empirical research

A strong theoretical link exists between innovation theory and valuation theory on a very high conceptual level (compare chapters 3.1 and 3.4). But with regard to valuation methodology or practices only few approaches exist (Damodaran, 2009; Granig, 2007). For example, DAMODARAN conceptualizes the valuation of young firms and separates cash flows from existing assets from cash flows from future assets or investments in his valuation models. GRANIG applies valuation methodologies to the valuation of innovation projects.

On an even more conceptual level, one can link valuation theory and innovation theory using corporate finance aspects of a theory of the firm. As ZINGALES states in his seminal *Journal of Finance* article "In search of new foundations" (2000), corporate finance and its three major areas, valuation being one of them, need to be tied closer to an accurate theory of the firm. The characteristics of many non-industrial firms represent rather collaborating smaller entities with intangibles as most important assets than they represent tangible, asset-intensive, and highly vertically integrated entities. ZINGALES understands hidden or intangible organizational assets as important resources and the capabilities to capture growth opportunities as critical for the success of a firm. Thus, innovation theory based on the foundations of the resource-based view should be a useful perspective to answer the fundamental question in this context: Which perceived characteristics of a firm should be analyzed to determine the capabilities of firms to capture these new profitable growth opportunities? How should they be appraised?

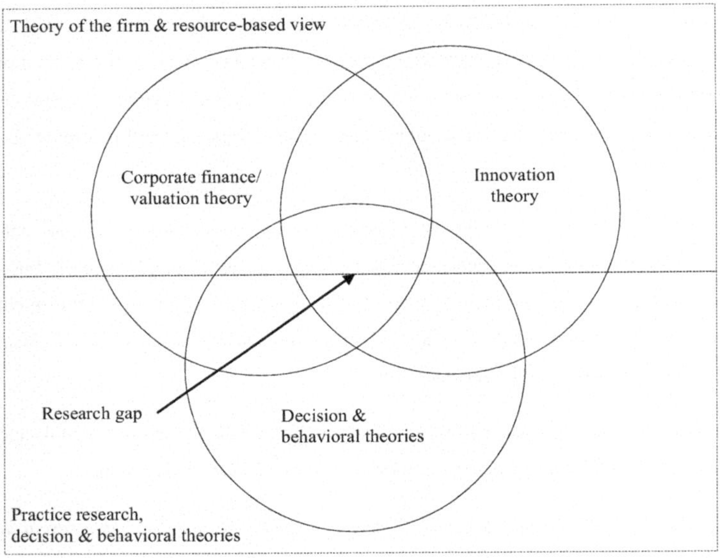

Figure 1. Research Gap

To conclude, this investigation closes a research gap that exists between valuation theory, innovation theory, and practice research/decision theory (compare Figure 1).

2.3 Research Objectives

Taking into account the previously depicted research gap, my investigation focuses on the practices to appraise a firm's innovation potential in the context of strategic investments and acquisitions. As the previous literature research has shown, the field of practices has not been covered by existing literature and therefore can only be guided on a framework-level by theory.

The focus of the investigation leads to the following research questions to extend available theory:

(1) What is the *relationship between a firm's valuation and its innovation potential* based on existing theory?

(2) What *methodologies and relevant information does theory suggest* with regard to the appraisal of innovation potential for different firm types ranging from idea to mature firms?

(3) What do practitioners do to value a firm's innovation potential for different firm types?

   a. What *valuation methodologies and practices* do equity and strategic investors use to value the innovation potential of firms they want to fund or acquire?

   b. Which *information* do they use as input for these models?

   c. How is this information *translated or interpreted* to be useful as inputs required by mathematical valuation methodologies?

(4) How can the differences between the innovation potential appraisal of different firm types and between theory and practice be used to *extend existing theory*?

An additional aspect of this work is to give more descriptive insights in the thinking and practices of firm valuators. Thus, many original statements are presented in chapter 6.

There exist two fundamental differences to the existing research mentioned in chapter 2.2:

(1) My research focuses on *equity and strategic investors* in contrast to focusing on financial stock market analysts. Additionally, I also focus on the *information* considered as inputs to the used valuation models.

(2) My research focuses on the *valuation of the innovation-related influence on a firm's value* in contrast to the valuation approaches used to appraise a firm as a whole.

These differences from the existing research constitute a research gap of not yet investigated relationships, which is, also because of its strong link to the resource-based theory and one of its major research fields, the valuation of resources, valuable to fill. This investigation is elaborating and complementing existing research on the resource-based view and explaining gaps and links between different fields of related theories, e.g. innovation theory, valuation theory, strategy as practice, decision theory, and the theory of the firm. By this approach to consider different existing theories combined with an explorative investigation of practices, my research "draw[s] from the several substantive areas that are frequently reflected in a given daily reality" (Suddaby, 2006, p. 635) and avoids the danger that prior knowledge contaminates the researcher's perspective or forces the researcher to unconsciously test hypotheses (Suddaby, 2006).

2.4 Research Strategy and Process

Based on the research gap and objectives depicted in the previous chapters, the overall research strategy was to combine existent theory with empirical insights about practices and extend existing theory thereafter (compare Figure 2).

As first step, I investigated the existing conceptual and empirical research by the means of *literature research* to identify and specify the research gap and depict theoretical foundations of the current investigation.

The following literature is considered in this dissertation:

(1) Existing conceptual and empirical research on innovation, innovation capability, innovation management & controlling, innovation performance, and innovation assessments
(2) Existing conceptual and empirical research on mergers & acquisitions, technology acquisitions, post merger integration, and company valuation methodologies
(3) Explorative empirical research on practitioners' use of company valuation methodologies, constraints of their valuations, data gathering and estimation, and implications for firm valuation.

The literature research was conducted by searching in peer reviewed and ranked journal publications in the three respective areas accompanied by valuation standard literature, e.g., DAMODARAN (2002) or KOLLER ET AL. (2005), and more practice oriented studies and innovation assessments.

Based on the identified and specified research gap, I chose a contingency approach to investigate theoretical implications, guide the empirical investigation of valuation practices, and facilitate a comparison of theory and practices. A typology is a useful tool in scientific research to investigate phenomena, which are contingent on their contextual embedment. In contrast to a taxonomy or classification, the *investigated types and their characteristics, named dimensions, are derived from existing theory* and are not clustered from empirical data as for example BENNETT & ELMAN state:

What differentiates a typological theory from a taxonomy designed to define types or classify cases is its theoretical content. The dimensions of the property space associated with a typological theory are provided by the theory's explanatory variables, and the content of the cells comes from the logic of the theory. (Bennett & Elman, 2006, p. 465).

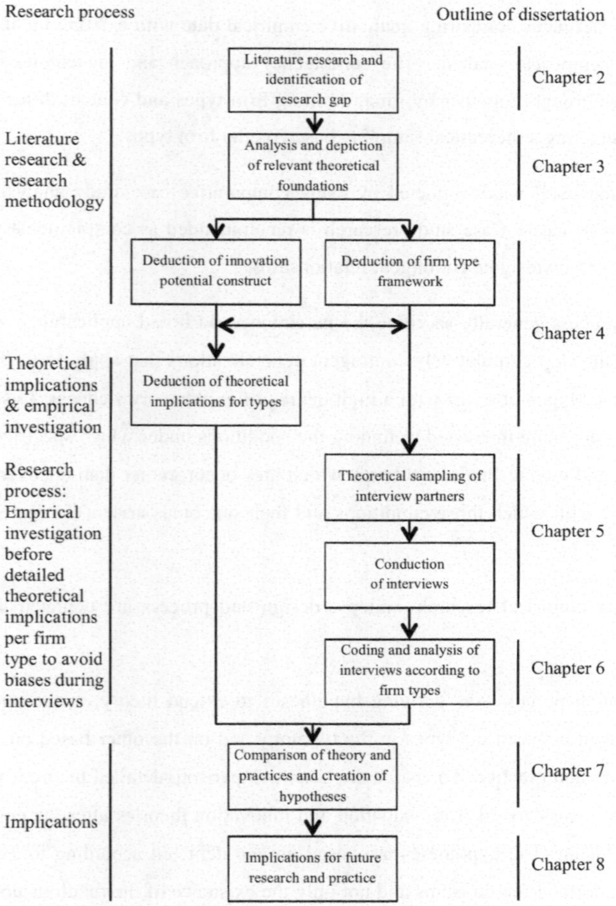

Figure 2. Research Process & Outline of Dissertation

Thus, a typology on the one hand provides a guiding framework to structure an investigation:

> If an investigator wishes to compare and contrast two or more different types of intervention, the study must be guided by clearly defined puzzles, questions, or problems that may be different from or similar to those of a study of a single subclass. (George & Bennett, 2005, pp. 78–79)

And on the other hand it facilitates comparing qualitative empirical data with existing theory and enables comparative empirical analysis. The contingency approach and the empirical comparative analysis were brought together by, first, defining firm types and content dimensions and, second, by conducting a theoretical sampling based on the firm types.

The empirical investigation itself was conducted by using comparative case study analysis utilizing expert interviews as cases. Case study research is recommended as complementary empirical research strategy to investigate contingent relationships:

> Case study researchers generally sacrifice the parsimony and broad applicability of their theories to develop cumulatively contingent generalizations that apply to well-defined types or subtypes of cases with a high degree of explanatory richness. Case study researchers are more interested in finding the conditions under which specified outcomes occur, and the mechanisms through which they occur, rather than uncovering the frequency with which those conditions and their outcomes arise. (George & Bennett, 2005, p. 31)

Details with regard to the empirical research strategy, design and process are depicted in chapter 5.

The last step in the research process was deriving hypotheses to extend theory on the one hand based on a comparison between the types in the typology and on the other based on a comparison between theory and practice. To enable the latter comparison, detailed theoretical implications per firm type were derived from valuation and innovation theories after the empirical research was conducted. The hypotheses are based on and depicted according to explaining the "why" of the derived relationships and not only the existence of the relationships to provide meaningful extensions to existing theory ("explain the arrows, not the boxes") (Thomas, Cuervo-Cazurra, & Brannen, 2011).

3 Theoretical Foundations

As stated in the previous chapter, this research draws from different fields of existing research to frame the explorative investigation of practices for valuing firms' innovation potentials. The major two fields of existing research setting the frame for such an investigation are the fields of existing innovation management research and existing corporate finance research. To investigate an integration of these two research fields and research valuation practices, it is necessary or at least useful to investigate common foundations of both research streams and define theoretical concepts in a way that helps readers to understand individual concepts and their distinctions from other theoretical concepts.

In the following chapters, I describe the theory of the firm as a useful perspective for my research propositions and clarify important theoretical concepts of decision theory, corporate finance and innovation research for the purpose of my investigation. Specifically, the following sub-chapters will depict based on existing deductive theory and existing empirical research

(1) that the resource-based view is a common basis of innovation and corporate finance research,
(2) that valuation is critical challenge within the resource-based view,
(3) how decision theory and valuation theory are linked together, and
(4) how the resource-based view and innovation theory are linked together.

Based on these foundations and the theoretical framework and typology developed in chapter 4, I deduce further theoretical links between valuation theory, innovation theory, and decision theory to enhance and crosslink existing theory in the chapters 3 and 4.

3.1 Basic Foundations

The following sections outline the basic underlying of the more specific theory presented in later sections. Specifically, it depicts the basics of the resource-based view that serves as major basis for both corporate finance and innovation theories.

3.1.1 Theory of the Firm

Researchers investigating the theory of the firm aim to answer fundamental questions in economics: Why do firms exist? What constitutes a firm? What are the boundaries of firms? Why are firms organized in a certain way? Why do firms act, perform, and grow differently?

Existence and boundaries of firms

COASE (1937) elaborated a theory that firms are established and continue to exist, if their hierarchical organization provides them with an efficiency advantage compared to individuals coordinating themselves via market mechanisms. Thus, a hierarchical organization, a set of activities, which are performed more efficiently within this hierarchical organization (instead purchasing the outputs of such activities from other individuals or firms), the people who perform these activities, and the assets that support them in performing these activities constitute a firm and, thus, define a firm's boundary. This theory was later advanced by WILLIAMSON (1975, 1981, 2010) to the so-called "transaction cost economics". This theory explains the constitution and existence of firms and their boundaries by the costs of internal transactions within a hierarchy versus the costs of external transactions via market mechanisms.

Growth of firms

PENROSE introduced a different view on the firm in the late 1950s to explain the growth of firms. She understands a firm as a bundle of tangible and intangible resources, which firms apply to create so-called *productive services* (Penrose, 1959). In her theory, the transformation of hitherto unused resources into new or enhanced productive services is supposed to be the origin of growth within a firm. Major researchers following this perspective advanced the theory to the understanding that a firm's growth originates from its resources and developed the so-called resource-based view (for example Barney, 1991; Wernerfelt, 1984).

Lifecycle of firms

Taking into account PENROSE'S growth theory, it becomes obvious that firms pass certain development paths while growing, which could be categorized in certain phases to facilitate theory building. Additionally, reality shows that firms do not always grow. Some stagnate, get distressed or disappear from the market finally. Both findings suggest that firms pass through a certain lifecycle and face different challenges on their way through this lifecycle (for example Holt, 1962; Zahra, Filatotchev, & Wright, 2009). Taking this thinking further, firms need different capabilities at different stages, which suggests that also capabilities within firms have lifecycles themselves (Helfat & Peteraf, 2003)

Link between theory of the firm and corporate finance theory

The theory of the firm offers a useful common ground for linking corporate finance and valuation research to innovation research because of two reasons:

(1) The object of valuation in the case of a firm acquisition or a major equity investment is a company, a firm, or a corporation with defined boundaries. Without a defined object boundary, an object's valuation would be impossible.

(2) The existence and growth of a firm is dependent on the economic advantage of a hierarchical organization with defined roles and processes as well as control over resources versus market transactions (compare previous paragraphs). Following this reasoning, firms are supposed to accumulate and control resources more efficiently than market mechanisms. This is also true in the case of innovation because accumulated resources and capabilities enable and support innovation processes (compare chapter 3.2.)[3] This understanding of innovation and resources is also reflected in the so-called resource-based view and its enhancements (compare chapter 3.1.2)

Thus, anchoring valuation as part of corporate finance in a suitable theory of the firm is also a necessary foundation to answer the following questions:

- What are the boundaries of a firm to delineate the valuation of this firm?
- What are the sources of growth within a firm, which have to be considered when valuing a firm?
- What determines, if value is created or destroyed for the acquirer by acquiring and integrating a firm?

This investigation contributes to answering these questions based on an explorative study of firm valuation practices.

3.1.2 Resource-Based View

PENROSE (1959) in the late 1950s and later in the 1980s and 1990s further researchers such as WERNERFELT (1984, 1995), RUMELT (1984), BARNEY (1986, 1991, 1996), DIERICKX & COOL (1989), GRANT (1991, 1996), PETERAF (1993), PRIEM & BUTLER (2001a, 2001b) and, in a more practice-oriented way, PRAHALAD & HAMEL (1990) introduced and developed an internal view of the firm to investigate the determinants of a firm's survival and growth. This so-called resource-based view (RBV) puts a firm's resources, knowledge, competences, and the capabilities to transform these into competitive products or services in the focus of strategy

---

[3] Negative effects on innovation from existing resources are supposed to exist as well. The existing structure of assets (i. e., an organization with defined processes and management incentive systems) can also hinder innovation. This is exemplary depicted in Clayton Christensen's book "The innovator's dilemma" (C. M. Christensen, 1997) or in Dorothy Leonard-Barton's contribution "Core capabilities and core rigidities" (Leonard-Barton, 1992).

research. According to BARNEY (1991, pp. 105–106), resources have to be (1) valuable, (2) rare, (3) imperfectly imitable, and (4) not strategically substitutable to lead to a sustainable competitive advantage. Thus, a firm's competitive advantage compared to other firms derives from the heterogeneity of the resource distribution between these firms.

HELFAT & PETERAF (2003, p. 999) define a *resource* as "an asset or input to production (tangible or intangible) that an organization owns, controls, or has access to on a semi-permanent basis". This highlights the relationship between a firm as an organization and its resources. Thus, a firm's resources must be under control of its management.

They also define a *capability* the following way: "An organizational capability refers to the ability of an organization to perform a coordinated set of tasks, utilizing organizational resources, for the purpose of achieving a particular end result." (Helfat & Peteraf, 2003, p. 999). LEONARD-BARTON (1992) defines a *core capability* as a (1) set of skills & a knowledge base, (2) values & norms, (3) managerial systems, and (4) technical systems. A capability can thus be understood as a mechanism and structure within a firm to utilize and transform resources.

In the light of strategic management research based on this resource-based view, "for managers, the *challenge is to identify, develop, protect, and deploy resources and capabilities in a way that provides the firm with a sustainable competitive advantage* and, thereby, a superior return on capital." (Amit & Schoemaker, 1993, p. 33) Capabilities can be developed, brought to maturity, retired or renewed within a firm and, thus, can be investigated on the base of a lifecycle view (Helfat & Peteraf, 2003). The development of capabilities can be understood as being based on learning and the codification in technology and formal procedures (Eisenhardt & Martin, 2000). It is important to mention at this point though that the lifecycle of a capabilities should not be understood as the lifecycle of a firm (for example Damodaran, 2009, p. 8). A firm should rather be understood as a set of resources and capabilities and, thus, the lifecycle of a firm should be understood as the sets of its capabilities' lifecycles. The typology developed in chapter 4.4 is based on the lifecycle of firms.

Another important characteristic of capabilities is that their existence and quality depend on *development paths*. Capabilities are so-called "*path-dependent*". This implies that capabilities are difficult to create, re-create, or imitate without running through a certain development path (Eisenhardt & Martin, 2000; Teece, Pisano, & Shuen, 1997). In the same context, EISENHARDT & MARTIN (2000) point out that *resource configurations* and not dynamic capabilities, which they define as well-known learning mechanisms, lead to competitive advantage: "More broadly, we conclude that long-term competitive advantage lies in resource configurations, not dynamic capabilities." (Eisenhardt & Martin, 2000, p. 1118)

Implications for innovation theory

In this dissertation, the resource-based view is a useful perspective and a common ground for both the innovation management and the corporate finance, M&A, and valuation theories. The resource-based view is a useful perspective in the field of innovation management, because it focuses on the resources necessary to develop and produce products or services (Wernerfelt, 1984).[4] A firm needs capabilities to be able to execute the whole basic innovation creation process, which starts with generating an idea and ends with bringing a product or service successfully to the market. One can interpret these capabilities as *meta-capabilities*, i.e., capabilities, whose existence lead to the best allocation of technology or product development resources and capabilities to perform efforts of innovation creation successfully.

Implications for valuation theory

In the context of existing valuation theory, ROBINS (1992) points out the need to anchor the valuation of assets in the resource-based view of the firm to avoid problems rooted in a market-oriented view of valuation (for example the use of the capital asset pricing model). Additionally, valuation is an important part of the resource-based view itself: "The price paid for the acquired resource(s) greatly affects that resource's contribution to the firm's ability to create value, especially in terms of owner's wealth." (Sirmon et al., 2007, p. 278)

It is important to mention that one can understand resource-based view (RBV) and market-based view (MBV) as complementary views. AMIT & SCHOEMAKER (1993) developed a framework, in which managers need to match strategic industry factors (resources & capabilities necessary to gather economic rents within an industry) derived from the MBV with strategic assets (firm-specific resources & capabilities) derived from the RBV. TEECE, PISANO, & SHUEN (1997) point out however that both views lead to two different processes of strategic decision-making. One process starts with identifying attractive industries and the other starts with analyzing the firm-specific base of resources and capabilities.

---

4 Wernerfelt explicitly mentions "technological skills" as an example for a resource (Wernerfelt, 1984, p. 171).

3.1.3 Complementary Theories

The following sub-sections depict the basics of two complementary theories to explain the development of firms: The market-based view and the relational view. During the course of the *investigation, those are used complementarily to discuss empirical results.*

Market-based view

The market-based view (MBV) derived from industrial economics theory and focuses on strategic positioning of product-market combinations within one or more industries. PORTER (1998) for example developed the prominent five-forces-framework to analyze a specific industry structure by analyzing five dimensions (he calls them forces): customers, competitors, new entrants, substitutes, and suppliers. All these forces are supposed to affect the industry a firm is acting in. MBV advocates try to explain competitive advantage mainly via a firm's positioning within its industry and investigate determinants such as market entry barriers, customer concentration, or a firm's product portfolio and product pricing. Nevertheless, it is obvious that this view is complementary to the RBV because to utilize these industry determinants for a firm's competitive advantage, capabilities and resources are needed. For example, to profit from an industry's price level, a firm must have the capabilities to create its products with a lower cost level than the industry price level. Market entry barriers are usually created, if it is to expensive for competitors to rebuild the resource configuration to be successful in this industry or they do not find alternative resource configurations that they can realize with less costs than the firms successful in the industry.

In the light of the innovation management and corporate finance theories, the MBV is important because only inventions, which find a market and customers who are willing to pay a price higher than the invention's development and production costs, are commercially successful and are regarded as innovations in the context of this dissertation (compare chapter 3.2). Those innovations in turn should be the basis of higher firm valuations or lead to higher returns than the average cost of capital in corporate finance theory.

Relational View

Followers of the resource-based view regard firm-internal resources or capabilities as sources of competitive advantage. An extension to the resource-based view is the relational view, which takes into consideration a firm's relationships to other entities outside the firm. For example, the relational view regards a firm's relations to competitors, suppliers, customers, or users of products as sources of competitive advantage. Thus, either these relationships themselves or the capabilities to manage them are considered as valuable resources (for example Das & Teng, 2000; Dyer & Singh, 1998; Gulati, Nohria, & Zaheer, 2000).

The relational view also affects COASE'S (1937) theory of a firm's boundary. Peer production by a network of individuals at least in information intensive industries might be more efficient than both market transactions and the hierarchical management that constitutes a firm (Benkler, 2002). Thus, a firm's boundaries, or a valuation object in the context of this dissertation, might contain also a firm's network of partners. A critical source of competitive advantage might be this firm's network of firms and individuals, which contribute value to this firm. For example, CHESBROUGH (2005) and VON HIPPEL (1988, 2005) introduced the concept of "open innovation" as the capability to leverage innovative capabilities of network partners such as customers or end-users. Another example is that the network heterogeneity of start-ups seems to complement their innovation capability (Zheng, Liu, & George, 2010).

3.2 Innovation Theory

To interpret the empirical results depicted in later chapters in the light of existing theory, it is necessary to elaborate on the theoretical constructs, which I use as guiding framework to investigate the research object. In the following chapters, I will elaborate in more detail about the understanding of innovation, innovation potential, innovation projects, and innovation capability in this dissertation.

Schumpeter understands innovation and economic development as the creation of new combinations of existing resources and defines "development" as the implementation or enforcement of such new combinations. He presents five different ways to create "development" or innovation as a firm (Schumpeter, 1997, pp. 100–101):

(1) Production of a new good or a new quality that was previously unknown to consumers
(2) Introduction of a new production method or a new way to deal commercially with a given good within an industry
(3) Development of a new market area for an industry
(4) Use of a new source of raw materials or semi-finished goods
(5) Implementation of a new organization, such as the creation of a monopoly position or the penetration of an existing monopoly position

One can differentiate existing research on innovation in a research area focused specifically on the development of new products and services and a research area investigating a much wider scope of innovation such as continuous improvement, process innovation or business model innovation.

In the case of the first research area, new product development (NPD) or new service development (NSD), I follow GARCIA & CALANTONE (2002, p. 112) for this dissertation and use a definition for the term "innovation" derived from a study conducted by the OECD (1991, pp. 303–314). The OECD defines innovation as an iterative process initiated by the perception of a new market or new service opportunity for an invention, which leads to development, production, and marketing tasks striving for commercial success of this invention.[5] It is important to point out that an invention does not become an innovation unless it is diffused into the marketplace (Rogers, 1976).

The theoretical foundations of the second research area, the wider scope of the innovation understanding, are conceptualizing and investigating processes and capabilities, which enable the sustained commercial success of a firm or an interconnected network of firms. In this view, innovation is generally regarded as a firm's major success factor that leads to competitive advantage (for example Lengnick-Hall, 1992). The successful development of new products and services is only one process or one capability of many in this understanding of innovation. Others are for example the development of more efficient business processes, new business models (for example Kim & Mauborgne, 2005), or management techniques (for example Birkinshaw, Hamel, & Mol, 2008). In this context, I build on the existing research on "dynamic capabilities" (Eisenhardt & Martin, 2000; Teece et al., 1997) to define this wider scope of innovation. The dynamic capabilities view "emphasizes the development of management capabilities, and difficult-to-imitate combinations of organizational, functional and technological skills" (Teece et al., 1997, p. 510) and thus, considers major factors to foster innovation within a firm.

3.2.1 Process View on Innovation

To create innovation within a firm or together with partners outside a firm, it is necessary to conduct a set of activities in a sequential or iterative process. Different proposed processes

5 The original definition included the term 'technology-based invention' instead of 'invention'. As my research does not focus specifically on technology-based innovation, I generalize this definition to all kind of inventions.

exist in innovation literature. The following two processes are exemplary for a process-oriented understanding of innovation.

COOPER (1990) proposes a stage-gate system with five stages of activities:

(1) Preliminary assessment of ideas
(2) Detailed investigation (business case)
(3) Development
(4) Testing & validation
(5) Full production & market launch

SONG & MONTOYA-WEISS (1998) identify six sets of critical activities:

(1) Strategic planning
(2) Idea development and screening
(3) Business and market opportunity analysis
(4) Technical development
(5) Product testing
(6) Product commercialization

An extension of this single-process-oriented view on innovation is a view on the management of a set of more than one innovation processes or innovation projects. This management activity can be understood as a process itself often denoted as innovation project portfolio management. COOPER, EDGETT, & KLEINSCHMIDT (1999, p. 335) define this management process as follows:

> "Portfolio management is a dynamic decision process, whereby a business's list of active new product (and R&D) projects is constantly updated and revised. In this process, new projects are evaluated, selected, and prioritized; existing projects may be accelerated, killed, or deprioritized; and resources are allocated and reallocated to the active projects."

Whereas the stage-gate process is suitable for the execution of individual innovation projects, SONG'S & MONTOYA-WEISS' approach and even more the portfolio management approach include aspects of strategically managing more than one innovation project.

Another relevant aspect of the process view on innovation is that building new or enhancing existing capabilities including innovation capability (compare next chapter) is itself regarded as a process or a "path" with the new or enhanced capability as the output: "Well known learning mechanisms guide the evolution of dynamic capabilities und underlie path dependence." (Eisenhardt & Martin, 2000, p. 1106)

3.2.2 Capability View on Innovation

As indicated in the previous subchapter, one can understand the effective and efficient execution of product, service, or capability development itself as a capability that leads to competitive advantages (Brown & Eisenhardt, 1995; Buganza & Verganti, 2006; Eisenhardt & Martin, 2000; Lawson & Samson, 2001). SONG'S & MONTOYA-WEISS' activity definitions in the previous section could in fact also be understood as capabilities to perform innovation activities, e.g., strategic planning or business and market opportunity analysis. I refer to this meta-capability as "innovation capability" in the following chapters (specifically, compare chapter 3.2.5). The overall "innovation capability" can be understood as path-dependent as well, if understood as a dynamic capability leading to competitive advantage: "The competitive advantage of firms is seen as resting on . . . the evolution path(s) it has adopted or inherited." (Teece et al., 1997, p. 509)

All of the mentioned approaches have in common that they transform inputs, such as ideas, competences, capabilities, or resources, into outputs, such as commercially successful products or new and advanced capabilities that lead to competitive advantages. The following subchapter depicts the desired outputs of innovation activities as existing literature characterize them and possible inputs and enabling factors to the delineated innovation processes.

3.2.3 Outputs of Innovation Processes or Innovation Capabilities

ABERNATHY & CLARK (1985) and HENDERSON & CLARK (1990) developed a framework based on SCHUMPETER'S "creative destruction" view with the two dimensions markets/customers and technology/production to differentiate between four kinds of innovation.

(1) *Regular innovation* conserves existing linkages to customers and markets and conserves existing competencies

(2) *Niche creation* conserves existing linkages to customers and markets but disrupts existing competencies

(3) *Revolutionary innovation* disrupts existing linkages to customers and markets but conserves existing competencies

(4) *Architectural innovation* disrupts both existing linkages to customers and markets as well as existing competencies

LENGNICK-HALL (1992) aggregates four characteristics of innovation that lead to competitive advantage:

(1) Innovations that are *hard to imitate* are more likely to lead to sustainable competitive advantage.
(2) Innovations that *accurately reflect market realities* are more likely to lead to sustainable competitive advantage.
(3) Innovations that *enable a firm to exploit the timing characteristics* of the relevant industry are more likely to lead to sustainable competitive advantage.
(4) Innovations that *rely on capabilities and technologies that are readily accessible* to the firm are more likely to lead to sustainable competitive advantage.

As one can see, both of these definitions include products or services as well as capabilities as outputs of innovation activities with the ultimate goal to receive competitive advantages. Both descriptions also include characteristics such as disruptive, revolutionary, hard to imitate, or regular to describe another quality of innovation outputs: The degree of newness or the impact of an innovation on a firm or an industry.

3.2.4 Sources of Innovation

The resource-based view (compare chapter 3.1.2) is a useful perspective in the field of innovation management, because it focuses on the resources and skills or capabilities necessary to develop and produce new products or processes (Wernerfelt, 1984).[6] PENROSE furthermore suggests that available resources or capabilities even influence the decision which direction of innovation a firm takes:

> "The type of product in which the consumer might be interested is in effect very often suggested to the entrepreneur by the firm's resources, and the possibilities of successfully introducing it largely depend upon them. The general direction of innovation in the firm (including innovation in production) is not haphazard but is closely related to the nature of a existing resources (including capital equipment) and the type and range of productive services they can render." (Penrose, 1959, p. 84)

Even the commercial success of an innovation, which can rather be related to the market-based view, can be understood as being based on a firm-internal capability: A firm needs resources or capabilities to be able to execute the whole innovation process chain from idea

[6] Wernerfelt explicitly mentions 'technological skills' as an example for a resource (Wernerfelt, 1984, p. 171).

generation to market entry. Such a capability could also be interpreted as a meta-capability, which controls the right allocation of technology development or product development resources and capabilities (Lawson & Samson, 2001).

Thus, a firm's sources of innovation are the resources and capabilities of this firm such as employees, laboratories, capital, capabilities to learn and exchange knowledge internally and with firm-external parties.

3.2.5 Innovation Potential

Innovation potential is an essential term and concept within this dissertation. I define the innovation potential as consisting of two sub-concepts:

(1) *Innovation projects* are a set of activities to develop and, where appropriate, commercialize potentially successful new products, services, processes, or capabilities. The outputs of innovation projects are objects such as products, services, technologies, knowledge, patents, processes, and capabilities.

(2) *Innovation capability* is a firm-, business unit-, or program-specific capability that enables or supports the start of new innovation projects and the successful, efficient execution of running innovation projects. Enhancing the innovation capability itself can also be the objective of innovation efforts.

On the one hand, HARMANCIOGLU, DROGE, & CALANTONE (2009) and JOHNE & SNELSON (1988) suggest such a distinction in their typology of "innovation" after having conducted an extensive literature and theory reviews of innovation literature to differentiate domains in innovation research. On the other hand, this distinction enables the identification of two valuation objects, innovation projects as one valuation object and firms as a portfolio of innovation capabilities leading to a sustained competitive advantage as the other.

In the following paragraphs, I will elaborate in more detail but in adequate conciseness what specifics constitute innovation projects and innovation capability.

Innovation projects

Innovation projects in most aspects refer to the process view of innovation (compare chapter 3.2.1). An idea is specified to become a development project and the result of the development process is a new or enhanced product, service, process, capability, or business model. Projects should in most cases be specified With regard to the result that is expected by their execution. If compared to the presented understandings of innovation, the concept projects would cover process steps two to five from COOPER (1990) or process steps three to six from SONG & MONTOYA-WEISS (1998) (for both concepts compare chapter 3.4.1):

COOPER (1990):

(1) Detailed investigation (business case)
(2) Development
(3) Testing & validation
(4) Full production & market launch

SONG & MONTOYA-WEISS (1998):

(1) Business and market opportunity analysis
(2) Technical development
(3) Product testing
(4) Product commercialization

With regard to the paradigm of exploring and exploiting ideas or opportunities (e.g. March, 1991), innovation projects would be more closely related to the exploitation of ideas by transforming ideas into implement projects. Out of a corporate finance view and with its terminology, innovation projects are about exploiting growth options (Myers, 1977; Zingales, 2000).

Innovation capability

A firm's innovation capability can be understood as the capability to generate novel and useful knowledge, products, or services (Hagedoorn & Cloodt, 2003; Lee, Lee, & Pennings, 2001; Zheng et al., 2010). Thus, innovation capability starts, enables, supports, or refines ongoing innovation processes.

It can be characterized as coordinating capability (Helfat & Peteraf, 2003). This capability (1) coordinates the use of capabilities that are necessary to conduct individual steps of a firm's innovation process (Froehle & Roth, 2007), (2) it coordinates the set of individual ongoing innovation processes including dependencies (portfolio management), and (3) it coordinates the coexistence of ongoing innovation processes and ongoing core business processes for already established businesses with established products and services within a firm. The last aspect is often referred to as duality, ambidexterity, or even solving an "innovator's dilemma" (Chandy & Tellis, 1998; C. M. Christensen & Raynor, 2003; C. M. Christensen, 1997;

Farjoun, 2010; Leonard-Barton, 1992; March, 1991; O'Reilly III & Tushman, 2004, 2008; Tushman & O'Reilly III, 1996). Hence, innovation capability itself consists or makes use of other capabilities that enable the exploration of new ideas, of capabilities that enable the exploitation of such ideas, and the capabilities to manage both exploration and exploitation together on a higher level.

How can innovation capability be further specified? Which more specific capabilities should be put into place to create innovations? For the purpose of this dissertation, I base a more detailed specification of innovation capability on the contribution of SAMMERL (2006, pp. 194–196). She bases her innovation capability conception on the dynamic capability conception of TEECE, PISANO, & SHUEN (1997). SAMMERL differentiates innovation capability into two dimensions: *Learning processes* and *coordination processes*. Learning processes consist of internal and external learning processes. The coordination processes consist of strategic coordination, operational coordination, and cultural coordination. SAMMERL'S notion of "processes" in this context should however rather be understood as the capabilities to perform the processes in focus instead of as the processes as set of activities themselves. She later also denotes them as dynamic meta-capabilities:

(1) *Internal learning* is the capability to develop and enhance a firm's knowledge internally.

(2) *External learning* is the capability to develop and enhance a firm's knowledge in collaboration with important external stakeholders and groups such as customers, suppliers, or universities.

(3) *Operational coordination* is the capability to manage projects, processes, tasks, and activities. In this context, those should be limited to innovation projects and innovation related processes.

(4) *Strategic coordination* is the capability to control strategic business activities, secure long-term competitive advantage and implement a suitable resource and capability structure to support strategic decisions.

(5) *Firm culture* is a non-structural form of coordination founded on values and believes that influence a firm's members' actions (for example R. Hall, 1992).[7] A firm's culture is also supposed to influence how likely firm-internal routines (Nelson & Winter,

[7] HALL states: "Cultural differential applies to the organization as a whole. It incorporates the habits, attitudes, beliefs and values, which permeate the individuals and groups which comprise the organization. When the organization's culture results in, for example: a perception of high quality standards, an ability to react to challenge, an ability to change, an ability to put the customer first etc.; then that culture is a contributor to competitive advantage." (R. Hall, 1992, p. 136)

1982) are supposed to change to support the development and implementation of new products, services, or processes. A resistance to change is considered as one of a firm's major obstacle to profit from innovation initiatives (for example C. M. Christensen, 1997; Leonard-Barton, 1992). Innovation capability is reinforced by "innovativeness", "the propensity . . . to innovate or develop new products . . . [or] to adopt innovations" (Garcia & Calantone, 2002, p. 113). This innovativeness is most likely rooted in a firm's culture as well.

These five dimensions give also only a top-level structural definition of innovation capability as a dynamic capability. As a meta-capability consisting and/or coordinating other specific capabilities "dynamic capabilities actually consist of identifiable and specific routines that often have been the subject of extensive empirical research in their own right outside of RBV." (Eisenhardt & Martin, 2000, p. 1107) As indicated at the beginning of this section, innovation capability itself can be enhanced and developed. Thus, its enhancement can be the objective of an innovation project that is enabled by the existing innovation capability (Lawson & Samson, 2001).

3.3 Valuation Theory

Damodaran (2002, p. 1) states: "A postulate of sound investing is that an investor does not pay more for asset than it's worth." Therefore, for investors the challenge is, to find out what an asset's worth is. In the following sub-chapters, I will give a short overview on valuation methodologies developed in corporate finance theory to determine an asset's or resource's value.

3.3.1 Investments, Valuation, and Risk

As depicted in the previous chapters, valuation is a critical sub-process of investment decision-making. While trying to estimate a value for a resource or an asset one has to consider the risks, chances, or uncertainty that the acquired resources do not lead to the expected benefits or lead to even more benefits then expected. "Investors who buy assets expect to earn returns over the time horizon that they hold the asset. Their actual return over this holding period may be very different from the expected, and it is this difference between actual and expected returns that is a source of risk." (Damodaran, 2002, p. 61)

Risk or uncertainty in the context of an asset valuation can originate from different sources. For example, DAMODARAN (2002, pp. 66–67) breaks down risk influence factors for the valuation of firms in a spectrum between firm-specific risk and market-wide risk:

- Projects may do better or worse than expected.
- Competition may be stronger or weaker than anticipated.
- Entire sector may be affected by unexpected events.
- Exchange rates and political risk change unexpectedly.
- Interest rates, inflation, and news about economy change unexpectedly.

This breakdown emphasizes a differentiation between firm-specific and non-firm-specific risk, which is used in some valuation approaches to handle the estimation of risk and uncertainty.

If risk is considered out of the perspective of an investor in a firm that is able to trade the asset (or his shares of the asset) at any given point and time, because he owns a diversified asset portfolio, this investor is often denoted as "marginal investor". The existence of such a "marginal investor" is pre-assumed by many risk-handling techniques within valuation approaches, such as the capital asset pricing model (CAPM) (Damodaran, 2002, pp. 60–83). In contrast, in the context of the acquisition of major stakes of firms or even complete firms opposed to the context of acquiring minor shares or stocks, one should not consider such an investor as "marginal investor".

3.3.2 Income Approaches

The income approach originates from the present value methodology used in capital budgeting and in the according mathematical model developed by MILLER & MODIGLIANI (1961). Several authors enhanced this approach and established it as widely used methodology (Bodie, Kane, & Marcus, 2008; Copeland et al., 2000; Damodaran, 2002; Myers, 1984; Penman, 2006b; Rappaport, 1979). The fundamental idea of the income approach is that the best estimation of an asset's value can be derived from the present value of future incomes generated with this asset: "Although focusing on the balance sheet can give some useful information about a firm's liquidation value or its replacement cost, the analyst must usually turn to expected future cash flows for a better estimate of the firm's value as a going concern." (Bodie et al., 2008, p. 605)

In the following paragraphs three variants of the income methodology are shortly depicted to clarify their specifics with a focus on how these methodologies deal with risk:

(1) Discounted cash flow methodology (and variations)
(2) Decision tree analysis
(3) Contingent claim methodology

Discounted cash flow methodology

The income approach uses expected cash flows (*E(CF)*) discounted by a discount rate *r* over an infinite number of future periods to compute the going concern value of a firm.

Since in most cases it is neither possible nor practical to compute expected cash flows for a large or even infinite number of periods, cash flows are usually estimated and discounted for a small number *N* of periods only and a separate *terminal value TV* is added for the periods beyond period *N*.

$$Value\ of\ Asset = \sum_{t=1}^{N} \frac{E(CF_t)}{(1+r)^t} + TV$$

Different approaches exist to estimate the terminal value. Most commonly used are two variants: Variant one is based on an *assumed constant growth rate g* of cash flows beyond year *N* to infinity.

$$TV = \frac{E(CF_{N+1})}{(r-g)}$$

Variant two is based on a so-called *exit multiple*[8] combining income and market approach. Investors willing to sell the acquired company within a limited timeframe use this variant to determine the exit value of their investment. The challenge with this approach is estimating a future multiple with current accrual data. If the asset or firm is not considered as going concern, other variants to calculate a terminal value are suggested by literature, for example, it is possible to use the liquidation value or calculate a replacement cost as terminal value (Damodaran, 2002, pp. 11–18).

In common discounted cash flow valuation models, the discount rate *r* becomes the vehicle for considering risk. Higher discount rates are used on riskier cash flows and lower discount

8 An introduction to the multiples methodology can be found in the next sub-chapter "Market Approach"

rates on more certain cash flows. In the case of marginal investors[9], which own a diversified portfolio of publicly traded assets, risk can be calculated by the capital asset pricing model (CAPM) (Lintner, 1965; Sharpe, 1964). Using the CAPM, only the risk within an asset that is influenced by the whole market or economy, and is not diversifiable, is considered in the discount rate of a discounted cash flow methodology. (Damodaran, 2009, p. 31) In the CAPM, the risk free rate is the expected return on an asset with guaranteed returns; the equity risk premium is the premium, investors demand for investing in risky assets as a class, relative to the risk-free rate; and β (beta) captures the asset's market risk exposure. Risk-free rate and asset risk premium are the same for all assets traded in a market. It is useful to point out that the risk of the expected cash flows, which can be attributed specifically to the characteristics of an individual asset is not considered in the CAPM.

A second way to handle risk is to use expected cash flows[10] and adjust them for risk, for example by using security equivalents as risk-adjusted expected cash flows or other cash flow variants such as capital cash flows (for example Ruback, 2002). Thus, risk can be handled in two ways within the DCF methodology:

(1) Risk is handled in the discount rate with approaches such as the CAPM.
(2) Risk is handled by adjusting the expected cash flows for risk.

Discounted cash flow approaches are supposed to be widely used in the context of firm acquisitions (Damodaran, 2009, p. 91): "Discounted cash flow techniques are more common in acquisitions and corporate finance. While casual empiricism suggests that almost every acquisition is backed up by a discounted cash flow valuation, the value paid in the acquisition is often determined using a multiple. In acquisition valuation, many discounted cash flow valuations are themselves relative valuations in disguise because the terminal values are computed using multiples." Quantitative investigations also show that DCF valuations approximate market prices quite well (for example S. N. Kaplan & Ruback, 1995).

Decision tree analysis

Decision tree analysis (DTA) extends the standard DCF methodology by allowing integrating sequential decisions or events with conditional probabilities and according conditional NPVs as outcomes to valuate an asset. A decision tree begins with a start node, which is followed by risk phases separated by event or decision nodes. Each of the phases is assigned a number of

9 Marginal investors own a diversified portfolio of investments to hedge the risk of single investments.
10 From a mathematical point of view, risk is already included in an expected value.

outcomes and according estimated probabilities. The last nodes in the tree are end notes which represent the final outcomes depending on the path taken through the previous nodes (for example Damodaran, 2009, pp. 68–76).

Contingent claim methodology

The contingent claim methodology using real options can also be classified as an income approach method. "The theory rests on a relatively simple argument. It starts with the observation that most firms are valued as going concerns, and that this value reflects an expectation of continued future investment by the firm. However, the investment is discretionary. The amount invested depends on the net present values of opportunities as they arise in the future." (Myers, 1977, p. 184) COPELAND & ANTIKAROV (2001, p. 5) define a real option as "the right, but not the obligation, to take an action (for example deferring, expanding, contracting, or abandoning) at a predetermined cost called the exercise price, for a predetermined period of time – the life of the option."

This definition of a firm's value points out two important aspects of real options. First, real options in contrast to DCF assume that a firm's value is depending on a discrete set of sequential and dependent decisions.[11]

Second, With regard to risk, a firm is considered as a set of real options (opportunities) and the valuation of single real options allows for considering flexibility in pursuing these opportunities. It is possible to valuate these opportunities depending on the outcomes of the pursuit of previous opportunities or external environmental factors. This is in contrast to the DCF methodology, which considers no flexibility and only downside risk reflected in the discount rate. Stated more clearly, riskier cash flows are valued less than safer cash flows. Chances to exploit riskier investments, if they are successful are not considered explicitly. Some proponents even state that the DCF methodology "systematically undervalues every project." (Copeland & Antikarov, 2001, p. 5) On the opposite, real option methodology rewards risk taking by positively taking into account the negative, but also the positive variance of expected incomes from an asset. DAMODARAN (2002) lists the affects of changes in factors that determine an options value.

---

11 It can be shown that the value of risky asset valued by real option methodology and valued by a decision tree with path-dependent discount rates is the same (Brandão, Dyer, & Hahn, 2005; Copeland & Antikarov, 2001).

Table 1. Summary of Variables Affecting Call and Put Prices for Real Options

Factor	Effect On	
	Call Value	Put Value
Increase in underlying asset's value	Increases	Decreases
Increase in variance of underlying asset	Increases	Increases
Increase in strike price	Decreases	Increases
Increase in dividends paid	Decreases	Increases
Increase in time to expiration	Increases	Increases
Increase in interest rates	Increases	Decreases

From Damodaran, 2002, p. 91

One of the main differences between the standard DCF approach extended by decision tree analysis (DTA) and the real option approach is the calculation of appropriate discount factors at each stage of the decision tree. DTA usually calculates with one fixed discount rate for all stages although the risk profiles are likely to change in each stage of the analysis. The real option methodology calculates individual discount rates for each stage and branch of a decision tree by using a replicating portfolio of marked-priced twin securities and risk-free bonds. As COPELAND & ANTIKAROV (2001, p. 94) state: "The frustrating part of the twin security approach is that it is practically impossible to find a priced security whose cash payouts in every state of nature over the life of the project are perfectly correlated with those of the project. Therefore it is nearly impossible to find market-priced underlying risky assets." They propose to take the NPV of the inflexible project as underlying twin-security and assume that this NPV is the market price of the project.

Alternative approaches

There exist other approaches as the method of excess returns or economic value added which focus on the difference between future returns and costs of capital to estimate the value of an asset (Stewart, 1991; Damodaran, 2002, pp. 15–16, 863–878). I do not elaborate on them in the context of this study because they share the same general idea of discounting future returns back to a present value, which is enough to understand the reasoning of my investigation.

3.3.3 Market Approaches

Market approaches valuate assets based on how similar assets are priced in a market that is assumed to be somehow efficient. DAMODARAN (2009, pp. 90–113) suggests three fundamental steps to conduct a valuation relative to a similar asset's market price:

(1) Find comparable assets that are priced by the market
(2) Scale the market prices to a common variable to generate standard prizes that are comparable
(3) Adjust for differences across assets when comparing their standardized values

The difficulties of this approach lie in steps one and three: What is a comparable asset and how can one adjust for differences? "Many analysts adjust for these differences qualitatively, making every relative valuation a storytelling experience; analysts with better and more believable stories are given credit for better valuations." (Damodaran, 2009, p. 91)

Regarding risk, all multiples regard only downside risk. DAMODARAN analytical derives risk behaviors of common multiples from their fundamental determinants. One can see that always less risk leads to a higher multiple (Table 2).

Table 2. Multiples and Risk

Multiple	Fundamental Determinants
Price/earnings ratio	Expected growth (↑), payout (↑), risk (↓)
Price-to-book equity ratio	Expected growth (↑), payout (↑), risk (↓), ROE (↑)
Price-to-sales ratio	Expected growth (↑), payout (↑), risk (↓), net margin (↑)
EV to FCFF	Cost of capital (↓), growth rate (↑)
EV to EBITDA	Expected growth (↑), reinvestment rate (↓), risk (↓), ROC (↑), tax rate (↓)
EV to capital ratio	Expected growth (↑), reinvestment rate (↓), risk (↓), ROC (↑)
EV to sales	Expected growth (↑), reinvestment rate (↓), risk (↓), operating margin (↑)

Adapted from Damodaran, 2009, p. 104

Even if a comparable asset can be found and the valuator is able to adjust the comparable with a multiple, a third challenge remains: Does the market appraise the comparable adequately? Especially: Does the market appraise the comparable adequately for the intended use of the acquisition? Most assets are not publicly traded, e.g., private firms or firm-internal assets) and, thus, one cannot assume that these assets are valuated by a market with a high degree of efficiency.

3.3.4 Cost Approaches

Cost approaches base the value of an asset on the costs that accrued from its creation. Prominent examples are the production costs or the replacement costs, the costs to replace an asset with a reasonable substitute or recreation. Risks can only be considered with difficulties with such an approach because with such an approach the value derives from past information with only little reference to possible future developments.

Another challenge is that this approach completely leaves out, if the asset might lead to earnings in the future. It only considers that the asset has been created and not, if the asset is of any use to anyone: "These considerations do not, of course, rule out a purely cost-based approach to valuation. With some effort, it is possible to measure the investment involved in the creation of a particular complex resource, although the result is partly determined by luck. Cost data, however, clearly cannot answer by themselves the question of what the resource is worth. The demand-side information is missing." (Denrell, Fang, & Winter, 2003, p. 980)

3.3.5 Hurdle Rate Approaches

Hurdle rate approaches, sometimes credited as IRR (internal rate of return) approaches, are rather different ways of using the previously depicted approaches, especially the income approaches, than completely different approaches to valuation. Valuation professionals use income approaches to determine the current value of an asset as dependent variable using a postulated internal rate of return (IRR) or discount rate derived from comparable risk profiles, risk-free rates, or methodologies such as the CAPM to discount the future value or future incomes. In contrast, with hurdle rate approaches the rate of return becomes the dependent variable and the future value of the asset becomes an independent variable.

Hurdle rate approaches can be used in two ways. On the one hand, one can use them to determine a present value using a future value and a postulated IRR, the hurdle rate. On the other hand, one can use them to investigate, if a postulated return rate is feasible under the conditions of a certain future value and a postulated acquisition price that has to be paid at the current time. Variant one can be used by venture capitalists to determine the present value of an asset using postulated hurdle rates for certain venture capital stages. Private equity investors determining, if investments in certain assets yield the return they promise their investors, can use variant two.

The mechanics of hurdle rate approaches are as follows:

(1) Postulate a time period for how long the investment in an asset should be held.
(2) Determine the future value of an asset at the end of the time period. For example, this can be done by determining a multiple as proxy for a price that can be obtained by selling the asset at the end of the time period from step 1.
(3) Discount the future value over the postulated time period using the postulated hurdle rate to derive the present value of the asset – or – use the future value and the probable acquisition price of the asset to determine, if a postulated hurdle rate is feasible.

With this approach, risk is reflected in the hurdle rate. Depending on the valuators attitude towards risk, he/she can postulate a higher or lower hurdle rate to determine a present value for an asset.

3.4 Decision Theory

Why is it important to elaborate some basic concepts of decision theory and behavioral aspects in this dissertation? On the one hand, valuations are usually part of decision-making processes. "A decision may be defined as the selection of a proposed course of action." (Butler, Davies, Pike, & Sharp, 1993, p. 6) Thus, the decision maker's challenge is to select a course of action from many possible courses of action that leads to favored outcomes or consequences: "To each alternative is a set of consequences – the events that will ensue if that particular alternative is chosen." (March & Simon, 1958, p. 137). Therefore, the major task of the decision maker while making a decision is to "evaluate" and compare the proposed consequences of his or her decision alternatives.

On the other hand, investigating decision-making without considering the decision makers themselves would leave an important factor out of the investigation. Humans perform valuations as part of a decision-making processes affected by bounded rationality, cognitive biases, and limited information processing capacity. I will depict some critical foundations possibly affecting valuations in the following paragraphs.

3.4.1 Decisions and Risk

MARCH & SIMON (1958, p. 137) define three contexts of available knowledge under which decisions can occur:

(1) *Certainty*: The decision maker has complete and accurate knowledge of the consequences of each alternative.

(2) *Risk*: The decision maker has accurate knowledge of the probability distribution of the consequences of each alternative.

(3) *Uncertainty*: The decision maker knows that the consequences of each alternative belong to some subset of all possible consequences, but he/she cannot assign definite probabilities.

These definitions suggest that most decisions regarding firm transactions or transactions of complex resource bundles are associated with risk or uncertainty because the complexity of such objects and their use in the future seem to be unlikely to be known completely. Especially, the outcomes of innovation projects are difficult to foresee and adequate knowledge about future developments is missing many times. Valuators certainly have to deal with *risk and uncertainty.*

A typical methodology to deal with risks is for example to use *decision trees*. With this methodology, each branch must be assigned a probability or a decision (for example Damodaran, 2009, pp. 68–76). A typical methodology to cope with uncertainty is *scenario analysis* (for example Cornelius, Van de Putte, & Romani, 2005). With this methodology, a certain number of scenarios as consistent bundle of assumptions are defined, but no probabilities are assigned for their probabilities of occurrence.

3.4.2 Information Asymmetry

Valuations in the context of firm acquisitions are likely to be made under information asymmetry (Akerlof, 1970; Leland & Pyle, 1977). Information asymmetry means that sellers are better informed about the internal characteristics and, thus, the quality of the asset they are selling than the potential buyer.

Closely related to information asymmetry are the concepts of *signaling* and *screening*. As in many cases, buyers are not able to assess the quality of an asset in detail, the look for signals (or proxies) to aid them in their decision-making. Signals can be either send by sellers or originate from other sources. Other potential investors' interest or investment in an asset could for example act as signal for that asset's quality (Leland & Pyle, 1977). The processes and approaches to look for signals is termed screening (Sanders & Boivie, 2004; Weiss, 1995).

3.4.3 Bounded Rationality and Behavioral Biases

As valuing a firm's innovation potential is about estimating a value that arises from a firm's future developments in a complex environment, it must be doubted that such valuations are made with all necessary information or with the individually needed information processing capability. This leads on the one hand to the conclusion that most valuations are made under risk or uncertainty (see above). On the other hand, valuations cannot be assumed to be independent from the context they are made in or independent from the decision-makers cognition and personal preferences. MARCH & SIMON state: "What a person wants and likes influences what he sees; what he sees influences what he wants and likes" (March & Simon, 1958, p. 151). Hence, it should be presumed that such valuations are made with bounded rationality (March & Simon, 1958, pp. 136–171).

I will shortly depict three main aspects to consider in the context of valuing a firm's innovation potential:

(1) Valuators in the investigated context of strategic investments prepare decisions with high financial impact and these decisions are usually made only one time for one investment. Hence, the assumption that valuators take a statistically expectancy value to consider risk in their valuation should be substituted by the assumption that these valuators are *risk averse* and prone to the so-called *certainty effect*. One million Euros without risk are of more value to these valuators as a risky amount of payout with "only" an expectancy value of 1 million Euro (for example Kahneman & Tversky, 1979, pp. 264–265; Penrose, 1959, p. 57).
(2) Since valuators can be assumed to neither possess the information nor the information processing capability to calculate a precise value in such a complex setting, they are likely to *use heuristics and their valuations become cognitively biased.*
(3) The information exchanged between buyer and seller is likely to be *framed* (S. Kaplan, 2008; Tversky & Kahneman, 1981, 1986) to the benefit of the party that is providing the information.

In the following paragraphs, I will describe in more detail the theoretical underlying of heuristics, biases, and framing.

Heuristics and biases

To judge alternatives under risk or uncertainty, managers use all kinds of *heuristics, which lead to cognitive biases*. Most of them are compiled in the so-called prospect theory (Kahneman & Tversky, 1979; Tversky & Kahneman, 1974, 1992). Common heuristics and biases that should be considered in valuation contexts are the following (Tversky & Kahneman, 1974):

(1) *Representativeness*: The decision-maker appraises the probability that an object's attribute is similar to another object's attribute higher, if the two objects are similar in other attributes even if there exists no reliable link between those other attributes and the appraised one.
(2) *Availability*: The decision-maker appraises decision alternatives from information that is available or retrievable, for example from experience. This can lead to a non-optimal decision because he/she does not take into consideration or even collect information that would support the decision to follow another alternative.

(3) *Anchoring*: The decision-maker makes an estimate starting on an initial value (that could be based for example on a value influenced by the availability bias). In the decision process all further estimates are biased towards this initial value.

(4) *Overconfidence*: The decision-maker overestimates an alternative's positive prospects and her/his influence on the chosen alternative's prospects.

Framing of decisions

The *framing concept* implies that decision makers are not able to transfer different representations of the same decision problem into a normalized representation. This means that not only the decision problem itself influences the decision, but also the presentation of this problem and especially the presentation of the according information (Tversky & Kahneman, 1981, 1986). Thus, a discussion about differing valuation results or a negotiation of a firm transaction price could for instance also be understood as a framing contest, in which each party tries to convince the other that its cognitive frame of the firm, of the firm's business environment and the firm's prospects is the "better" one (S. Kaplan, 2008).

3.4.4 Decision-Making Processes for Investments and Acquisitions

Acquiring a complex resource bundle or a firm should be considered as strategic investment decision for a firm's management. RAPPAPORT (1979) defines the stages planning, search & screen, and financial evaluation as critical in the process of analyzing acquisitions. BUTLER ET AL. (1993, p. 52) identify four steps in investment decision-making.

(1) Identification of investment opportunities
(2) Preliminary project review
(3) Evaluation and selection including financial valuation of the project
(4) Control of the project's implementation

The financial evaluation activity (process step 3) has the objective to answer a fundamental question in investment decision-making: What are the maximum costs or what is the maximum price that should be invested in the acquisition of a target company to still be able to benefit from this investment? The answer to this question depends on the answers to three more detailed questions: (1) "What are the principal areas of risk?", (2) "What are the earnings, cash flow, and balance sheet implications of the acquisition?", and (3) "What is the best way of financing the acquisition?" (Rappaport, 1979, p. 100)

Several authors elaborated on the first two questions. They point out to evaluate the acquisition and integration process and the changes to the target firm that are caused by the acquisition to better understand implications and risks (Hunt, 1990; Jemison & Sitkin, 1986; Pablo, Sitkin, & Jemison, 1996; Sitkin & Pablo, 1992; Sitkin & Weingart, 1995). HUNT (1990, p. 74) states that "a behavioural process within a context is the determinant of success or failure." In his understanding the context contains factors such as strategy, industry, relative size, and experience. JEMISON & SITKIN (1986) depict that strategic fit, organizational fit, and the acquisition process should influence the investment decision-makers evaluation.

3.4.5 Decisions as Practices

In this dissertation's empirical part is investigated, how valuators conduct valuations, which practices and methodologies they use, and which information and data they take into consideration. So *the "how"-question is in focus of the investigation* to answer "why"-questions. How a valuation is conducted influences the result of the valuation, by that the investment decision that relies on this valuation as information, and, in the end, it influences the economic success as result of this investment decision.

This investigation focus on practices is very similar to the strategy-as-practice view on strategy research, which is very well accepted in the scientific community. In the light of the strategy-as-practice view, strategic decision makers use practices to come to strategic decisions. Therefore, a valuable research area in management and strategy research is the investigation of these practices. This is in contrast to the investigation of what the right strategic decisions under different circumstances might be. (Balogun, Huff, & Johnson, 2003; Eisenhardt, 1999; Jarzabkowski & Kaplan, 2008; Spee & Jarzabkowski, 2009; Whittington, 1996, 2003; Whittington et al., 2003; Whittington, Molloy, Mayer, & Smith, 2006). This view on strategy research includes investigations how the process of strategic decision-making works, which tools and methodologies decision-makers use, and how they use them to come to their decisions. This view represents a fundamental basis for the following investigation.

4 Theoretical Framework and Implications

Having depicted the foundations of the theory of the firm and the resource-based view on the one hand and on the other hand innovation, valuation, and decision-making theories, the question arises: *How can these theories be integrated to build an adequate framework to guide the empirical research?* What are the integral characteristics of valuation practices for valuing innovation potential? The framework should be structured enough to allow a classification of empirical results to guide theory enhancement, but at the same time open enough to respect the explorative character of this investigation (compare chapters 2 and 5).

4.1 Value of Resources and Innovation

Several theoretical foundations with regard to resources, innovation, and valuation have been depicted in chapter 3. How do they link together to facilitate the investigation of the chosen research objectives? The following sections depict the relationship between innovation and the value of resources on a general level and on the level of resource acquisitions.

4.1.1 Innovation and the Value of Resources

How are innovation theory and valuation theory linked on a theory level? Taking into account the previously depicted theories, one can define the creation of *value through innovation* as the positive difference in value between an asset's future new use and its current use. This understanding is very close to DRUCKER'S definition of innovation: "Whatever changes the wealth-producing potential of already existing resources constitutes innovation." (Drucker, 1985, p. 31)

> [Innovation] is the act that endows resources with a new capacity to create wealth. Innovation, indeed, creates a resource. There is no such thing as a 'resource' until man finds a use for something in nature und thus endows it with economic value. Until then, every plant is a weed and every mineral just another rock. (Drucker, 1985, p. 30)

Thus, "for managers, the challenge is to identify, develop, protect, and deploy resources and capabilities in a way that provides the firm with a sustainable competitive advantage and, thereby, a superior return on capital." (Amit & Schoemaker, 1993)

This value difference introduced above can materialize in different ways such as:

- New differentiated, and thus, high-margin products, whose development is enabled by complementary technology, capability, or patent acquisitions
- Cost-reduced processes in the case of a production technology or capability acquisition
- Revenue and cost synergies in the case of a firm merger or acquisitions
- Reduced corporate overhead and reinforcement of an entrepreneurial culture in the case of a corporate business unit's leveraged buyout by a private equity investor
- Enabled technology development by venture capital financing (complementary capabilities and financial resources)

4.1.2 Acquisition of Resources

One way of enabling new uses of resources is to acquire resources such as firms, which themselves can be understood as bundles of capabilities and resources (compare chapter 3.1.2). These assets then can be brought to a new use or brought into a new combination that enables a new use.

Existing literature points out that following this way, value creation for the acquirer is enabled by acquiring related or complementary assets, which fit strategically and organizational (Jemison & Sitkin, 1986), lead to synergistic cash flows (Barney, 1988), or allow for new unique resource combinations (Harrison et al., 1991; Harrison, Hitt, Hoskisson, & Ireland, 2001).

Arguing from a RBV perspective, *resource acquisitions are strategic opportunities, if they can be acquired for a price lower than their rent-generating capacity*. A strategic opportunity exists whenever prices fail to reflect the value of a resource's best use (Barney, 1986; Denrell et al., 2003). This RBV argument is mirrored in corporate finance theory: "A positive NPV must be explained by a short-run deviation from equilibrium or by some permanent competitive advantage." (Myers, 1984, p. 130). DENRELL ET AL. state the link between innovation in the sense of new resource uses and valuation very comprehensively:

> The proposition that truly deserves a serious claim on our attention, and that Barney correctly highlighted, is much weaker than the claim that the market always has the price right. It says that existing resources are correctly valued in relation to their existing uses. If that is the case, then valuable strategic opportunities cannot be found

> unless some element of novelty is introduced into the situation - either new resources, or new uses for existing resources; since the latter usually involves the creation of new complex resources it is typically the same thing as the former. (Denrell et al., 2003, p. 981)

Following this argument, WERNERFELT states with regard to valuation: "A key implication of the latter is that a given target will have different values for different buyers, with particularly big variance among those who can obtain some sort of fit (synergy) between their resources and those of the target." (Wernerfelt, 1984, p. 175)

Additionally, in the case of complex resources and capabilities, capabilities that are idiosyncratic or even "unique", one can imply imperfect markets (Denrell et al., 2003; Dierickx & Cool, 1989). Thus, a fundamental challenge of strategic opportunities is "*imputing a resource's value in the absence of explicit price guidance*" (Denrell et al., 2003, p. 977). The reason for this is that complex resources and capabilities are often the result of path-dependent and not easily imitable combinations of other commodity or complex resources and capabilities (Eisenhardt & Martin, 2000; Teece et al., 1997).

As stated already in chapter 2.1, existing research about the success of firm acquisitions for the acquirer show mixed results (compare Table 3). Acquisitions do not reliably yield desired financial returns for the acquirer (Agrawal et al., 1992; Barney, 1988; Bradley et al., 1988; Capron & Pistre, 2002; Healy et al., 1992, 1997; King et al., 2004). Combining the discussion about value creation through resource acquisitions and empirical results about firm acquisition success/failure, it can be inferred that misleading valuations are one of the major reasons why acquisitions don't yield the desired returns. A study of HITT ET AL. state that "inadequate target evaluation was a factor in 11 of the 12 acquisitions with low performance." (M. Hitt et al., 1998)

With regard to innovation potential, the complementary new use of an acquired resource is limited by the absorptive capacity of its acquirer (Cohen & Levinthal, 1990; Lichtenthaler, 2009; Nooteboom, Haverbeke, Duysters, Gilsing, & Oord, 2007; Zahra & George, 2002). Thus, even, if a resource theoretically could be brought to a new use by the acquirer, he would not be able to profit from the acquisition, if he has not the capacity available to implement the resource's new use or "absorb" and transform the acquired capabilities and knowledge. Hence, effects of an acquisition on the innovation potential are also often mixed, sometimes credited even as poison pill, or contingent on certain aspects (Ahuja & Katila, 2001; Cassiman, Colombo, Garrone, & Veugelers, 2005; Chiara Di Guardo & Valentini, 2007; K. S. Christensen, 2006; Cloodt, Hagedoorn, & Van Kranenburg, 2006; Desyllas & Hughes, 2008; Graebner, 2004; M. A. Hitt, Ireland, Harrison, & Hoskisson, 1991; Paruchuri, Nerkar, & Hambrick, 2006; Prabhu, Chandy, & Ellis, 2005; Puranam & Srikanth, 2007; Tsai & Wang, 2008).

Table 3. Quantitative Studies and Meta-Studies on Acquisition/Takeover Success

Study	Development of Acquirer's Value After Acquisition
Lubatkin (1983, p. 221) (meta-study including research from 1971 to 1980)	Even / Only slightly positive (0.0-7.9% stock price increase)
Jensen & Ruback (1983)	Even
Bradley, Desai, & Kim (1988)	Slightly positive (17.3% market value increase, but 107.1% for targets (before transaction)
Agrawal, Jaffe, & Mandelker (1992)	Negative
Datta, Pinches, & Narayanan (1992) (meta-study)	Even (for acquirers, but positive for targets)
Healy, Palepu, & Ruback (1992)	Positive (cash flow growth & asset growth rate higher than industry)
Capron & Pistre (2002)	Mixed (positive, when transferring own resources to target, even, when transferring resources from target to acquirer only)
King, Dalton, Daily, & Covin (2004) (meta-study)	Slightly negative

4.2 Typology as Theoretical Framework

Originating from the implications depicted in the previous sub-chapters, I develop a typology framework linking valuation and innovation theory as basis for the following empirical qualitative investigation. A typology is a useful tool in scientific research to investigate phenomena, which are contingent on their contextual embedment. In contrast to a taxonomy or classification, the *investigated types and their characteristics, named dimensions, are derived from existing theory* and are not clustered from empirical data as for example BENNETT & ELMAN state: "What differentiates a typological theory from a taxonomy designed to define types or classify cases is its theoretical content. The dimensions of the property space associated with a typological theory are provided by the theory's explanatory variables, and the content of the cells comes from the logic of the theory." (Bennett & Elman, 2006, p. 465).

In the following sub-chapters I depict a typology based on the previously presented theoretical foundations. The typology differentiates between *three firm types* (*idea*, *growth*, and *mature* firms) according to a firm's lifecycle and is filled with the *two dimensions* for empirical investigation: *methodology* and *information*. Both of those two dimensions contain the same three sub-dimensions *innovation projects*, *innovation capability*, and *transaction effects*. Additionally, the methodology dimension contains a fourth sub-dimension *risk and uncertainty*. The reason for that addition is that dealing with risk and uncertainty is a methodology problem in its core. Risks and uncertainty can be assessed for all of the other three dimensions innovation projects, innovation capability, and transaction effects. Thus, information with regards to risks can be mapped to these three sub-dimensions and no separate sub-dimension in the information dimension is required.

Both, innovation theory and valuation theory suggest that investigating innovation potential or valuation contingent on a firm's position in its lifecycle is a valuable approach. CRISCUOLO ET AL. for example state: "The analysis demonstrates that start-ups do differ considerably from established firms in their innovative performance, indicating that considering the role of firm age in shaping patterns of innovation remains a valuable approach." (Criscuolo, Nicolaou, & Salter, 2008, p. 5). The typology used and further developed in this dissertation is based on a typology by DAMODARAN, a valuation expert.

4.2.1 Firm Types

DAMODARAN developed distinct firm types as typical valuation objects based on the development stages of firms in their lifecycle (Damodaran, 2009, p. 8). He defines five types from idea firms to declining firms. In the context of this investigation and in respect to the more open qualitative research approach (compare chapter 5), a simplification to three types (*idea*, *growth* and *mature firms*) seems reasonable. Another reasonable assumption about firms that are supposed to have innovation potential is that they are not in the declining stage of their lifecycle. Taking this assumption even further, firms, which are able to continuously innovate, change, and adapt themselves to current or future market demands, should theoretically never reach the declining stage in their lifecycle. Therefore, the investigation of declining firms is out of the scope of this investigation. DAMODARAN also differentiates between idea, young growth firms and mature growth firms. To facilitate a more open approach to the empirical investigation, a simplification to the two types of idea and growth firms seems acceptable. With regard to growth, the major difference between growth and mature firms is that growth firms grow faster or more than the industry they act in while mature firms grow with their industries or the economy. Table 4 summarizes the three chosen firm types including valuation key questions and typical valuators for each type.

Table 4. Firm Types and Their Characteristics

Firm Type / Characteristics	Idea Firms	Growth Firms	Mature Firms
Key questions revenue / earnings	What is the potential market? Will this product sell and at which price? What are the expected margins?	Can the company scale up? How will competition affect margins? As growth declines, how will the firm's reinvestment policy change? Will the financing policy change as the firm matures?	Is there the possibility of the firm being restructured? Will business units be brought to a better use within other firms?
Key questions survival	Will the firm make it?	Will the firm be acquired?	Will the firm be taken private?
Investors	Venture capital Owners Angel investors	Venture capital Corporate venture capital Strategic investors	Private equity Strategic investors

Adapted from Damodaran, 2009, p. 8

Additionally to the definitions above I also assume that a firm's position in the lifecycle does not only describe its "age" or lifecycle phase, but that it also allows implications about its size, product portfolio complexity, and organizational complexity. Thus, the adapted typology considers also that a firm's innovation characteristics, processes, strategy, and "performance" might change with the position within a firm's lifecycle (Criscuolo, Nicolaou, & Salter, 2012; A. D. Henderson, 1999; Zahra et al., 2009; Zheng et al., 2010).

The reasons for this change in performance are supposed to be for example on the one hand core rigidities that have been developed in an organization over years, which restrict innovation in established firms (Leonard-Barton, 1992; MacCormack, Baldwin, & Rusnak, 2012), and, on the other hand, core capabilities and complementary assets such as access to financial means or distribution channels, which idea and growth firms do not possess (Leonard-Barton, 1992; Prahalad & Hamel, 1990; Teece et al., 1997; Teece, 1986).

4.2.2 Dimensions

The three firm types give the structure to the theoretical and empirical research in the following chapters. The dimensions within the types give structure for the investigation itself and guide which topics to address in the following theoretical and empirical research.

The dimensions selected to be in scope for this investigation are (1) *methodologies* that practitioners use to appraise the value of a firm's innovation potential and (2) the *information* they use to apply those methodologies. It is obvious that applied methodologies and used information and data are tightly linked together. If a methodology requires a growth rate g then this growth rate has to be determined from the available information. But which data is used to estimate that growth rate? On which information are assumptions based on? Which data can act as proxy information for innovation potential? All these questions support the explicit investigation of the information and data that practitioners use to apply their methodologies of choice.

For both dimensions the three sub-dimensions *innovation projects*, *innovation capability*, and *transaction effects* build the framework to discuss differences between firm types. *Risk and uncertainty* is introduced as a fourth sub-dimension for the methodologies dimension only as dealing with risk and uncertainty is dominated by methodological questions and not so much by questions of information and data. The main reason why risk and uncertainty occur is incomplete or unreliable information (compare chapter 3.4.1).

The first two sub-dimensions *innovation projects* and *innovation capability* directly refer to the definition of *innovation potential* in chapter 3.2.5. Thus, their depiction is straightforward according to the definitions in this chapter.

Innovation projects

The sub-dimension *innovation projects* considers the valuation of concrete projects with a defined scope, objective and ideally an explicit business case.

Innovation projects are a set of activities to develop and, where appropriate, commercialize potentially successful new products, services, processes, or capabilities. The outputs of innovation projects are objects such as products, services, technologies, knowledge, patents, processes, and capabilities (compare chapter 3.2.5)

The definition fits very well with the key questions that DAMODARAN (2009, p. 8) depicts for the valuation of idea firms:

- What is the potential market?
- Will this product sell and at which price?
- What are the expected margins?

These questions reflect the key business case questions to evaluate a product or service development project proposal as one of the first steps in the innovation process (Cooper, 1990; X. M. Song & Montoya-Weiss, 1998).

Innovation capability

Innovation capability is a firm-, business unit-, or program-specific capability that enables or supports the start of new innovation projects and the successful, efficient execution of running innovation projects. Enhancing the innovation capability itself can also be the objective of innovation efforts (compare chapter 3.2.5).

Typical questions derived from theory to assess innovation capability should be depending on the firm's lifecycle stage (Lengnick-Hall, 1992; Sammerl, 2006):

- How is internal learning organized?
- How is external learning organized and knowledge from outside absorbed in the firm (Cohen & Levinthal, 1990)?
- How are innovation programs, projects and tasks organized?
- Are the capabilities or technologies to develop new products/services readily accessible for the firm or are there capability contingencies to consider (Brush & Artz, 1999)?
- How are strategic plans developed and according capabilities built?
- Does the firm culture facilitate or support innovation activities?
- Are market realities reflected in the project selection?
- Are the innovation systems adequate for the velocity of the market the firm acts in (Eisenhardt & Martin, 2000, p. 1111)?

If a valuator intends to consider the answers to these theory-deduced questions in his valuation approach, two challenges arise:

(1) *Access to information and data*: Is she/he able to get information and data to answer these questions at all? Does he get access to this data? What investigations does he perform to answer those questions (the according information might not even be reported or documented within the firm itself)?
(2) *Quantification of information and data*: Is she/he able to transform qualitative data such as answers to those questions to quantified information that can be used to quantify the value of a firm?

For both, innovation projects and innovation capability, even the *outputs of those could be intangible or hard to quantify* such as patents, capabilities, competencies, or processes. Thus, not only investigating the capabilities themselves, but also their aspired outputs are difficult to appraise and quantify.

Transaction effects

The sub-dimension *transaction effects* covers the anticipated effects of the transaction or the investment that is the reason to perform the firm valuation. Existing research shows mixed results of the success of such transactions not only on the firm level, but also with regard to innovation potential (compare chapter 4.1.2). Therefore, this sub-dimension should give valuable theoretical and empirical insights for the overall research objective.

Risk and uncertainty

Risk and uncertainty are in a broad sense caused by incomplete information (compare chapters 3.3.1 and 3.4). They are relevant aspects for the appraisal of innovation potential because of the following reasons:

(1) A firm's future prospects as major input to all valuation methodologies (except the cost approach) in general are risky or uncertain. Valuators have to deal with assumptions and approaches of risk mitigation.
(2) The output of innovation activities is risky and sometimes uncertain.
(3) The valuation of an external complex resource such as a firm is conducted under information asymmetry, as the seller knows ore about the resource than the potential buyer.

The first two mentioned reasons imply that valuing the innovation potential of firms is prone to behavioral biases such as the ones depicted in chapter 3.4.2.

Overview

Key rationale for integrating the depicted sub-dimensions is to investigate the *methodologies* to appraise such projects and the *information and data* that need to be acquired and applied with the chosen methodologies.

The following table depicts the framework of dimensions and sub-dimensions:

Table 5. Overview of Typology Dimensions

Dimensions	Sub-dimensions	Description
Methodologies	Innovation projects	Methodologies used to valuate single innovation projects
	Innovation capability	Methodologies used to appraise or account for a firm's innovation capability
	Transaction effects	Methodologies used to anticipate the effects of the acquisition or major investment
	Risk and uncertainty	Methodologies to anticipate risk and uncertainty and consider those for a firm's valuation and for the interpretation of information and data
Information	Innovation projects	Collected and analyzed data used to valuate single innovation projects
	Innovation capability	Collected and analyzed data used to valuate a firm's innovation capability
	Transaction effects	Collected and analyzed data used to anticipate the effects of the acquisition or major investment

4.2.3 Typology Framework

The combination of the identified generic firm types according to a lifecycle approach and the dimensions derived from innovation and valuation theories constructs the typology framework. This framework structures on the one hand initial theoretical implications of how valuations should been done and on the other hand the analysis of the empirical investigation in chapter 6. The following table depicts the conceptual model of the typology.

Table 6. Conceptual Model of Typology

Firm Type / Dimensions	Idea Firms	Growth Firms	Mature Firms
Methodologies	Innovation projects	Innovation projects	Innovation projects
	Innovation capability	Innovation capability	Innovation capability
	Transaction effects	Transaction effects	Transaction effects
	Risk and uncertainty	Risk and uncertainty	Risk and uncertainty
Information	Innovation projects	Innovation projects	Innovation projects
	Innovation capability	Innovation capability	Innovation capability
	Transaction effects	Transaction effects	Transaction effects

4.3 Implications from Theory

In the following sub-chapters, I will shortly depict on the one hand what common literature on valuation suggests methodological-wise for each firm type. On the other hand, I will depict the characteristics that common innovation theory suggests investigating to appraise innovation potential per firm type (compare chapter 3). As described in the overall research process (chapter 2.4), most of the detailed theoretical implications have been derived after the empirical investigation has been conducted to enable an open and unbiased conduction of the qualitative investigation. The following sub-sections' purpose is rather to support the comparison of theory and practice based on relevant common theory and basic concepts than to provide a detailed or half-way complete elaborated discussion of innovation or valuation theories.

4.3.1 Idea Firms

As DAMODARAN states, the core challenge of valuating an idea firm is to estimate and make assumptions about such a firm's prospects. "There can be no denying the fact that young companies pose the most difficult estimation challenges in valuation." (Damodaran, 2009, p. 262)

Methodologies

With regard to methodologies, DAMODARAN questions the use of highly sophisticated detailed valuation models as he supposes the effect of such models on the valuation quality to be minor in comparison to providing good estimations and assumptions: "In valuing young companies less (detail) is often more (precision)." (Damodaran, 2009, p. 227) Nevertheless he *suggests using conventional income approaches* and *market approaches* to value idea firms and discourages the use of hurdle or venture capital approaches:

> While it is understandable that analysts, when confronted with the myriad of uncertainties associated with valuing young companies, look for shortcuts, there is no reason why young companies cannot be valued systematically. (Damodaran, 2009, p. 225)

> While these [income and market] approaches require us to estimate inputs that are often difficult to nail down, they are still useful insofar as they force us to confront the sources of uncertainty, learn more about them and make our best estimates. While we may be tempted to add premiums to these values for potential opportunities that we see in the future, the use of real option premiums should be limited to those companies that have some degree of exclusivity in exploiting these opportunities. (Damodaran, 2009, p. 262)

In particular, he proposes using three conventional methodologies:

(1) *Discounted cash flow* (income approach in chapter 3.3.2)
(2) *Contingent claim*, e.g., real options (income approach in chapter 3.3.2)
(3) *Transaction/private multiples or public multiples* (market approach in chapter 3.3.3)

Further standard valuation literature does also suggest to use those conventional methodologies (for example Damodaran, 2002; Koller et al., 2005).

For the *discounted cash flow methodology*, the following approaches are recommended to estimate or calculate the three major components *future cash flows*, *discount rate*, and *terminal value*. Literature suggests two methodologies to estimate future cash flows for idea firms:

(1) *Top-down approach*: The top-down-approach suggest starting with estimating the potential market for the new product service (including evolution of the market over time). After this first assessment potential market share, operative expenses & margins and investments for growth are derived. DAMODARAN suggests checking anticipated growth and reinvestment rate for internal consistency (Damodaran, 2009, pp. 226–228). The suggested approach starts from an anticipated future market share for the steady state of the firm, e.g. a market share in 10 years, details out the development path to that future market share, and quantifies the development of revenues, costs, margins, and investments.
(2) *Bottom-up approach*: The bottom-up approach in contrasts is in its basis an investment plan starting with an investment in capacity and after that estimating the devel-

opment of sales and costs for the next periods. Production capacity size, investments, unit sales, revenues, operating costs, and additional reinvestments are considered.

Discount rates are the means to cover risks and the value of money in discounted cash flow methodology. Idea firms are often held by either undiversified owners or partially diversified venture capitalists. Thus, it makes no sense to consider only the market risk, e.g. in a beta factor derived from stock prices (compare chapter 3.3.2), in the valuation. Further issues exist for estimating the cost of debt and the debt ration as an idea firm's debt is neither traded as bonds nor rated, but mostly provided through bank or other loans. Thus, no market values can be derived to value debt. DAMODARAN (Damodaran, 2009, pp. 237–238) suggests alternatives to estimate discount factors: Sector averages for other firms that idea firm aspires to make business in, adjustments for the missing diversification of the owners, and industry averages or founders target debt rates for costs of debt. All of these factors should be expected to change over time and these changes should be considered in the model as well.

The last calculation factor is the *terminal value*. For idea firms this value component considering the stable state of the firm most likely can represent most of the value. Literature offers generally three approaches (Damodaran, 2009, p. 242):

(1) Value the firm as *going conc*ern and make reasonable assumptions about cash flows growing in perpetuity
(2) Estimate the present value of *further cash flows beyond the forecast horizon*
(3) Assume that the *firm will be liquidated after the forecast horizon* (most conservative assumption)

It is obvious that using a multiple to calculate the terminal value is inconsistent with the idea of income approaches, which are based on the intrinsic valuation paradigm.

The other mentioned income approach is to use *contingent claims* (real options) to value idea firms (compare for example also Schwartz & Moon, 2000, for internet companies). The *option to expand* into new products or markets can be used to augment intrinsic valuations with a value premium. This should only be done, if the valued idea firm has this option exclusively, i.e., learning and adaptive behavior is restricted to the valued firm and not open to competitors in the market.

> Why can't we build expectations about new products and new markets into our cash flows and value? We can try, but there are two problems. The first is that our fore-

> casts about these potential product and market extensions will be very hazy at the time of the initial valuation and the cash flows will reflect this uncertainty. In other words, neither Microsoft nor Apple would have been able to visualize the potential markets for Microsoft Office or the iPhone at the time that they were introducing MS-DOS or the iPod. The second is that it is the information gleaned and the lessons learned during the initial product launch and subsequent development that allows firms to take full advantage of the follow-up offerings. It is this learning and adaptive behavior that gives rise to the option value. (Damodaran, 2009, p. 259)

The last suggested methodology is to use *multiples* to value idea firms. Two ways of using multiples are suggested (Damodaran, 2009, pp. 253–257):

(1) *Private or transaction multiples* (also compare Corvello, Iazzolino, & Ritrovato, 2013): Though databases for those seem to be available, problems exist with regard to comparability: Different understandings of what the transaction prices considered as inputs or what they cover exactly, different times or economic environments of the transactions, different scales and sizes of firms, non-standardized equity, or international differences.

(2) *Public firm multiples*: Public multiples pose a major challenge as idea firms have to be compared with publicly traded firms, which are based on their lifecycle mostly more mature.

How is *innovation potential* considered by idea firm valuation approaches? Though the valuation object for the income approaches is a complete firm, theory seems to consider this firm majorly in the sense of a product/service development project and not in the sense of the innovation capability definition developed in chapter 3.2.5. The innovation capability could be valuated by the use of the expand real option as depicted above. The multiples valuation approaches could implicitly consider innovation capability as they compare the idea firm to other firms. With the comparison it should be possible to compare by the means of analogy also, which development path the firm might take in its lifecycle supported by innovation capability.

Transaction effects can be considered in two ways using a DCF methodology: Key person discounts and the use of post-money-valuation. *Key person discounts* adjust the value for the risk that key personnel leaves the idea firm and by this, the anticipated business plan cannot be realized. *Post-money-valuation* describes an approach that values a firm by taking into consideration investments made possible by equity provided by the transaction, e.g. a venture capital infusion. Originally developed to calculate the value of the invested money and the distribution, if the firm is successful, it seems logical that in many cases idea firm valuations can only be done post-money because without the provided equity the idea firm will not be able to do the necessary investments to do business.

With regard to *risk and uncertainty*, idea firms do not only bear the risk or uncertainty that their business plans do not realize to full extend, but also that the young idea firm might not *survive* at all. To cope with that risks and uncertainties two approaches are suggested by theory: Taking *sector averages* of survival if available or using *advanced mathematical models, i.e. a probit model, or simulations.* Another source of risk and uncertainty is information asymmetry:

> Determining the value of new firms in emerging industries is a vexing problem for investors because of asymmetric information and its associated risks of adverse selection and moral hazard. While these are two distinct forms of risk, both types of risk arise because of the asymmetry of information between a principal and an agent (Hertzel & Smith, 1993; Stiglitz, 1985). In the case of adverse selection, the asymmetry is about qualitative differences in initial conditions, while for moral hazard the asymmetry is about unobserved actions. When information asymmetry is high, prices are typically discounted (Riley, 1989). However, price premiums can still be achieved in such markets if buyers have access to alternative types of data that reduce information asymmetry and which help differentiate new firms of varying quality (Spence, 1974). (Sanders & Boivie, 2004, p. 168)

It makes sense to differentiate between risks and uncertainty based firm-internal and firm-external factors. For firm-internal risks, such as the quality of the management team, the idea firm's founder or management team is better informed than the investor. For firm-external risks, such as the innovation projects market size or customer adoption, the investor can be less, equal or even better informed (Gompers & Lerner, 2004, p. 162)

All of the above mentioned risk and uncertainty challenges should lead to discounted and, thus, lower valuation results. The only way that risks and uncertainties should lead to higher values is the use of the expand option mentioned above in the description of contingent claims.

Information

"In virtually all cases a critical role of venture capitalists is generating information about the firm's prospects." (Gompers & Lerner, 2004, p. 160) The methodologies mentioned above are quantitative in nature, but what information and data should be considered as proxies to derive the necessary numbers about the future prospects of an idea firm and where does this data come from? First of all, financials and operating data is only of limited use:

> Thus, in emerging market sectors with high levels of uncertainty investors are likely to shift emphasis from objective financial and operating data, which is lacking or not well understood, to indirect, secondary information sources that are better understood (Sanders & Boivie, 2004, p. 168).

The information that can be used can be clustered into three areas:

(1) *Business idea*: As stated above, an idea firm's value should be highly dependent on the commercial success of a *single innovation project or a single innovative idea*. Most idea firms should are single idea or single product firms. Taking into account the top-down or bottom-up approaches the following information should be relevant for a valuation: Market size, targeted market share, planned developments of revenues, costs, margins, and necessary investments (Damodaran, 2009, pp. 226–228; J. Hall & Hofer, 1993).

(2) *Team of developers/managers*: A team of founders, very often with technical and not necessarily business expertise, works on the development of a technology or an innovative business model. Thus, collecting information about the capabilities of this team seems to be relevant for the valuation (X.-P. Chen, Yao, & Kotha, 2009; MacMillan et al., 1985; M. Song, Podoynitsyna, van der Bij, & Halman, 2008).

(3) *Utilization of advanced technologies*: As for young growth firms, assessing the firm's utilization of advanced technologies should facilitate appraising the value of an innovation project (Siegel, Siegel, & MacMillan, 1993).

(4) *Relationships and network*: Theory suggests that an idea firm's relationships within an industry, to investors, or to potential customers should be relevant for its economic success (Andersen, 2013; Gilsing, Nooteboom, Vanhaverbeke, Duysters, & Oord, 2008).

(5) *Observable corporate governance characteristics*: Additional information in the case an idea firm that has already been founded or is in the process of being set up are cor-

porate governance characteristics such as executive and director stock-based incentives or venture capital participation (Sanders & Boivie, 2004, p. 168).

Most of the depicted information categories are relevant to value *innovation projects*, but the team of developers/managers and the idea firm's governance and financing can also be related to the *innovation capability* in the sense of executing such projects successfully and enabling a firm's capability to continuously develop innovations.

With regard to *transaction effects* innovation theory suggests that acquired firms might lose their innovation potential, if certain idea firm characteristics such as entrepreneurial freedom or limited organizational boundaries for employees cannot be kept and key inventors lower their performance or leave the firm after the acquisitions (K. S. Christensen, 2006; Ernst & Vitt, 2000; Paruchuri et al., 2006). These effects could be anticipated in a valuation by investigating the *fit between firm culture and organization of the acquirer and firm culture and organization of the acquisition.*

4.3.2 Growth Firms

Idea firms that made it "through the rigors of the marketplace" (Damodaran, 2009, p. 263) become growth firms at the next stage in their lifecycle. From a valuator's view growth firm valuation is challenging because of those firms' dynamic financials, mixture of private and public debt, limited significance of operational financial data, and a short and shifting market history. (Damodaran, 2009, pp. 265–266). From an innovation theory perspective, growth firm's challenges should lie in the later stages of their innovation processes, i.e., "full production & market launch" (Cooper, 1990) or "product commercialization" (X. M. Song & Montoya-Weiss, 1998), and aspects of innovation capability such as operational and strategic coordination as well as firm culture (Sammerl, 2006, pp. 194–196) should be considered as relevant information for the valuation (compare chapters 3.2.1, 3.2.2, and 3.2.5).

Methodologies

Comparing standard literature (Damodaran, 2002; Koller et al., 2005), growth firms seem to have fitting characteristics to be valued by income approaches as those income approaches fit best to growing or stable firms. A common approach to deal with growth firms is to split the firm's future income periods in a growth and a stable phase. Specialized literature suggests majorly the following methodologies to appraise growth firms (Damodaran, 2009, p. 281):

(1) *Discounted cash flow* (income approach in chapter 3.3.2)

(2) *Public multiples* (market approach in chapter 3.3.3)

Contingent claim analysis seems not to be suggested for growth firm. Instead it is recommended for individual strategic investment appraisals (Bowman & Moskowitz, 2001; Copeland, 2001; Reuer & Tong, 2007).

To appraise growth firms and their innovation potentials with *discounted cash flow methodologies* it is recommended to *differentiate between a high growth and stable (growth) phase*. HOLT (1962) for example indicates from his investigation that a firm's value depends on the duration of its growth phase.

To operationalize this approach for the *high growth phase* one should estimate and verify revenue growth rates for the high growth phase on a per-year level and estimate a terminal value for the stable growth phase. To check for reasonable growth rates it is recommended to *compute absolute revenue changes* from year to year to visualize the growth. The next step is to derive operating incomes by the use of calculating operating margins. This step is a challenge for growth firms as it is expected that these margins change over time. They can be even negative for the first periods. DAMODARAN recommends the use of *target margins* to determine the development of operating margins. As sustainable growth does not come for free, the valuator should consider reinvestments over time majorly based on fixed formulas taking changes in revenues, growth rates, (return on) capital, and efficiency growth as inputs (Damodaran, 2009, p. 284).

To estimate the *stable (growth) phase* component the use of the *terminal value* is recommended. For growth firms the terminal value is a larger proportion of value than for mature firms. Thus, more uncertainty about the assumptions underlying the terminal value exists. Nevertheless, DAMODARAN recommends using a DCF methodology to value growth firms.

> The nature of the cash flows at growth companies – low or negative in the early years and higher later – will ensure that the terminal value is a high proportion of value, accounting for 80, 90 or even more than 100% of value. Some analysts use this as ammunition against using discounted cash flow valuations, suggesting that assumptions about the high growth phase will be drowned out by the terminal value assumptions. This is not true, since the base year value for the terminal value calculation (earnings and cash flows in year 5 or 10) is a function of the assumptions during the high growth phase; changing these assumptions will have dramatic effects (as it should) on value. (Damodaran, 2009, p. 286)

With regard to estimating the stable growth component DAMODARAN (2009, p. 286) emphasizes two topics. First: Being realistic valuing the length of the growth phase. And, second: Valuation characteristics of a stable (growth) firm with regard to discount and reinvestment rates should be used to value the stable component of the DCF valuation.

When valuing growth companies with *public multiples*, controlling for differences in growth and risk seems to be essential as well as steering away from multiples on current book value or current earnings as these numbers are likely to be small and unstable. Instead of using future revenues using expected future profits is recommended as the basis for multiples valuation. To adjust differences in growth and risk, a multiple regression approach is recommended instead of assuming that multiples increase proportionally with growth. (Damodaran, 2009, pp. 303–304)

How is *innovation potential* influencing such a valuation? The revenue changes might be linked to the firm's capability to develop a product or service that hits customer demand and its capability to commercialization this product or service. Target margins in the DCF methodology or future profits used with the multiples methodology should be closely tight to the differentiation potential and the time that differentiation potential can be protected from competitors. Future revenues, profit margins and their changes over time reflect more or less a business case for a product/service development and commercialization and seem to be tight more to individual products or services and, thus, *innovation projects*, rather than to the whole firm. In contrast, the calculation of reinvestments obviously should have a link to *innovation capability* in the sense of new product/service development or product/service improvement and could be connected to investments in innovation capability.

From a methodological perspective *transaction effects* do not seem to be addressed in a special way for growth firms. They should be similar to idea firms for younger growth firms (compare last chapter) and similar to mature firms for more mature growth firms (compare next chapter).

With regard to *risk and uncertainty* the risk profiles for the high growth and stable growth phases of the DCF methodology should be held consistent with growth and operating numbers according to the corresponding phase. The risk of non-survival seems not to be perceived as a growth firm risk in DCF valuation. Nevertheless, if non-survival is regarded as a risk, the methodologies for idea firms should be used. The use of sophisticated valuation methodologies such as decision trees or simulations seems to only promise limited support as those methodologies only support estimating value ranges or value distributions and not a single value for the firm at hand:

> Note, though, that much of this uncertainty comes not from the quality of the information or the precision of the valuation model used, but from the real world. The future is full of surprises, and for growth firms, where so much of the value lies in the future, this will translate into big changes in value. . . . [W]e presented probabilistic approaches including decision trees, simulations and scenario analysis that can be used to enrich valuations. These approaches offer some promise with growth companies, not because they provide more precise estimates of value or even because they generate risk measures but because they allow analysts to be more comfortable with their own estimates of value. They are, however, not particularly useful for a simple reason. The uncertainty in the estimates will result in distributions in value that reflect that uncertainty. . . . A more useful technique for grappling with uncertainty, with growth companies, is to focus on the one of two key drivers of value for that company and look at not only the effects on value of varying assumptions about those drivers but also breakeven points in terms of the current price. For instance, assuming that revenue growth is the key determinant of value for a firm, we can ask the question: What would the revenue growth rate have to be to justify the current market price? We can then follow up by looking whether we are comfortable as investors, with the market-implied revenue growth rate. (Damodaran, 2009, p. 301)

In the case of multiples valuation and forward earnings multiples, the risk of survival should be covered, as the firm might not make it to the forward year the multiple is based on. Taking into account IPO literature, which is closely tied to growth firms, another tool to deal with uncertainty is to *appraise a firm's network ties* such as endorsement relationships with venture capital firms or strategic partnerships (Gulati & Higgins, 2003; Gulati et al., 2000).

Information

Based on the characteristics of growth firms the key question for a growth firm is, if the firm can "scale up" (compare chapter 4.2.1). This can be achieved by taking two paths: (1) exploiting the existing market with the developed product or service or (2) developing new or improved products or services for the currently handled, adjacent, or completely new markets (Kim & Mauborgne, 2005).

With regard to innovation potential the first path should match to the commercialization phase of an *innovation project* and the second path should match to the *innovation capability* defined in chapter 3.2.5 whereas the first path should be the major case for younger growth firms and the second for more mature growth firms. "These results seem logical in that smaller companies have fewer resources and therefore may perform better by focusing their effort. Conversely, more mature companies need to expand growth prospects and hedge against overreliance on any particular opportunity." (Siegel et al., 1993, p. 170) SIEGEL ET AL. (1993) investigated the characteristics of high growth firms and recommend to investigate the following factors that support high growth: Industry experience of the management team, focus on one product (younger growth firms) or capabilities to broaden product portfolio (more mature growth firms), composition of the management team (lean team for younger growth and balanced team for mature growth firms), utilization of advanced technology (younger growth firms), and customer relationships (more mature growth firms).

Comparable to idea firms, but much more relevant to growth firms, observable corporate governance characteristics could be used to assess innovation capability. For growth firms those could be executive and director stock-based incentives, institutional and blockholder stock ownership, or board structure (Sanders & Boivie, 2004, p. 168)

With regard to *transaction effects* the effect of losing innovativeness could be considered similar to the valuation of idea firms (compare chapter 4.3.1). An additional component though could be the augmentation of necessary capabilities by the buyer. A buyer could for example augment the growth firm's management team to tailor it to the business needs of a more mature growth firm (commercialization capability) or provide access to relevant strategic partners, investors, or customers.

4.3.3 Mature Firms

In contrast to idea and growth firms, mature firms derive most of their value and income from existing assets. They can be characterized as having their revenue growth rates approaching the growth rate in the economy, yielding stable margins, and being likely to grow inorganically (Damodaran, 2009, pp. 313–314).

Methodologies

Most of the existing literature on valuation describes the standard methodologies to appraise mature stable firms (for example Bodie et al., 2008; Damodaran, 2002; Koller et al., 2005; Reilly & Schweihs, 2000). Recommended are the

(1) *discounted cash flow* and
(2) *public multiples*

methodologies depicted in detail in the "standard" valuation literature. Additionally to the application of those standard methodologies, DAMODARAN (2009, pp. 325–343) points out two major topics to consider in mature firm valuations: growth by acquisitions and changing management.

Similar to growth firms, *innovation potential* in the sense of *innovation capability* is on the one hand majorly considered by the anticipated reinvestment rate, in this case including acquisitions by the mature firm as capital expenditures. On the other hand, DAMODARAN (2009, pp. 329–343) recommends assessing potentials deriving from changing the way the firm is run, e.g., changing the management. This potential is derived from three dimensions (excluding non-operating assets and financial restructuring): (1) Increased cash flows from assets in place, (2) increased expected growth, (3) a longer high growth period. *Innovation projects* do not seem to be valued on an individual level. For mature firms with high dependency on major high-risk innovation projects, such as pharmaceutical firms, *real option* valuation is suggested by literature (Bowman & Moskowitz, 2001; Cassimon, De Backer, Engelen, Van Wouwe, & Yordanov, 2011; Hartmann & Hassan, 2006; McGrath & Nerkar, 2004).

Transaction effects can be appraised by calculating a *value of control* based on the *value of changing management*, e.g., value of management change = optimal firm value - status quo value, and the *probability of changing management*, majorly based on determinants such as institutional concerns, firm-specific constraints, or corporate holding structures. It is obvious that the probability of changing management is only of concern, if the firm is not acquired with full control rights.

To deal with *risk and uncertainty*, practitioners seem to use the standard instruments recommended in valuation literature, e.g., the discount rate in the DCF methodology.

Information

From a financial perspective, relevant information about the reinvestments of revenues (reinvestment rate and reinvestment quality) in assets supporting innovation projects or innovation capability should be collected and interpreted to assess the innovation potential of a mature firm. Investigating a firm's acquisition strategy with regard to innovation capability should be part of the appraisal (Damodaran, 2009, pp. 325–326).

From an innovation theory perspective, mature firms should feature many of the *innovation capability* aspects discussed in chapter 3.2.5. Innovation processes should be in place as well as supporting capabilities such as internal and external learning, operational and strategic coordination, and a supporting firm culture. Continuing the development path from maturing growth companies, the focus of relevant information should move from appraising individual innovation projects to the innovation capabilities to manage a portfolio of innovation activities. As mature firms are likely to maintain a larger base of (core) capabilities, they are prone to losing their dynamics to innovate into new markets or changing market dynamics. Their capabilities become rigidities hindering them to cannibalize existing products or services by developing new architectural innovations or new technological paradigms (Chandy & Tellis, 1998, 2000; Dosi, 1982; R. M. Henderson & Clark, 1990; Leonard-Barton, 1992). Thus, investigating a mature firm's capability to overcome such restrictions should lead to valuable information.

Following last paragraphs argumentation, *transaction effects* with regard to innovation potential should be investigated majorly via investigating the capability to overcome rigidities, e.g., by changing the management team or policy. SØRENSEN ET AL. (2008) for example indicate that patent citations increase for firms after having conducted a leveraged buyout (LBO) and, thus, conducted a change in management. To appraise the probability that a change in management could unlock such a kind of innovation potential DAMODARAN (Damodaran, 2009, pp. 344–360) suggests to critically assess stock price, earnings performance, and the manifestations in Table 7 (next page). Many of them directly relate to innovation capability facets such as reinvestments or the exploitation of strategic opportunities by developing adequate products or services.

Table 7. Ways of Increasing Value

Potential problem	Manifestations	Possible Fixes	Value Consequence
Existing assets are poorly managed	Operating margins are lower than peer group, and return on capital is lower than the cost of capital	Manage existing assets better. This may require divesting some poorly performing assets.	Higher operating margin and return on capital on existing assets, leading to higher operating income. Efficiency growth in near term as return on capital improves.
Management is underinvesting. (It is too conservative in exploiting growth opportunities)	Low reinvestment rate and high return on capital in high growth period.	Reinvest more in new investments, even if it means lower return on capital (albeit > cost of capital).	Higher growth rate and higher reinvestment rate during high growth period, creating higher value because growth is value-creating.
Management is overinvesting. (It is investing in value destroying new investments)	High reinvestment rate and return on capital that is lower than cost of capital.	Reduce reinvestment rate until marginal return on capital is at least equal to cost of capital.	Lower growth rate and lower reinvestment rate during high growth period, resulting in higher value because growth is no longer value destroying.
Management is not exploiting possible strategic advantages.	Short or non-existent high growth period with low or no excess returns.	Build on competitive advantages.	Longer high growth period, with larger excess returns, leading to higher value.
Management is too conservative in its use of debt.	Debt ratio is lower than optimal (or industry average).	Increase debt financing.	Higher debt ratio and lower cost of capital, resulting in higher firm value.
Management is overusing debt.	Debt ratio is higher than optimal.	Reduce debt financing.	Lower debt ratio and lower cost of capital, generating higher firm value.
Management is using wrong type of financing.	Cost of debt is higher than it should be, given the firm's earning power.	Match debt up to assets, using swaps, derivatives or refinancing.	Lower cost of debt and cost of capital, creating higher firm value.
Management holds excess cash and is not trusted by the market with the cash.	Cash and marketable securities are a large percent of firm value. Firm has poor track record on investments.	Return cash to stockholders, either as dividends or stock buybacks.	Firm value is reduced by cash paid out, but stockholders gain because the cash was discounted in the firm's hands.
Management has made investments in unrelated companies.	Substantial cross holdings in other companies that are being undervalued by the market.	As a first step, try to be more transparent about cross holdings. If that is not sufficient, divest cross holdings.	Firm value is reduced by divested cross holdings but increased by cash received from divestitures. When cross holdings are undervalued, the latter should exceed the former.

Based on Damodaran, 2009, pp. 344-346

4.3.4 Cross-Type Implications

The following section sums up the theoretical implications from theory for the defined firm types, discusses cross-type patterns and differences between valuation and innovation theories.

Before going into details with regard to the dimensions methodologies and information, it is valuable to enrich the general definitions of the firm types in chapter 4.2.1 with implications from both valuation and innovation theories and findings of the last chapters. Table 8 depicts major characteristics of the three firm types with regard to product portfolio, revenue and earnings development, and information & data collection issues.

Table 8. Valuation Characteristics of Firm Types

Firm Type / Characteristics	Idea Firms	Growth Firms	Mature Firms
Products/services	One idea One product or service	One or few products and/or services	Portfolio of products and/or services
Revenue / earnings	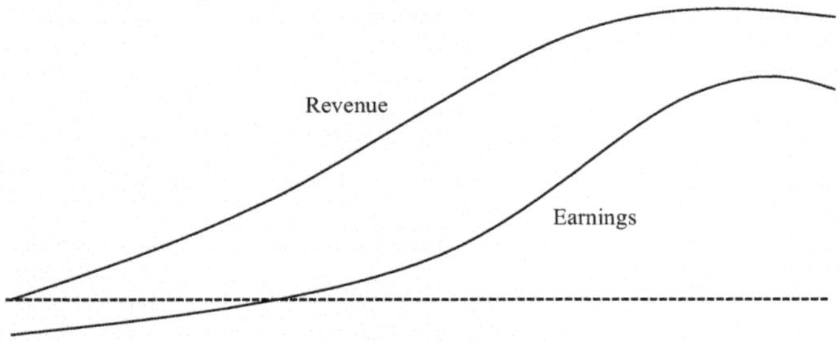		
Major Source of Value and Income	Future assets	Future assets / growth assets	Existing assets
Information & Data Collection Issues	No history No financials	Low revenues Zero or negative earnings Changing margins Past data reflects smaller firm	Stable earnings Numbers can change if management changes

Adapted from Damodaran, 2009, p. 8, extended by author

Following this depiction, one can generally infer that an idea firm's innovation potential should be dependent on the success of a single idea, product, or service whereas a mature firm's innovation potential should depend on the development and management of a portfolio of products & services. Thus, the major source of value should shift from anticipated future assets that create anticipated income (idea firms) to existing assets that create the majority of income (mature firms). With regard to useful information, generally, idea firms should be difficult to appraise by existing or past financials such as revenue or earnings whereas those financials should be more meaningful for the appraisal of mature firms.

Methodologies

A closer look at the methodologies implied by theory is depicted in the following table.

Table 9. Implications From Theory – Proposed Valuation Methodologies

Firm Type / Characteristics	Idea Firms	Growth Firms	Mature Firms
Innovation projects	Discounted cash flow - Top-down approach - Bottom-up approach Contingent claim Private or transaction multiples	Discounted cash flow (differentiation between high and stable growth phase) Public multiples	*Generally not valued on individual level* *Real options for firms with high dependency on high-risk innovation projects*
Innovation capability	Contingent claim (expand option) in addition to discounted cash flow valuation	Consideration of reinvestments in DCF Public multiples	Discounted cash flow / consideration of reinvestments in DCF Public multiples Assessing probability of changing management and its effects
Transaction effects	Post-money valuation Key person discounts	*Compare idea firms for younger growth firms* *Compare mature firms for more mature growth firms*	Pre-transaction valuation Appraising value of control based on value of changing management
Risk and uncertainty	Discount rate (DCF) Advanced mathematical models or simulations for risk of non-survival	Discount rates for high and stable growth phases (DCF) Risk of non-survival (compare idea firms) for multiple methodology Appraisal of firm network ties / other parties' appraisals	Discount rate (DCF)

From the point of valuation theory, *innovation projects* should be valued on an individual level for idea and growth firms. For mature firms that depend on the success of a only a few products, brands, or R&D activities such as pharmaceutical firms, contingent claim methodology is recommended (Girotra, Terwiesch, & Ulrich, 2007; Hartmann & Hassan, 2006). The valuation of innovation projects could be done by DCF, contingent claim, and multiples. Despite of the challenges to estimate cash flows or contingent claims, DAMODARAN suggests to use tools of fundamental valuation such as DCF and only to complement those with other methodologies such as contingent claims (Damodaran, 2009, pp. 225, 262).

Innovation capability in the sense of managing more than one innovation project begins to become a valuation object for growth and mature firms and should be appraised with DCF on one hand and on the other with public multiples as comparable public firms become available for those firms. Reinvestments are the key input factor that considers innovation capability in a DCF valuation though they are majorly considered as costs by a reinvestment rate that decreases the valuation. Top-line effects should then be considered via adapted revenues and operating margins in a DCF valuation. The probability and effects of changing management as indicator for increasing innovation potential can also be valued quantitative by a DCF valuation.

Transaction effects should be considered in differently for idea firms on the one hand and mature firms on the other hand. For idea firms, the valuation is generally from the post-transaction perspective in the case of a capital infusion or equity investment. In the case of an acquisition the threat of losing innovation potential could be appraised by key person discounts. For mature firms, the methodology proposed to appraise transaction effects is to estimate a value of control or value of changing management, e.g., influencing how the firm is run (in this case the effect on the innovation potential) through the acquisition or investment. For growth firms, methodologies from both idea and mature firms could be used dependent on the firm at hand.

In the case of using the DCF methodology, the discount rate becomes the vehicle to deal with *risk and uncertainty* for all firm types. For growth firms, the discount rates and hence the reflected risk used to value growth firms should be higher in earlier periods and decrease in later periods towards mature company levels (Damodaran, 2009, pp. 268–269).For idea firms, the risk of non-survival should be appraised by simulation models. For growth firms, an interesting approach to appraise risks is to use the endorsements of other investors or strategic partners. This approach includes other parties' appraisals in the own appraisal to assess risks and deal with uncertainty.

Information

The following table gives an overview of valuation key questions and valuation inputs based on DAMODARAN'S work.

Table 10. Implications From Theory – Key Valuation Questions & Inputs

Firm Type / Characteristics	Idea Firms	Growth Firms	Mature Firms
Key Questions Revenue / Earnings	What is the potential market? Will this product sell and at which price? What are the expected margins?	Can the company scale up? How will competition affect margins? As growth declines, how will the firm's reinvestment policy change? Will the financing policy change as the firm matures?	Is there the possibility of the firm being restructured? Will business units be brought to a better use within other firms?
Key Valuation Inputs	Potential Market Margins Capital investment Key person value	Revenue growth Target margins Return on capital (ROC) Reinvestment rate Length of growth period	Current earnings Efficiency growth Changing cost of capital

Adapted from Damodaran, 2009, p. 8

Those key questions should be answered by collecting relevant information and data. The acquired information must then be translated into the key valuation inputs to apply the suggested methodologies depicted in the previous section. Table 11 depicts the suggested relevant information and derived from innovation theory per firm type.

Information about *innovation projects* should be majorly relevant for idea and young growth firms developing and commercializing majorly a single new product or service. An exception to this could be mature firms dependent on the success of a few products or brands such as pharmaceutical firms, which could be valued for example by contingent claim methodologies (Girotra et al., 2007; Hartmann & Hassan, 2006). The essential information about an innovation project for both idea and young growth firms is its business case based on the idea itself. Utilization of advanced technology could act as proxy for the differentiation potential of the product or service as major influence factor on the business case. For idea firms, the founder or developer team's capabilities can act as proxy to assess the technical feasibility of developing the product or service and commercializing it. To appraise the validity of the business case and the valuators could pull up secondary information such as corporate governance characteristics including executive incentives and venture capital participation in the idea firm. For young growth firms, team capabilities such as industry experience, management focus, and a lean team become more important as the idea has to be commercialized and brought to the market.

Table 11. Implications From Theory – Relevant Information

Firm Type / Dimensions	Idea Firms	Growth Firms	Mature Firms
Innovation projects	Idea / business case Team of developers/managers Observable corporate governance characteristics, e.g., incentive systems and VC participation Utilization of advanced technologies	*Younger growth firms:* Team's industry experience Focus Lean team Utilization of advanced technologies	*Not valued on individual level, except firms depending on major innovation projects*
Innovation capability	Team of developers/managers Observable corporate governance characteristics, e.g., incentive systems and VC participation	*More mature growth firms:* Team's industry experience Capabilities to broaden product portfolio Balanced team Customer relationships Observable corporate governance characteristics, e.g., incentive systems, investors, board structure	Aspects of innovation capability: Internal & external learning processes, operational and strategic coordination, firm culture supporting innovation and change Reinvestment rate and reinvestment quality
Transaction effects	Retention of key personnel Acquirer's firm culture and organization	Retention of key personnel Acquirer's firm culture and organization Acquirer's augmentation capabilities	Probability and possible effects of changing management

The information relevant to appraise *innovation capability* changes over a firm's lifecycle. For idea firms, two proxies seem best suited to assess innovation capability: On the one hand the team of developers and founders and on the other hand the firm's observable governance characteristics. Observable governance characteristics such executive incentive systems, ownership structure, or venture capital participation should be a proxies to support the valuation: "One type of secondary indicator that may convey valuable information to investors about both hidden information and hidden actions is corporate governance." (Sanders & Boivie, 2004, p. 168)

For more mature growth firms trying to develop further adjacent or completely new products or services complementary to the original idea, valuable proxies with regard to innovation capability should be very similar to the ones facilitating the valuation of innovation projects. Differences should majorly exist related to capabilities and composition of the management team on the one hand and on the switch from a technology focus to a market focus. For mature growth firms, commercializing and extending the markets for their products become more important. Thus, management teams should be more balanced and open (compared to lean and focused for idea and young firms) and customer relationships should move into focus (compared to focus on advanced technologies for idea and young growth firms).

Mature firms should feature sophisticated processes and structures to support their innovation capability. Thus, proxies to assess innovation capability should be the existence and quality of internal and external learning processes, coordination processes, and a firm culture that supports change and overcoming structural rigidities. Further proxies could be the firm's total (re)investment rate or investments in innovation projects or capability.

With regard to *transaction effects* the relevant information for idea and growth firms should be very similar. Information about the acquiring firm's ability to retain key personnel and, related to this, to preserve the innovation potential of the acquired firm should be relevant. For mature firms, information about the ability to and effects of triggering changes in management such as depicted in Table 7 should be considered.

5 Design of the Empirical Study

According to BRYMAN'S classification of research approach elements (Bryman, 2004), the following chapters contain the chosen research strategy, research design, and the according research process for the empirical study, which is the core part of this dissertation. They also contain the reasoning why the research strategy, design, and process are suitable to investigate the research objectives stated in chapter 2.3 and why they fit in the overall research strategy depicted in chapter 2.4.

5.1 Epistemological Position

The theory of science underlying this dissertation is *interpretivism* sometimes also credited anti-positivism, which is underlying most qualitative research methodologies such as grounded theory, from which this dissertation draws substantial methodological approaches (Glaser & Strauss, 1967; P. Y. Martin & Turner, 1986; Morgan & Smircich, 1980; Suddaby, 2006). Qualitative research in the tradition of interpretivism focuses on causal explanations instead of statistical correlations. The latter are often associated with positivism. Comparable to *ethnomethodology*, reality is understood as a social construction (Morgan & Smircich, 1980, p. 497). This understanding is fitting the research objective quite well as researching the practices of firm valuation requires to investigate how valuation practitioners perceive a firm, its environment, and its prospects, how they construct mental representations of these aspects and how they draw conclusions from this construct to determine a value for a firm.

Additionally, qualitative research also allows *falsifying* theory or evaluating the contexts, in which theories are valid or not, by collecting and investigating observations in conflict with existing theory: "Case study findings can have implications both for theory and development and for theory testing. On the inductive side of theory development, plausibility probes and studies of deviant cases can uncover new or omitted variables, hypotheses, causal paths, causal mechanisms, types, or interactions effects." (George & Bennett, 2005, p. 109) This aspect of qualitative research can be theoretically based on the *critical rationalism* proposed by POPPER (2002).

The epistemological position creates the basis for the investigation, but should not be regarded as strict dogma. In general, I follow a pragmatic approach best suited to achieve the research objectives. SUDDABY (2006, p. 639) states in this context: "But being aware of one's epistemological position does not justify dogmatism about conducting grounded theory research. Ultimately, questions of when saturation is achieved, how coding should be done, or when counting is appropriate can be resolved pragmatically."

5.2 Research Strategy

The following paragraphs depict the empirical study's research strategy based on the chosen epistemological position, the research objectives, and the general research strategy depicted in chapter 2.4.

The core of this investigation is investigating valuation practices and extending existing based on the results of this investigation. Investigating practices requires researching *how* and *why* processes or methodologies are applied and by this identifying *why* practitioners come to certain results using the investigated practices. In order to investigate *how* and *why* questions literature on research strategies recommend the use of qualitative research (Bryman, 2004; Eisenhardt & Graebner, 2007; Eisenhardt, 1989; Gephart, 2004; Helfat, 2007; Suddaby, 2006; Whittington, 1996; Yin, 2003). HELFAT for example states:

> Qualitative research, however, has an important role to play in uncovering interesting or unexpected phenomena that statistical analysis may miss, because such research provides fine-grained detail and insights that can only come from case analysis. Findings from qualitative research in turn can form the basis for larger scale data collection and analysis. (Helfat, 2007, p. 189)

Especially with regard to investigating the mentioned *how* and *why* questions, I take up RYNES ET AL. assumption: "Tacit assumptions of practitioners can be made explicit through interaction academics employing case analysis, grounded theory, or protocol analysis. . . . Higher levels of direct contact with practitioners should improve the quality of academic research." (Rynes et al., 2001, pp. 348–349)

To go into more details, I chose a qualitative research strategy because of the following reasons:

(1) No empirical research on the use of valuation methods by practitioners has been conducted with regard to *how* and *why* questions (compare research gap in chapter 2.2).
(2) The valuation of innovation potential by practitioners has not been investigated before (compare research gap in chapter 2.2).
(3) Professional service firms and equity investors such as venture capitalists, auditors, investment bankers, or other corporate finance professionals dominate the community

of valuation practitioners. Many community members change employers within the community (also compare my sample in Appendix A) and are likely to have a close range of valuation approaches. Thus, a more detailed, open, qualitative research approach incorporating a smaller number of experts is likely to yield better results than a structured confirmatory quantitative investigation and at the same time is likely to have reasonable reliability and validity.

Discussion of research strategy alternatives

The following paragraphs depict two alternatives to the chosen research strategy and discuss the disadvantages compared to the chosen research strategy.

Using a *structured survey* to confirm hypotheses derived from existing theory:

(1) There exists no research with stated and confirmable hypotheses/scales about the application of existing valuation methodologies in the context of innovation potential.
(2) The use of a highly structured survey is not recommended to research such a complex phenomenon and to reveal answers to *why* and *how* questions.
(3) Experts with the expertise in valuation work in a very demanding job environment; thus, a real danger of a very low response rate exists, if no personal contact to those experts has been built.
(4) The population of professional service firms offering valuation services is little; thus, a representative return of surveys suitable for statistical analysis is unlikely.
(5) As the investigation revealed, many experts changed jobs between the professional service firms in focus, which on the one hand further reduces the variety within the sample population on the other hand raises the validity of implications for the smaller group of interviewees.

Using an *ethnographical approach* and investigate only very few detailed valuation cases:

(1) Existing theory in the field of valuation methodologies such as the respective valuation standard literature does not justify the completely explorative extent of a single or two case study approach.
(2) Ethnography for only one or two cases does not allow the investigation of valuation practices contingent on the defined firm types and, thus does not allow a comparative investigation (compare chapter 4.2).

5.3 Research Design

The empirical investigation's research design builds on the contingent research approach that utilizes a typology depicted in chapter 2.4. Comparative empirical research based on case studies should have a good fit to the chosen theory-guided overall contingent research design because a comparative empirical research design allows a better understanding of social or business phenomena due to the logic of comparison between two or more contrasting case studies (Bryman, 2004, pp. 53–55). Case study research in general offers the following strengths: Potential for achieving high conceptual validity; strong procedures for fostering new hypotheses and identifying new variables; value as a means to closely examine the hypothesized role of causal mechanisms, and capacity for addressing causal complexity (George & Bennett, 2005, p. 19). In the context of theory-building or theory-extension, comparative research is well-suited to generate hypotheses from empirical data, as "the elements of theory that are generated by comparative analysis are, first, conceptual categories and their conceptual properties; and second, hypotheses or generalized relations among the categories and their properties." (Glaser & Strauss, 1967, p. 35)

Combining the theory-driven contingency design (typology) and the empirical-driven comparative design should enable analytic induction of decision-making and valuation processes and practices as George & Bennett state:

> The procedure makes use of an inductive approach for theory-building, but it is analytic induction not raw empiricism. The black boxes of decision-making and strategic interaction are opened up and efforts are made to study actual processes of decision-making and of strategic interaction insofar as available data permitted (George & Bennett, 2005, p. xi).

The following paragraphs will describe unit of analysis and construction of cases in more detail.

Unit of analysis

The units of analysis within my research are valuation practices to appraise the innovation potential of different target firm types. Those practices are defined as a combination of methodologies and information used to appraise the innovation potential of firms within the context the valuation is conducted in.

Construction of cases

According to GEORGE & BENNETT (2005, p. 17), I define a case as an instance of a class of events. In the context of this investigation, those instances are valuations that practitioners have conducted during their professional careers.

To access those instances I interviewed valuation practitioners and asked them to elaborate about their firm valuation practices with the focus on considering the firms' innovation potential. Expert interviews offer the advantage that the expertise of more than one valuation case and the reflection and learning based on those cases can be leveraged in the empirical investigation. Relating this to the unit of analysis, thus, a single interview is likely to contain information about more than one instance of the unit of analysis depending on the experience of the practitioner. A disadvantage of expert interviews is that they can be considered as secondary data as the investigator was not present at the time the valuations actually happened. This might lead to biases that have to be taken into account and dealt with (see chapter 5.4.3).

5.4 Research Process

The following sub-sections describe the three major qualitative research process steps *sample selection*, *data collection*, and *data analysis*.

5.4.1 Sample Selection

I built the sample of experts based on the typology framework developed in chapter 4.2 as "the construction of deductive typological theories can suggest an initial list of variables and point out cases whose study is most likely to provide theoretical insights." (George & Bennett, 2005, p. 240) Experts were selected according to the lifecycle stage of their typical valuation targets, e.g., venture capital practitioners were selected because they appraise idea firms and investment bank practitioners because they majorly appraise mature firms. Thus, the empirical sample was selected according to theoretical sampling (Glaser & Strauss, 1967, pp. 45–77).

I did not restrict the sample to valuators dealing with certain industries. The reason for this decision is that innovation potential as defined in the chapters 3.2.5 and 4 is on an abstraction level that should be applicable to firms of all industries. A division into three groups characterizes the selected sample:

Group 1: I gathered information by leveraging the expertise of valuation experts from companies valuing firms as important part of their core business as professional service firms. Those are investment banks, corporate finance advisors, auditors, and a lawyer specialized on intellectual property (IP). HAUNSCHILD'S investigation (1994) also suggests that acquiring firms turn to professional service firms in case of valuation uncertainty, which is especially true for firms whose commercial success depends on innovation and the risks and uncertainties associated with innovation.

Group 2: I included venture capital investors, corporate venture capital investors, private equity investors, and a business angel investor. The valuation of high-risk/high-return companies is one of their core processes (Franke, Gruber, Harhoff, & Henkel, 2008; Gorman & Sahlman, 1989; MacMillan et al., 1985; Sanders & Boivie, 2004). I assume that venture capital investors invest majorly idea firms, corporate venture capital investors invest in later stage idea firms or growth firms (Dushnitsky & Shapira, 2010), and private equity investors invest majorly in growth or mature firms.

Group 3: I included two experts from industry firms' business and development departments to allow for the fact that valuation experts in the previously mentioned professional service firms often work closely together with their industry principals.

Table 12 summarizes the mapping from experts to the three firm types investigated in this dissertation. The mapping in this table is the result of the descriptive information about the practitioners' valuation expertise with certain firm types taken during the interview. It was not possible to determine the exact mapping in advance of the interviews as experts might have had expertise with different types of firms.

Table 12. Allocation of Experts in Data Sample and Firm Types

Firm Type	Idea Firms	Growth Firms	Mature Firms
Experts	Business angels Business developers (industry) Venture capital investors	Auditors Corporate finance advisors Corporate venture capital investors Business developers (industry) Investment bank professionals Intellectual property specialists Private equity investors	Auditors Corporate finance advisors Investment bank professionals Intellectual property specialists Private equity investors

By using the lifecycle concept, the sample contains both extreme cases (valuation of idea and valuation of mature firms) as well as cases between those both extremes or even between two of the three defined firm types.

Using the theoretical sampling and the descriptive data captured in the interviews, I was able to populate all three firm types with according statements for all typology dimensions. I took repeating statements of the experts mapped to the same firm type as proxy for empirical saturation of each firm type (Glaser & Strauss, 1967, pp. 45–77).

As I focus on strategic investments majorly based on equity investments and acquisitions of resources with this dissertation, I left out providers of loans and credits such as regular banks. Literature indicates especially in the context of idea and growth firms that banks might not have the necessary skills to evaluate projects or firms with few collateralizable assets and significant uncertainty (Gompers & Lerner, 2004, p. 163).

5.4.2 Data Collection

I collected the empirical data by conducting semi-structured interviews with the experts mentioned above in the years 2009-2012. The interviews took from 45 to 90 minutes and were conducted in most cases at the expert's office (some per telephone). I consider three interviews as pre-test (one industry interview, one venture capital interview, and one auditor interview) because after conducting these interviews, I complemented the interview guideline slightly and adapted it to the information gathered. Due to the explorative nature of this study, which should be considered as an iterative research process with the possibility to adapt the research process to new information, it makes sense to include all available information gathered to draw conclusions for my investigation (Bennett & Elman, 2006; Corbin & Strauss, 1990; Eisenhardt & Graebner, 2007; Eisenhardt, 1989; Gephart, 2004; Suddaby, 2006; Yin, 2003). Therefore, I did not exclude the information gathered during the pre-test from my final analysis. All interviews were recorded with a voice recorder except the pre-test interviews for which I used notes. After conducting the interviews, I transcribed interviews statement by statement into a spreadsheet database and coded them (compare next sub-section).

The interviews covered the following main topics (the original interview guideline can be found in Appendix B):

(1) *Descriptive data* about the expert (education, years of experience, valuation targets (lifecycle-phase and/or size). Existing research suggests that an expert's experience and expertise influence the way he considers data and makes strategic decisions (for example Melone, 1994)

(2) The *significance of the innovation potential* during a company valuation (closed and open questions)

(3) The *way the innovation potential is considered* in a company valuation (open questions)

   a. The way concrete innovation projects are considered in a valuation (derived from a conceptual model about innovation potential)

   b. The way innovation capability is considered in a valuation (derived from a conceptual model about innovation potential)

   c. The way the effects of changes to the company are valuated (for example due to additional resources in the case of a VC-investment or dys(synergies) due to a merger integration)

   d. The methods that are used for the valuations of the innovation potential and its conceptual parts

   e. The data that is considered in the valuation

   f. The dealing with risks associated with the outcomes of the innovation potential

(4) The *context (for example time and resources)* in which valuations take place (open questions)

(5) The *parties involved in the valuation process* (open questions)

(6) The *possibilities of improving* the used methodologies, their application, or the information that should be considered additionally (open questions)

5.4.3 Data Analysis

"In discovering theory, one generates conceptual categories or their properties from evidence; then the evidence from which the category emerged is used to illustrate the concept." (Glaser & Strauss, 1967, p. 23) Following that approach, I condensed and interpreted the empirical data by conducting the following steps:

(1) Expert-statements were transcribed in the order they have been made during the interview in a spreadsheet database (one statement per row, mapped to the firm type they are associated with) and compared with the notes taken. Statements were transcribed very close to what was said; with few exceptions, the original quotes are used.

(2) Expert-statements were associated with the dimensions of the typology main topics of the interview guideline (see last sub-section) by the use of codes.

(3) New codes were introduced, if statements did not fit into the main topics

(4) A new level of codes on a different abstraction level was introduced to allow grouping statements to newly created groups within or across the main topics (compare step 2)

(5) Step 4 groupings were than taken as 1st order constructs in the tables in chapter six of the dissertation and further abstracted to 2nd order constructs.

This coding allowed forming themes, concepts, and hypotheses about the research gap in a pragmatic way. Additionally, original statements are used throughout the following sections to illustrate the derived constructs and relationships.

As qualitative research is prone to biases by the researcher at least two biases should be addressed: Biases with regard to the selection of cases and biases during the collection and interpretation of data.

Selection bias

Selecting cases or in this case interview partners is a well-known challenge in qualitative research (Bennett & Elman, 2006, pp. 460–463). The most common critique is the selection of cases by a proposed result of a dependent variable, for example selecting only "successful" firms to investigate factors for a firm's success. By this methodology, it is not possible to differentiate between the necessity and the sufficiency of an investigated independent variable for a proposed value of the dependent variable.

The theoretical sampling was not made with a specific dependent variable in mind, but according to the firm types in chapter 4.2. This dissertation is an open investigation of what practitioners do. Thus, a selection bias rooted in selecting cases by observing specific outcomes can not be given.

Furthermore, I'm not affiliated with any of the interviewees' companies. The only interaction with the interviewees regarding the investigated topics took place during the interviews and never in a work context. Interviewees were acquired by using my personal network, career fairs or non-personalized inquiries addressed to companies in accordance with the sample criteria.

Data collection and interpretation bias

With regard to data collection & interpretation, researches are prone to several biases caused by themselves or their interview partners:

(1) Asking leading questions with implicit hypotheses.
(2) Transcribing and coding interviews in a way that implicit hypotheses are confirmed.
(3) Experts perceive or present their valuation expertise in an idealized way.

I dealt with these possible biases the following way:

(1) An open interview atmosphere was created. Answers are treated in an anonymous way. The results and publication of results do not pose a threat to the perception of others regarding interviewee or her/his company.
(2) In most cases, open questions have been used.
(3) Factual questions have been used. The self-evaluation of a practitioner's expertise has been asked in a separate question block at the end and not in between factual questions.
(4) The interviews are transcribed statement-wise/quote-wise. No condensation or interpretation has been made in the first step of collection.
(5) The coding of results has been examined, reviewed, revised with several breaks (sometimes more than half a year) during the time of the research to facilitate an unbiased interpretation of the collected data.

5.5 Data Sample

To investigate the research objectives, I composed a data sample by the way of theoretical sampling that reflects the need to consider valuations of companies in different stages of their lifecycle. I created this sample by selecting valuation experts from professional service firms offering valuation services on the one hand or equity investors on the other hand. The sample consists of experts from venture capital companies, corporate venture capital companies, investment banks, auditors, and a private equity investor. I enriched the sample by a business development and acquisition professional from an engineering company, a head of business development from an Internet trading company, and a lawyer with special expertise on intangible assets. Altogether, I conducted interviews with 21 experts from 20 companies. The experts' experience in valuation topics ranged from one to more than 20 years with an average of about 7 years. The interested reader will find detailed information about the interviewed experts in Appendix A.

Table 13. Experts and Statements in Data Sample

Company Type	Industry	Business Angel / Venture Capital	Corporate Venture Capital	Private Equity	Investment Bank	Auditor
Number	2	4	2	1	6	5
Number of statements	83	179	188	67	454	380

With the selected interview partners I was able to get expertise for all three firm types (compare chapter 4.2.1) and populate the typology with statements mapped according to those types.

Table 14. Interview Statements per Firm Type

Company Type	Idea firm	Growth firm	Growth or mature firm[12]	Mature firm
Number of statements	190	260	502	399

As can be seen in Table 14 the collection of data led to a reasonable saturation of statements per firm type.

The validity and reliability of the qualitative empirical investigation should be at a reasonable level. On the one hand, the large majority of interviewees either work for professional service firms or equity investors that should be involved in the majority of relevant firm valuations and conduct valuations as their profession (validity). On the other, the interviewees are equipped with an average experience of about seven years in their valuation jobs and should have participated in a significant number of valuations (reliability).

[12] Statements in this category could not be mapped clearly to only one of the two firm types. They were mapped to either both firm types or according to the context the statement was made in, e.g., the valuation projects the interviewee mentioned or the major firm types, he has dealt with in her/his career.

6 Empirical Findings and Discussion

In the following chapters, I present and discuss only empirical statements and findings of the conducted empirical study, which are most relevant to the research objective and for theory enhancement.[13] The presentation of the empirical results is split in five sections: In the first section, I present a depiction of the valuation process with enhancements based on the empirical research. In the sections 6.2, 6.3, and 6.4, I present and discuss empirical results with regard to used methodologies and data for each of the developed firm types (compare chapter 4). After presenting these results, I present and discuss a cross-firm-type analysis (section 6.5) before I present and discuss implications for existing theory in the following chapter 7.

The presentation of used methodologies and data is divided into the according two dimensions. Within these dimensions the sub-dimensions

(1) *innovation projects*,

(2) *innovation capability*,

(3) *transaction effects*, and

(4) *risk and uncertainty* (only in methodology dimension)

are presented and discussed.

The sub-chapters 6.2-6.4 show rich data, i.e. interview statements. The purpose of this kind of depiction is to enable the interested reader in getting a comprehensive and interesting overview of the descriptive empirical data and evidence and to enable him/her in understanding the reasoning for the discussion at the end of each sub-chapter by illustrating the derived concepts. As GLASER & STRAUSS state: "In discovering theory, one generates conceptual categories or their properties from evidence; then the evidence from which the category emerged is used to illustrate the concept." (Glaser & Strauss, 1967, p. 23)

This approach to presenting empirical data is also quite useful to present differences between valuation practices and valuation theory according to the "as practice" approach (compare chapter 3.4.5) In the tradition of ethnographic work, the depiction of rich data is also quite valuable to get a better understanding of how valuators proceed and think (compare chapters 5.1 and 5.2) and out of the view of "good" qualitative research, enough data should be shown

---

13 The gathered interview data contains many more findings and artifacts, which can neither be presented nor discussed in the scope of this dissertation. The collected data is available for fellow researchers though (compare Appendix C).

in order to give interested readers the chance to follow and understand the analysis (compare chapter 1.3).

If the reader is mostly interested in the discussion and analysis of the empirical results as discussed in chapter 5.4.3, but not so much in the exemplary but still comprehensive empirical data, he/she is advised to jump directly to the chapters 6.1.1, 6.2.3, 6.3.3, 6.4.3, and especially 6.5 that sum up and discuss the empirical results with regard to used methodologies and information.

Relationship between methodologies and information

Because there exist strong relationships between used valuation methodologies and required information on the one hand but also between the different typology dimensions (innovation projects, innovation capability, transaction effects, and risk and uncertainty) on the other, interview statements supporting a particular implication are usually only presented in the first section they are of relevance.

Differentiation between calculation and interpretation

One of the results of the empirical investigation is an extended valuation process (compare chapter 6.1). This process separates the process of interpreting information and applying a valuation methodology into two steps. This separation is mirrored in the analysis of methodologies in the following key findings sections. Methodologies used for interpretation of information are marked as *interpretation*, mathematical valuation methodologies as *calculation.* Furthermore, also with regard to the drafted valuation process, the data interpretation can influence either the calculation directly, if the result is *quantified information,* or it can influence the calculation indirectly or lead to an adjustment after the calculation, if the data interpretation leads to *qualitative information.* Both types of interpretation are marked accordingly in the 2nd order construct abstractions in the following chapters that deal with the methodologies.

6.1 Valuation Process and Context Factors

The empirical investigation allows proposing a general process model that describes how valuators appraise the value of a firm's innovation potential (compare Figure 3). The two main results of the investigation with regards to the general valuation process are on the one hand a more detailed investigation and of the process itself and on the other hand the identification of context factors influencing the process.

> In der Unternehmensbewertung gibt es anwendbare Methoden, aber es bleibt vieles im Ermessen des Beraters, wie er damit umgeht. Man kann Bewerten nicht methodisch abhaken. Es gibt kein Kochbuch dafür. (Auditing professional)

The result of the findings is an extended valuation process considering several context factors illustrated in Figure 3. The process steps in the light grey area represent the process steps that are covered by common existing valuation literature. The existing literature is focusing mainly on the selection and application of the suitable valuation methodology (compare especially Benninga & Sarig, 1997, pp. 79–86; compare also Damodaran, 2002; Koller et al., 2005).

The following sub-sections depict the process steps and context factors in more detail.

6.1.1 Process Steps

The following descriptions sum up the identified basic process steps for a valuation process.

Methodology selection

The first step in a valuation seems to be the selection of a suitable valuation methodology based on the context factors *existing data*, *understanding of* value, *comprehensibility of the methodology*, and *application costs of the methodology*. This process step is in accordance to existing literature on valuation as this literature is usually describing the rationales and application of different valuation methodologies as starting point (e.g., Damodaran, 2002; Koller et al., 2005).

Detailed data collection and interpretation

Based on the selected methodology (or methodologies, if more than one is selected for the valuation) valuators decide on the data to collect and to apply with the valuation methodology. This process step also includes the interpretation of the collected data, the creation of assumptions and the identification of relevant proxy data to derive those assumptions from. The identification and interpretation of proxy data is an important step for the appraisal of complex constructs such as innovation capability or risks. As such constructs are difficult to measure directly, valuators try to identify proxy data that allows them via interpretation to estimate required values and input factors for the valuation methodology.

> Die meiste Arbeit steckt im Daten heranschaffen und bewerten, plausibilisieren drin. Das Bewerten ist dann nur der Knopfdruck. Der wesentliche Aufwand ist schon das Daten-Zusammentragen, Überlegen, passt es, passt es nicht, Rückfragen, Sich-

Versichern und so weiter. Das Bewerten ist ja dann nur noch eine Formel. (Auditing professional)

In the case of innovation potential, the detailed data selection and collection can be assumed as to work with the following two steps:[14]

(1) Identifying proxy data for the innovation capability
(2) Identifying data to appraise the probability that already defined innovation projects are completed successfully (or the risk that they are not) and to assess the impact of these projects on the firm

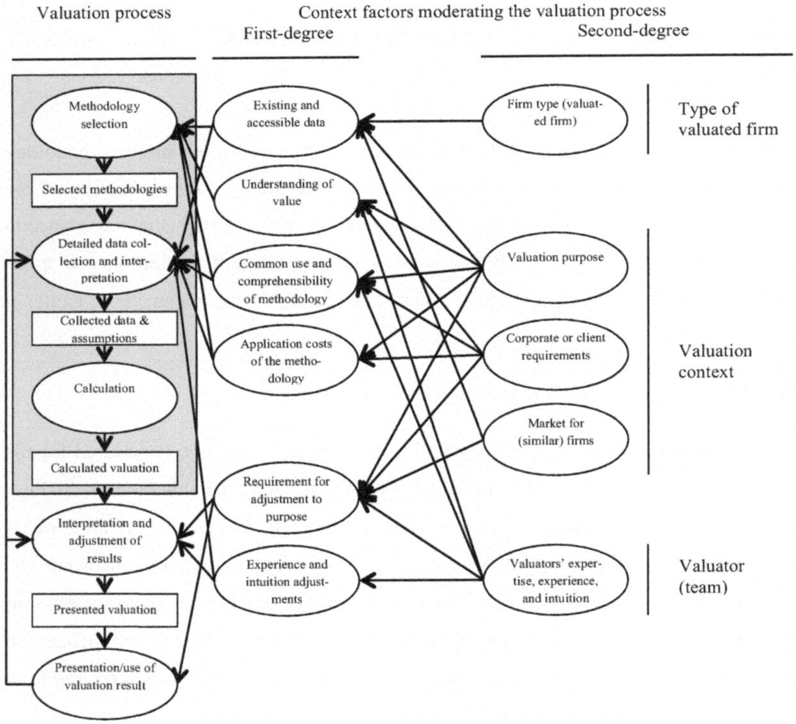

Figure 3. Valuation Process

14 These steps are according to the concepts of innovation potential as defined in chapter 3.2.5.

Calculation

Following data collection and creation of assumptions, the next process step is the application of the chosen methodologies with the collected data and with the assumptions built on the collected data. The result of this calculation is, in many cases, understood as being "the valuation" within the respective valuation literature.

Interpretation and adjustment of results

The next process step after the calculation of the valuation according to the selected methodology has not been covered in detail by existing literature. This study's empirical results indicate that after a quantitative calculation has been conducted, its result is interpreted, judged and adjusted based on qualitative considerations.

One of the factors that influence this adjustment could for example be the price that is demanded by the selling party in the context of a firm acquisition.

> *Die Bewertung wird also dem geforderten Preis angepasst?* Genau, das ist ja ein Klassiker. *Das heißt, die wissenschaftlich angehauchte Methode mit ihrer extremen Scheingenauigkeit dient dann dazu, das zu rechtfertigen?* Ja. Das ist kein Problem der Methode. Das ist immer ein Problem der Annahmen." (Corporate venture capital professional)

Another interviewee references that a strategic premium is added after the quantitative calculation, which he describes as difference between "value", the result of a calculated valuation and "price", understood as the value that is an external party willing to pay at the end of the valuation and negotiation process.

> Und dann gibt es noch einen Unterschied zwischen Wert und Preis. Es gibt immer noch eine strategische Prämie. (Auditing professional)

Interpretation and adjustment of the calculated value seem to be especially important for valuating innovation potential of a combined firm after an acquisition.

> Da gibt es schon solche Überlegungen und die sind auch durchaus in Business Plänen hier abgelegt. Die sind aber quasi ein Backup zu dem anderen Business Plan, der wesentlich mehr „down to earth" ist. (Industry business development professional)

Also, in the case of a strategic investment, effects of the transaction are valued separately, understood as "justification" (German: "Rechtfertigung"), and not put in the original value calculation.

> *Die Vorteile, die sich aus dem anteilmäßigen Besitz ergeben, stellen sie dann nur qualitativ da?* Nein, auch quantitativ. Wir sagen z. B.: Durch das Produkt kann die . . . [Firma] 10 Millionen einsparen. Das ist allerdings keine belastbare Zahl und entspricht natürlich auch nicht dem Gedanken einer Synergieberechnung. Man kann nur sagen: Wenn wir da nicht investieren, kommen wir vielleicht gar nicht so einfach an die Technologie dran oder, wenn wir da nicht investieren, würden wir mit denen gar nicht kooperieren und Umsätze von XY machen. Für die Investition machen wir dann eine Standalone-Bewertung und für die Rechtfertigung gibt es dann den Business Case mit Kooperationswertbeitrag. Der steht aber isoliert daneben. Es gibt keinen Business Case, wo das dann drin ist. *Das bedeutet, er steht auf der nächsten Folie?* Genau, fände ich auch sehr grenzwertig, das anders zu machen, weil wir den Einfluss nicht haben und weil uns das Ding nicht gehört. (Corporate venture capital professional)

Presentation/use of valuation results

The last process step that has also not been identified or investigated in current literature is the use of the documented valuation results. Those results are usually used in the context of the purpose they have been created. In the case of an acquisition, the valuations are used in most cases to support the negotiations of the price to acquire or sell an asset.

The investigation indicates that each negotiating party tries to frame the common understanding of a firm's prospects to achieve a targeted price (compare chapter 3.4.2). Creating and highlighting according assumptions before or in the negotiation are a major way to influence this common understanding.

> Der Eine glaubt halt, dass das Produkt in 2011 rauskommt, der Andere glaubt 2012, aber das sind halt die Annahmen, die jeder Bewertung zugrunde liegen. Der eine hat aus bestimmten Gründen, weil er eben dieses Unternehmen als Vergleichsunternehmen oder diese Produkte als Vergleichsprodukte herangezogen hat oder die Marktentwicklung so sieht, eben die Entscheidung getroffen und der andere die. Die richtige Lösung gibt es nicht. Jeder basiert Dinge auf seinen Annahmen, die er dann zu rechtfertigen hat. Klar kann es divergieren. Aber man versucht natürlich im Rahmen

> der Verhandlung mögliche Käufer in die Richtung zu treiben, die man selber sieht, um den Wert zu bekommen, den man erzielen möchte. D.h. man versucht Überzeugungsarbeit zu leisten für die eigenen Annahmen. Und dafür helfen Informationen. (Investment bank professional)

> Ich möchte vermeiden, dass der potentielle Käufer einen Abschlag in der Bewertung macht, weil er bestimmte Potenziale nicht sieht. *Sieht er die Potenziale nicht oder glaubt er sie nicht?* Beides. Deswegen gibt es ja dann auch nochmal Management Präsentationen. Das ist auch das Thema Glaubwürdigkeit im Prozess. (Investment bank professional)

> Und letztlich muss man das für den Kunden auch, denn man wird dafür bezahlt, dass man Gewinnmaximierung betreibt und die positiven Aspekte hervorhebt, ohne natürlich das Negative unter den Tisch zu kehren. (Investment bank professional)

It is obvious that the targeted price for the negotiation is able to influence the assumptions underlying the valuation and thereby the result of the valuation.

6.1.2 First-Degree Context Factors

As described above, certain process steps are moderated by context factors. What are these context factors and how do they influence certain process steps?

Existing and accessible data

Existing data influences the selection of appropriate methodologies and in a later valuation process stage the detailed selection of data to consider within the valuation. The data in this case comprehends all available data or data that can be generated by analyses, e.g. historical financial data, organizational data, or market analyses.

The investigation also highlights that the scope accessible information might change during the valuation process as the selling party is handing out more information to the valuators. This process is able to influence valuation results as for example bidding parties in the early stages of an acquisition proposal do not get access to all relevant information compared to the ones still present in later stages. Thus, information asymmetry with regard to the target firm's quality (Akerlof, 1970) seems to decrease during the valuation and negotiation process. This should be especially relevant for information about the innovation potential as this information can be regarded as either more confidential or complex to collect.

> Es muss grundsätzliches Interesse an einem Kauf bestehen. Man möchte vermeiden, dass Wettbewerber Informationen durch den Prozess rausziehen. . . . Als Käufer möchte ich so viel möglich über das Unternehmen wissen, weil, je mehr Infos ich habe, um so genauer kann ich meine Bewertung machen. Als Verkäufer möchte ich auch den Maximalpreis bekommen in einem Verkauf. Und jetzt habe ich einen schmalen Grat: Wie viel Information gebe ich dem Käufer, damit er auch auf den Wert kommt, den ich haben möchte, und was kann ich ihm nicht geben, weil es einfach zu confidential ist auf mein eigenes Business bezogen. Weil, wenn jemand etwas über mein Unternehmen nicht weiß, übersieht er vielleicht Wertpotenziale, die er in seine Bewertung nicht mit einrechnet, und kommt zu einem niedrigeren Preis. Ich muss ihm helfen zu meinem Preis zu kommen. Und helfen kann ich ihm mit Informationen. Da muss ich natürlich abwägen: Was kann ich ihm geben und in welcher Stufe des Prozesses kann ich es ihm geben? Wenn noch zehn Bieter im Prozess sind, dann wird die Information natürlich weniger sein. (Investment bank professional)

Understanding of value

The understanding of what “value” means, is essential for the selection of the valuation methodology. Generally, one can differentiate between two understandings:

(1) Value derives from the expected incomes that an owner receives from having control over an asset. This understanding leads to the so-called “intrinsic value” of an asset or a “fundamental valuation”.
(2) Value is the price that another party is willing to pay for an asset.

These two views are reflected in the chosen methodologies as described in chapter 3.5 and the respective literature referred to in that chapter. This study’s empirical data indicates that these two different understandings of value are on the one hand existent in practice and on the other are also a decisive factor in the valuation process and should majorly influence the choice of the according valuation methodology.

> Man muss bei einer Bewertung zwei Dinge sehen: Das Eine ist das, was Sie bewerten im Sinne einer Innenbetrachtung und das Zweite ist: Welchen Preis bieten Sie dafür? Das unterscheidet sich substanziell. Das Eine ist: Was steckt theoretisch da drin. Und das Zweite ist: Was erkennt einer von außen? (Auditing professional)

> Letztlich ist ein Unternehmen das wert, was der Markt oder jemand bereit ist zu bezahlen. Alles, was wir tun, ist im Prinzip eine Annäherung daran. (Investment bank professional)

Thus, the choice of the applied valuation methodologies seems to be influenced not only by the perceived precision or accuracy of the methodology, but also on the purpose of the valuation. That relationship is explained in further detail in the following sub-section about the second-order context factors.

Common use and comprehensibility of methodology

The comprehensibility of the methodology seems to be a major factor influencing methodology selection as they seem not only to be easier to apply, but their results seem also be better communicable within a negotiation or client presentation.

> Dieses Verfahren [Entscheidungsbäume] hat den Vorteil, dass sie viel besser verständlich sind und sicherer in der Anwendung, weniger Fehlerquellen. (Investment bank professional)

In this context, the selection of the methodology seems also to be influenced by corporate or client requirements. Corporate standards and clients of professional service firms that offer valuation services seem to use most common methods to valuate firms.

> Aber das gibt halt auch den gewissen Komfort. Das ist dieses Herdenelement vielleicht auch, dass man es nicht so viel anders macht wie die Anderen. Da ist was Gefährliches drin, das sehe ich auch so, aber das ist ein gängiger Ansatz zu sehen, was machen die Anderen. (Investment bank professional)
>
> *Kann man sagen, dass man mit NPV- oder DCF-Berechnungen wesentlich näher an in Konzernen gängigen Investitionsrechnungsverfahren, die auch einem Aktionär vorgelegt werden müssen, liegt und Methoden wie die Venture Capital Methode nicht vermittelbar sind?* Genau. Völlig richtig. . . . Wenn wir dem Komitee einen Fall vorstellen, haben wir den vorher mit den Controllern diskutiert und im . . . Konzern sind die DCF und die Multiple Methode die Methoden der Methoden. Wenn sie da nichts haben, brauchen Sie gar nicht weiterreden. Das ist schlicht ein Konzern-Methoden-Thema und ich vermute mal, dass es in anderen Konzernen auch keine anderen Methoden gibt. (Corporate venture capital professional)

Application costs of the methodology

The selection of the applied methodologies seems to depend on the existing data. The availability of data seems to depend on the time effort that valuators are putting into the data gathering and analysis. Sometimes, the time for the valuation is restricted by external factors:

> Die Quintessenz ist, dass vieles von dem, was wir tun, vom Zweck des Projektes und dann auch, - ganz offenes Visier -, von der Zahlungsbereitschaft des Mandanten abhängt. Natürlich kann es manchmal sinnvoll sein, Realoptionen zu rechnen. Wenn der Kunde aber nur 30.000 € bezahlt, werde ich das nicht tun. (Auditing professional)

> Es ist die Frage, ob man alle nötigen Informationen aus den Management- und Experteninterviews und genug Zeit zur Anwendung einer Sicherheitsäquivalenzmethode bekommt. In einem exklusiven Verfahren schon eher. (Auditing professional)

> In ganz, ganz seltenen Fällen kommt es dann mal zu einer Monte-Carlo-Simulation. Aber das ist auch wirklich relativ selten. . . . Ich hab das selbst erst einmal gemacht. *Hat das der Kunde gefordert oder hätten Sie das auch selbst gemacht?* Jaja, der Kunde hatte das gefordert. *Hätten Sie das auch gemacht, wenn er das nicht gefordert hätte?* Es war so 'ne Situation, wo man nicht wusste, in welche Richtung das geht und da war es für uns gut, das Ganze mal so zu machen, aber für die meisten Fälle ist das einfach over-engineered. Damit gewinnt man am Ende auch nicht mehr. Wie Sie sagen: GIGO [garbage in – garbage out]. Man weiß es einfach nicht besser. Man kann es nicht besser greifen. (Investment bank professional)

> Sie arbeiten schon oft unter Zeitdruck, weil oft gesagt wird: Das Unternehmen braucht jetzt Geld. Jetzt ist die Finanzierungsrunde. Steigt jetzt oder in den nächsten zwei Monaten ein! Ansonsten ist das Fenster zu und der Zug fährt. (Corporate venture capital professional)

Requirement for adjustment to purpose

Adjustments made afterwards to the calculated valuation are something that DAMODARAN describes as: "The market must know something I don't: The market price magnet" (Damodaran, 2009, p. 278). Based on the empirical investigation it is obvious that market price considerations and the supply of money in the market for firms can influence, bias, or adjust the results of the valuation.

> Und das ist das Spannungsfeld, in dem bei uns die Akquisitionen laufen, dass der Verkäufer mit [Umsatz oder EBITDA] Multiples daherkommt, von einer Rating- oder Bewertungsagentur, die sagt, das und das wäre ein gerechtfertigter Kaufpreis. Wir haben auf unserer Seite die Überlegung: Was macht das Unternehmen an NPV, wenn es ohne uns, und wie würde es ausschauen, wenn es mit uns geht? Irgendwo dazwischen findet man sich dann, was man bereit ist zu zahlen. Und wenn die Erwartungshaltung des Käufers unterhalb dieses Wertes ist, dann wird es ein Geschäft. Wenn sich das nicht ausgeht, dann wird es kein Geschäft. So simpel ist das. (Industry business development professional)

> Es gibt immer wieder Marktphasen, wo es erhebliche Irrationalitäten in der Bewertung gibt. Das hatten wir 2000/2001 und im Vorjahr. Und immer wenn der Controller Bauchgrimmen kriegt und meint, die Werte sind gehypt, dann ist normalerweise die Zeit für eine Blase die platzt. *Liegen diese Hypes daran, dass bestimmte Firmen dann knapp sind?* Nein, ich glaube, das ist mehr so dieses Lemminge-Thema. Es war die letzten Jahre unheimlich viel Geld im Markt und das Geld ist ja jetzt vielen ausgegangen. Prompt gehen die Bewertungen nach unten. Geld schafft Luft in den Bewertungen. Liquidität. (Corporate venture capital professional)

Experience and intuition adjustments

The last identified influence factor is the valuator's experience to deal with risk and uncertainty and create reasonable assumptions. Also referred to as "gut feeling" by one of the interviewees. It seems that this "gut feeling" is able to influence valuation decisions especially in the context of innovation potential.

> Man hat irgendwie so ein „gut feeling", dass man sagt: Die schaffen das. Und wenn ich am Ende meinen Preis abgebe, dann basiere ich meinen Preis vielleicht eher auf dem Upside-Case als auf dem Base- oder dem Downside-Case. Das sind dann so versteckte Dinge, die irgendwo mein Gefühl für die ganze Sache beeinflussen. Man kennt das ja auch: Wir haben unterschiedliche Kunden beraten, die dann irgendwann gesagt haben: Ich muss das Unternehmen haben. Wir sagen dann: Hmm, das ist ein bisschen teuer. Aber die haben ein gutes Gefühl dabei und ich glaube, dann spielt das eine Rolle. (Investment bank professional)

6.1.3 Second-Degree Context Factors

The first-degree context factors can be compiled to three major second-degree context factors (compare Figure 3): The *type of the valuated firm*, the *valuation context*, and the *valuator as person or team* with his/her/their personal capabilities.

Type of valuated firm

As stated in the previous section, the valuated firm's type according to the types described in chapter 4.2.1 seems to be a major influence factor on the valuation approach and especially on the choice of the valuation methodology. Details on the differences according to these firm types are depicted in the chapters 6.2-6.5.

Valuation context

The valuation context can be divided into three major context factors: The *valuation purpose*, *corporate or client requirements*, and the *market for similar firms*.

The first important factor that influences methodology selection, but also other process steps in a valuation seems to be the *valuation purpose*. The purpose of a valuation can for example be to facilitate buying or selling an asset or providing a neutral value assessment. The implications of this purpose can be found in the understanding of what value is (Does the value derive from fundamental capabilities and income expectations or from the price the market is willing to pay?), the comprehensibility of the methodology (Does the methodology facilitate justifying a certain targeted price?), application costs (Do the benefits from using a methodology compensate for the costs to apply it?), and the market adjustment (Does the valuation facilitate justifying a certain targeted price? Should the calculated valuation be reevaluated and revised, as it does not seem to reflect the market price?) It seems obvious that the valuation purpose therefore majorly influences the selection of certain valuation methodologies.

Corporate or client requirements with regard to comprehensibility, application costs, and even the understanding of value seem to be foremost a major influence on the selection of certain valuation methodologies and data collection efforts.

The *market for (similar) firms* influences valuation in two ways: First it enables the use of marked-based valuation methodologies such as multiples. If a market exists, it should be easier to find comparable firms or firm transaction and to perform conclusions by analogy. Second, the market for similar firms is able to bias valuations or adjust them after the valuation calculation as valuators are influenced by market prices or easy or cheap access to financial means.

Valuator (team)

The last major impact factor seems to be the valuator him/herself or the team of valuators and his/her experience and/or "intuition" to appraise complex resources, deal with risk and uncertainty, appraise the trustfulness of information providers, and create reasonable assumptions. Further personal characteristics such as education with regard to valuation should also influence which methodologies he/she prefers or expects to be common ground or his/her understanding of value.

Summing the discussion up, the valuation process seems to be influences by several context factors with effects on methodology selection, application of methodologies, data collection, or after-valuation-adjustments.

6.2 Valuation of Idea Firms

As stated in chapter 4.2.1 an idea firm can be characterized as a firm in the very early stage of its lifecycle. In many cases, only an idea and a team of founders exist at the time of a valuation. At this time in their firm's lifecycle, the team of founders is often looking for funding to implement their product, service, technology, or business model idea. Venture capital professionals valuate the future prospects of such idea firms to determine, if an investment in an idea firm has the chance to lead to positive returns in the future. They also valuate such a firm to determine how much of an idea firm's future value they should receive at the end of their investment period in exchange for their current investment and the risks they take.

6.2.1 Methodologies

The following sections depict the methodologies that idea firm valuators use to appraise an appropriate value for such a company.

Innovation projects

(1) For early business ideas, some valuators do not seem to rely on formal mathematical methodologies too much. Instead they try to appraise the future prospects of these ideas by *patterns and/or experience*.

> I think, end of the day, it is a lot of personal intuition when you invest and then, once you invested, getting the right team and getting the right people involved. . . . A lot

> of what they say they do in venture capital is pattern looking. We see so much that when we see patterns and are building on these patterns. (Venture capital professional)

> *Do you use some kind of formal method like DCF?* Not normally because of the stage we are investing in, at least in my group. It's too early. . . . If it's a later stage investment, which we don't do as much, we might look at a financial model, but not typically. (Venture capital professional)

Another venture capital professional states: “Wir machen ‘Finance for Babys’”.

(2) This study’s empirical data indicates that *hurdle rate approaches* seem to be widely used to valuate idea firms quantitatively. This methodology starts with the fundamental question: “How big can that business be?” (Venture capital professional). Valuators appraise the business situation of an idea firm in a future period or estimate its future value by determining an “exit multiple” as potential sales price using the market approach. This means, they take the future state of the idea firm and compare it with more or less similar firms, which are at their present state comparable with the future state of the idea firm. After this, they discount this future value: “Wir machen eine Exit-Bewertung nach 8-10 Jahren Investment. . . . Wir erwarten einen IRR [internal rate of return] von 50%.” (Venture capital professional)

(2a) One methodology to determine the future business situation is to *estimate the possible market size top-down* from a customer’s perspective.

> Also man versucht erst mal über eine Wettbewerbsanalyse herauszufinden, wie groß der Markt überhaupt ist. Also über eine Abschätzung der Marktgröße machen wir das, gerne bottom-up. Wie viele Kunden gibt es, die das benötigen? Was wären die bereit dafür zu bezahlen? Wo sitzen die? Und dann multipliziert man das aus und kommt auf eine Marktgröße. Und da muss man auch schon mal den Wert abschätzen, den das Produkt bei den Kunden potenziell generiert. Bei uns wird immer aus Kundensicht überlegt. (Venture capital professional)

> Einer der wichtigsten Indikatoren sind die Google Such-Volumina für uns. Wir schauen uns an: Jemand möchte jetzt beispielsweise einen Online-Shop für Schuhe aufbauen. Dann ist das noch lange nichts Innovatives, weil es könnte sein, dass den die Welt nicht braucht. Wenn aber ein Google Such-Volumen in dem Kontext da ist, dann ist das auf jeden Fall eine relevante Idee. . . . Das ist der erste Indikator, den wir

> uns angucken. Auch vor allem, um die Größe des Marktes einzuschätzen. Nicht nur die Frage: Ist da überhaupt ein Markt? Sondern es geht auch um die Frage: Wie groß ist der? . . . . *Ihr geht strikt von der Nachfrage aus?* Ja. (Business angel investor)

(2b) The second one is the *use of product analogies*. Valuators compare the characteristic of the innovation in development with other successful or less successful innovations:

> Man hat zwar ein paar Eckdaten. Es gibt Produktverwandschaften. Aber man muss schon irgendwie selber feststellen, ob zum Beispiel eine Trader-Plattform zukünftig benutzt wird oder nicht. (Venture capital professional)

> Wenn es woanders funktioniert, warum soll es nicht dort funktionieren? Also dieser Transfer über Landesgrenzen hinweg von Ideen oder Innovationen. Meiner Meinung nach auch ein starker Indikator dafür, wie viel die Wert ist, die Innovation oder auch, ob es eine Innovation ist. Das wären meine ersten Gedankenschritte. (Business angel investor)

(2c) The third one is the *market approach* as basis for a financial valuation. Another valuator puts it that way: "We look at comparables in the market." (Venture capital professional).

(3) Additionally, business cases based on *bottom-up planning* seem to be used to quantify the revenue, cost, and margin development of an innovation project.

> *D.h.: Ihr habt so eine Art Finanz- und Liquiditätsplan*? Ja. Genau. Der wirklich die einzelnen KPIs abbildet bzw. die Methoden und ein Gesamtbild liefert. . . . Ganz vereinfacht gesagt: Machen wir beides: Also wir machen Top-Down, Bottom-Up. (Business angel investor)

Innovation capability

Valuators seem to understand and, thus, *value innovation capability as the capability to execute an innovation project from product development to commercialization*. This capability, credited as "execution capability" by an interviewee, comprises the capability to develop the product or service and enables the firm to commercialize and implement a technically developed product, a conceptually developed service or a new process.

> Also Erfolg wird wie folgt definiert oder parametrisiert: Erstens: Man versucht, das Unternehmen versucht, bestimmte Marktanteile zu gewinnen und Umsätze aufzubauen, wenn es ganz jung anfängt - über ein Produkt oder eine Dienstleistung oder

> sonst eine innovative Situation, die es im Unternehmen gibt. Marktanteile und Umsatz zu gewinnen. Wie geht das? Einerseits durch die Produkteigenschaften bzw. die Innovation selbst und dann auch die Fähigkeit des Unternehmers, die sogenannte Execution, also die Möglichkeit des Management die PS, wenn man es mal einfach sagt, auf die Straße zu kriegen. Also das umzusetzen, was sich im Business Plan vorgenommen worden ist. (Venture capital professional)

(1) One approach to value this innovation capability is to estimate, if an idea firm's management is able to support the needed revenue growth. Necessary management skills comprise developing the idea firm from a firm with only a conceptual idea via a firm with first small revenues to a profitable growth or mature firm. This capability can be included in a valuation by using an *income approach and determining a growth curve* in dependence on the estimated management capabilities and market environment.

> Da wenden wir DCF an und sagen: Wenn wir jetzt da reinwachsen, dann würden wir mit einer angenommenen Wachstumskurve, die wir über das Unternehmen legen, die Umsätze steigern. Da gibt es wieder zwei Parameter: Einerseits ist es wieder die Fähigkeit des Managements, überhaupt ein Unternehmen zu organisieren, dass überhaupt ein Wachstum zustande kommt. Die Prozesse richtig aufsetzen, egal, ob das Lieferprozesse, Entwicklungsprozesse, ob das die Buchhaltung ist oder auch Mahnverfahren plus Verwaltung der Ersatzteile. Was es halt alles so gibt. Würde da die Wahrscheinlichkeit überlegen. Da ist ein wachstumsbegrenzender Faktor gegeben auf der Umsatzkurve. Und würde dann nochmal abschätzen, wenn wir die Marktgröße wissen, wie lange es dauert, um von Marktseite da überhaupt rein zu kommen. (Venture capital professional)

(2) To evaluate the management's capabilities, detailed data does not seem to be available many times; therefore, *assessing the credibility of the management team* seems to be an important methodology in idea firm valuation.

> Das zweite Thema ist: Wie gut sind die Leute, die es anfangen? Das sind auch nur lauter weiche Faktoren, die man zwar durch Referencing einigermaßen erhärten kann, aber faktisch muss man glauben, dass der Hans-Jürgen Schmidt das dann auch liefert, was er in seinem Business-Plan drinstehen hat. (Venture capital professional)

> Bei Management-Teams, die komplett sind, kann man über die einzelnen Persönlichkeiten Referencing machen. Man kann mal schauen: Sind die im Markt bekannt?

> Man spricht mit denen mit bestimmten Interview-Methoden, um rauszufinden, ob sie das alles, was in ihrem Lebenslauf steht, auch gemacht haben und bekommt dann, wenn man das oft genug gemacht hat, auch ein Gefühl dafür, ob er das, was er sich in seinem Business-Plan vorgenommen hat, auch leisten kann oder nicht. Da wird man ab und zu überrascht, aber die Wahrscheinlichkeit nimmt stark zu, wenn man es ab und zu gemacht hat, dass man die Leute schon einigermaßen einschätzen kann. (Venture capital professional)

Transaction effects

(1) Valuation professionals seem to value idea firms with the effects of the transaction or investment already anticipated. They do a so-called "*post money valuation*". The investment or transaction is anticipated in the future states that serves as the basis for valuation methodologies such as the hurdle rate approach depicted in the innovation projects section above.

> Es gibt eine Advanced-Dreisatz-Methode: Man rechnet ja in Zukunft irgendwas aus. Was das für einen Umsatz machen wird. Dann irgendwie Peer-Group-Umsatz-Multiples oder EBIT-Multiples. Kommt dann auf eine Unternehmensbewertung und macht dann mit der vereinfachten Rückwärtsrechnung und Abzinsungsfaktoren einen Unternehmenswert fest. Der Wert, den man dann festmacht, ist dann quasi der jetzige Wert plus das Investment schon, weil: Ohne das Investment kann der zukünftige Wert ja gar nicht erreicht werden. Also hat man jetzt eine Post-Money-Bewertung. Jetzt nehmen wir mal an, das Unternehmen ist jetzt 10 Millionen wert, wir geben 5 Millionen rein, um das zu erreichen. Dann kriegen wir 50% des Unternehmens und 50% ist die Idee wert oder das Setup oder das, was es jetzt schon gibt. Dann hat jeder 50% und so wird dann im Endeffekt eine Unternehmensbewertung durchgeführt. (Venture Capital Professional)

Risk and uncertainty

(1) Risk seems not only to be mitigated by a venture capital investor's portfolio[15], but the valuation of each single investment includes the riskiness of future prospects by the means of a demanded *discount or hurdle rate*.

[15] Venture capitalists seem to hold a portfolio of investments usually. Because the portfolio is an external factor to the valuation of a specific asset, the portfolio methodology itself is not listed as risk valuation or mitigation methodology.

> *Das heißt, das Risiko des Portfolios wäre dann in den 50% [hurdle rate] mit drin, aber der wesentliche Aspekt ist eher, welche Unternehmen ich für das Portfolio aussuche?* So ist es. Das heißt, die müssen alle das Potenzial auf einen Verzehn- oder Verfünffacher haben. Aus allen, die das Potenzial haben, dahin zu kommen, tritt das dann doch nur bei zwei bis drei ein. (Venture capital professional)

> Die Wahrscheinlichkeiten liegen in der Umsatzentwicklung. Diese Wahrscheinlichkeit schätzen wir dann auf zwei Ebenen ab und generieren daraus einen Abzinsungszinssatz für die Unternehmensbewertung. (Venture capital professional)

(2) The second methodology that practitioners seem to use is the *assignment of different risk profiles and discount rates to different stages of an idea's tangibility* or to different development stages of single product company's product. Especially for evaluing young pharmaceutical firms, practitioners seem to use average probabilities known for different stages of pharmaceutical development to estimate the success probability of a new pharma product. Venture capitalists differentiate between seed stage and later stage or to put it another way, they consider, if there still exists a risk that a technology as an intermediate step to a sellable product cannot be developed.

> We use a hurdle rate of 30-40% at least, usually at least 40%. It depends on how early it is. . . . *So the hurdle rate is going up, depending on how early it is?* Yes. Usually, cause there is still technology risk. *Technology risk is the risk that the technology can't be developed?* Yes. (Venture capital professional)

> *Wie beziehen Sie Risiko zum Beispiel in eine DCF mit ein?* Es gibt ja generell den WACC, den ich bei Seed sehr hoch ansetze und bei Later Stage etwas niedriger. Das ist ein genereller Risikofaktor. Den nutzen wir sehr intensiv. Wir haben da auch ganz genau definierte Stufen. Also wir machen keine beta-Analyse. Wir kalkulieren jetzt den WACC nicht, wie er im Lehrbuch vorgeschrieben ist. Wir sagen halt: Seed ist 25% und Buy-Out [Later Stage] ist 15% und das passen wir über die Jahre immer mal wieder an, weil sich die Marktzinsen ja verändern. Aber das wort „beta" ist hier im Hause schon lange nicht mehr gefallen. (Corporate venture capital professional)

> *Wie kommen Sie auf den Kaufpreis?* Das ist ein Henne-Ei-Problem. Wenn gar kein Kaufpreis feststeht, würden wir „straight forward" eine Diskontierung machen. Da gehe ich mit einem Satz rein, wo ich sage: Das ist Early Stage, 50%, wupp, und dann kommt ein Kaufpreis. (Corporate venture capital professional)

(3) The methodology practitioners use to handle uncertainty is the *scenario analysis*. In contrast to risk, no probabilities can be assigned to uncertain outcomes. The scenario approach accompanies the methodologies mentioned before by valuing firms under the preconditions of different assumption bundles (compare chapter 4.3).

> *Nehmen Sie auch auf der Cash-Flow-Seite Risikoabschätzungen vor, indem sie zum Beispiel Szenarien bilden?* Ja, da werden meistens drei Szenarien gebildet: Worst Case, Realistic Case und Best Case. Wir wollen immer komplette Planung haben, das heißt, da ist die Bilanz drin, die GuV und die Cash-Flow-Rechnung. Da werden die Top-Lines, um die es ja hauptsächlich geht, unter Annahmen geplant, das heißt: Wie viel Stück Dioden werden wann verkauft? In welchem Jahr? Dann kommt die Kostenseite. Wie viel sind die Fertigungskosten? Wie viele Leute brauche ich da dazu? Wie viel Support muss ich geben? Wie ist der zeitliche Verlauf? Und dann gibt es ja dann ein Ergebnis und das Ergebnis wird mit bestimmten Zahlungszielen versehen und kommt dann zum Cash-Flow und dann kann man daraus auch die Bilanz entwickeln. Solche Planungen gibt es eben in Worst, Best und Realistic Case. Und dann muss man sich in Diskussionen mit dem Management an den Case annähern, den wir alle glauben zum Schluss. (Venture capital professional)

(4) Another approach to assess and value the potential of *management team augmentation*. Venture capitalists use management enhancement and staff augmentation measures to mitigate risks and uncertainties associated with an idea firm's future development. On the one hand, these measures could be reflected on the cost, investment, and margin sides of all valuation approaches, on the other hand, this kind of risk mitigation seems to be assessed only qualitatively in many cases and not considered in a quantitative valuation.

> *How do you deal with risks?* That is what our business is about: Mitigating risk along the way. Bringing in a new CEx. We have a lot of times, where we change out the CEO or we're bringing a new sales force on or we know someone from the technical side and bring them in. It's part of connecting people. Even in terms of science: If we feel, they could be complemented by some research going on in another lab at an another university or something like that, we'll make that connection. *Do you primarily mitigate risk after you have invested?* Well, before we make the investment, we negotiate on valuation and things like that, but after we made the investment that's not for discussion anymore. Maybe in another round the valuation might be discussed.

> But, once you're in a company, you already negotiated on valuation and other similar preferences. (Venture capital professional)

(5) As shown in the innovation capability section, *assessing the credibility of the management team* is another important methodology in assessing and dealing with risks. One investment bank interviewee describes this mechanism exemplarily:

> Und bei diesen kleineren Unternehmen, wo das wirklich der Fall ist [bei denen Innovation eine große Rolle spielt], denke ich, ist es so, dass selbst die Leute, die diese Innovationen vorantreiben, das nicht genau beziffern können. Und von daher habe ich auch keine Erwartungen an irgendwelche Zahlen oder Material, das mir hilft, das Ganze besser zu verstehen. Ich muss dann auf die Einschätzung dieser Person vertrauen und dann selber nochmal darüber nachdenken und abwägen, was die Wahrscheinlichkeit betrifft, dass diese Zahlen, so wie sie mir präsentiert wurden, auch wirklich eintreffen. (Investment bank professional)

(6) An unexpected approach is *the assessment of the future business environment* that the idea firm is making business in. This approach seems to make sense though because a young company trying to implement an innovative idea might be much more sensible to macroeconomic changes than a large mature corporation. A venture capital professional puts it this way: "The wave is bigger than the boat."

(7) The last used approach to assess risk and uncertainty is to *leverage the knowledge of other parties* that evaluate the same idea firm. These can be other investors competing for the same investment share or a different, additional investment share in the idea firm. The challenge for the investment professional lies in the appraisal, if different valuations are caused by market dynamics or by better information or methods.

> Ich bin zu meinen fünf [als Bewertung] gekommen, weil ich das Risiko als äußerst hoch einschätze, dass das durchkommt. Man könnte auch acht sagen, wenn die Risikofaktoren nicht so hoch angesetzt werden. Jetzt kümmern sich viele der Investoren um das Thema, das heißt, manche haben acht berechnet, manche sechs, manche fünf und dann bildet sich so ein Preis und dann kann ich mir überlegen: Vielleicht ist der objektive Preis doch ein bisschen höher, weil... Da tun sich ja auch manchmal Syndikate zusammen, bezahlt ein bisschen mehr . . . der Exitwert ist doch, potenziell kann man was daraus bauen, was mehr Wert ist. Oder das Risiko ist nicht so hoch, ich muss das nicht so hoch abzinsen. *Das ist ja dann nochmal eine neue Datenquelle?*

> Das macht man unbewusst. Da wird zwar jeder sagen: Was soll denn das sein? Aber das ist irgendwie in der Praxis zuhause. Der sagt: Das eine Produkt, das du bei deiner Bewertung hast hinten runterfallen lassen, das sehe ich als absolutes Killerprodukt an. So werden die Diskussionen dann geführt. Oder er hat einfach Anlagedruck. Dann sollte man es nicht machen. Jeder Investment-Manager ist ein kleiner Sherlock Holmes da. Angucken, wie sich der ganze Markt bewegt. (Venture capital professional)

(8) Going back to the general approach to appraise idea firms, *experience* seems to play a major role for investment decision-making and evaluations of risks.

> I think, end of the day, it is a lot of personal intuition when you invest and then, once you invested, getting the right team and getting the right people involved. . . . A lot of what they say they do in venture capital is pattern looking. We see so much that when we see patterns and are building on these patterns. (Venture capital professional)

6.2.2 Information

The following sub-sections depict, which information idea firm valuators use to provide the previously presented methodologies with input data.

Innovation projects

(1) The first information valuators are looking for is the *use or value of an invention for potential customers*. This information serves as proxy for an invention's estimated success on the desired market.

> Das Schwierigste ist es, den Kundennutzen rauszukriegen. Dafür wird am Schluss bezahlt. (Venture capital professional)

> Wenn ich eine Laserdiode habe, die eine höhere Lichtleistung hat, dann kann ich mir überlegen: Was spart der Kunde durch die höhere Leuchtleistung ein oder kann er zusätzliche Produkte generieren? . . . . Dann kann ich aus dem Produktwert, den die Diode beim Kunden generiert, einen Umsatz für die Diode ausrechnen. (Venture capital professional)

(2) This customer value also comprises collecting information about the potential *customers' product lifecycles*.

> . . . und würde dann nochmal abschätzen, wenn wir die Marktgröße wissen, wie lange es dauert, um von Marktseite da überhaupt rein zu kommen. Das heißt: Wie lange braucht es, um Design in Phasen beim Kunden zu organisieren? Bei der Laserdiode zum Beispiel: Wie lange dauert es, bis die in ein Gerät reinkommt? Wie sind die Produktzyklen des Kunden? Und aus den Faktoren kann man dann eine potenzielle Wachstumsgeschwindigkeit des Unternehmens ausrechnen. (Venture capital professional)

(3) The other critical information is *the grade of differentiation that a new product or technology has to distinguish itself from competitors' products or technologies* and how long this differentiation will hold: ". . . and to see how differentiated it is. We take a look at the competitors in this case." (Venture capital professional)

(4) Further important data to consider when valuing running or started innovation projects is, if the result of the innovation project can be *protected against a quick margin erosion by patents*, if the result is technically easy to imitate. On the opposite, a critical question in innovation is, if the product in development infringes patents, which belong to other firms. Those can defer or impede the development.

> Und da ist es eher so, dass wir sagen: Schön, dass wir eigene Patente haben, die uns auch helfen können an ein paar Stellen. Aber manchmal ist es auch so, dass man aufpassen muss, dass man nicht auch in so ein paar Patentfallen reinkommt eher, dass alles irgendwie vermint ist in bestimmten Umfeldern. Und für die Patente gibt es keine Bewertung. Die führen ja zum Cash-Flow und sind dann in der Unternehmensbewertung mit drin, implizit mit drin. (Venture capital professional)

(5) Valuators collect information about *the state within the innovation process* of the innovation in development: "Wie weit ist das Produkt im Entwicklungsstadium? Ist ein Prototyp vorhanden?" (Venture capital professional)

Innovation capability

The major proxy to appraise the innovation capability of an idea firm seems to be the management and developer team. As mentioned in the methodologies section, valuators try to appraise the team for their "execution capability" and do this by investigating the credibility of the management team's claims in its business plan.

(1) Valuators seem to investigate or at least assume the *product development capabilities of the idea firm's team* (see statement below (2)).

(2) They also investigate, if the idea firm's team is able to *build a working firm* by implementing core business processes.

> *Welche Daten erheben Sie?* Von den Kernwertschöpfungsprozessen bis zu den banalen Dingen. Wenn das ganz junge Teams sind, dann muss man schon mal überlegen. Dann sind die meistens in der Produktentwicklung ganz stark drin. Das kann man denen auch zutrauen, dass sie das hinbekommen. Die ganzen banalen Prozesse, die eigentlich gar nicht so banal sind im Unternehmen ablauffähig und kosteneffizient hinzukriegen. (Venture capital professional)

(3) As can be seen in the next statement, valuators try to verify the team's capabilities by investigating the *management team's members' track records and references.*

> Bei Management-Teams, die komplett sind, kann man über die einzelnen Persönlichkeiten Referencing machen. Man kann mal schauen: Sind die im Markt bekannt? Man spricht mit denen mit bestimmten Interview-Methoden, um rauszufinden, ob sie das alles, was in ihrem Lebenslauf steht, auch gemacht haben und bekommt dann, wenn man das oft genug gemacht hat, auch ein Gefühl dafür, ob er das, was er sich in seinem Business-Plan vorgenommen hat, auch leisten kann oder nicht. Da wird man ab und zu überrascht, aber die Wahrscheinlichkeit nimmt stark zu, wenn man es ab und zu gemacht hat, dass man die Leute schon einigermaßen einschätzen kann. (Venture capital professional)

> Das zweite Thema ist: Wie gut sind die Leute, die es anfangen? Das sind auch nur lauter weiche Faktoren, die man zwar durch Referencing einigermaßen erhärten kann, aber faktisch muss man glauben, dass der Hans-Jürgen Schmidt das dann auch liefert, was er in seinem Business Plan drinstehen hat. Da kann man sagen: Die letzten fünf Jahre hat er die Ziele immer einigermaßen erreicht. Jetzt ganz neues Game. Wird das hinhauen? Weiß ich nicht. Da ist viel persönliche Einschätzung immer mit drin. (Venture capital professional)

Transaction effects

(1) Idea firm investors are often able to provide potential investment firms with their *network of contacts to other investors, distributors, or potential customers*. The value deriving from

this resource is included in the valuation as part of the underlying business case and the cash flows derived from the business case.

> Wenn [der VC-Investor] investiert, und Sie sind vorher nicht besonders bekannt gewesen und wollen jetzt einen Termin haben im Forschungszentrum bei BMW, dann helfen wir da meistens als Investoren mit, über unsere Kontakte und sagen: Lass den mal zur Tür rein zum Reden und nicht vom Pförtner wieder abweisen. Das heißt, die Investorennetzwerke gerade was das Finanzieren angeht, weitere Investoren finden oder auch bei der Personalsuche sind wirklich auch was wert, weil man eben schneller vorwärts kommt in dem ganzen Umfeld. Das richtig zu bewerten ist schwierig. Deswegen bewerten wir nur die Cashflows und sagen: Das ganze Netzwerk unterscheidet uns von den anderen Investoren und wird dann eher auf der weichen Schiene als Value miteingebracht. (Venture capital professional)

(2) Another information that seems to be considered in idea firms' valuation is the *network of potential buyers at the end of the investment*. This consideration can be associated to a market approach of valuation. Fundamental questions are: Is there a market for such firms or their developed technologies and capabilities at the end of the investment period? What price can be achieved for such a firm? "Wir sehen uns unser Netzwerk bekannter möglicher Käufer an." (Venture capital professional)

(3) Furthermore, the potential of *augmenting the management or founder team* can be brought in as relevant information.

> Da machen wir ab und zu mal Managementergänzungen. Das heißt, wir nehmen da bei so jungen Teams einen erfahrenen CFO oder COO mit rein, der sagt, er organisiert den Rest vom Unternehmen außerhalb des Produktumfelds und damit kriegen wir es einigermaßen in den Griff. (Venture capital professional)

Data sources

The information to valuate an idea firm seems to derive from three sources. Data given by the investment target's management, data gathered internally by the valuators at the investing firm, and data gathered from external sources.

(1) The information deriving from the acquisition target includes the idea firm's management's business plan and management interviews.
(2) The valuator's information seems to consist of his own industry experience.

(3) To check the consistency of their assumptions, professionals consult other idea firm investors' opinions. The venture capital investment process facilitates the exchange of information between investor and valuators of an idea firm because in many cases more than one investor bids or invests in an idea firm.

6.2.3 Key Findings and Discussion

The following paragraphs contain the summary of the empirical findings of how practitioners value idea firms.

Methodologies

Table 15 summarizes the 1st and 2nd order constructs as results of the empirical investigation. In the following paragraphs I will depict and discuss the 2nd order constructs as abstraction of the empirical investigation.

With regard to *innovation projects* practitioners seem to use majorly *qualitative assessments and analogical thinking*, such as searching for patterns based on their experiences. Methodological they also seem to base the valuation on a *future picture* of the firm and its business environment, i.e., they use an estimated market potential (total market size and market share for the new product or service) as basis for the valuation. To do so they seem to use majorly *analogical thinking on the product/service level* and compare the valuated idea firm's products with comparable products or the whole idea firm with comparable firms.

Innovation capability seems to be appraised by appraising the management or founder of the idea firm. This assessment seems to be done in two dimensions. The first dimension is the team's capability to continuously innovate further products or services for the idea firm and transform the firm from a single-product/service firm to a firm with a portfolio of products and services or keep the single product up-to-date. The second dimension is to assess the credibility of team with regard to its plans. The second dimension adds a trust component to the first dimension.

Table 15. Methodologies for the Valuation of Idea Firms

Dimensions	Valuation methodologies	
	Empirical data (1st order construct)	Abstraction (2nd order construct)
Innovation projects	(1) Patterns and/or experience	*Interpretation (qual.)*: Product/service development analogy
	(2) Hurdle rate approach	*Calculation*: Start from future state
	(2a) Top-down estimation of future market size	*Interpretation (quant.)*: Top-down market potential
	(2b) Analogies with comparable product developments	*Interpretation (quant.)*: Product/service development analogy
	(2c) Analogies with other firms (market approach)	*Interpretation (qual.)*: Firm analogy
	(3) Bottom-up revenue/cost/margin analysis	*Interpretation (quant.)*: Bottom-up/break-even analysis
Innovation capability	(1) Income approach with revenue growth curve in dependency on the team's capability	*Interpretation (qual.):* Team assessment
	(2) Assessment of team's credibility	*Interpretation (qual.):* Team assessment[16]
Transaction effects	(1) Firm state after the investment is appraised	*Calculation*: Post-transaction valuation
Risk and uncertainty	(1) Hurdle rate	*Calculation*: Hurdle rate
	(2) Assessing certain innovation projects' maturity state in the innovation process as proxy of riskiness (technology risk)	*Interpretation (qual.)*: Product/service tangibility assessment
	(3) Scenario analysis	*Interpretation (qual.)*: Scenarios
	(4) Potential for management team augmentation	*Interpretation (qual.)*: Team assessment
	(5) Assessment of management's credibility	*Interpretation (qual.)*: Team assessment
	(6) Assessment of future economic situation	*Interpretation (qual.)*: Business environment assessment
	(7) Consulting other investors' evaluations	*Interpretation (qual.)*: External opinions
	(8) Valuator's intuition	*Interpretation (qual.)*: Intuition

As most idea firms lack the necessary resources to implement their "idea" at the time of the valuation the appraisal is done assuming that the transaction, in most cases for idea firms, a capital infusion, has been conducted. Thus, *transaction effects in the sense of financing seem to be fully considered.*

With regard to *risk and uncertainty* valuators of idea firms seem to deal majorly with uncertainty and use *scenario techniques* as major methodology, i.e., they develop different scenarios (pictures) of an idea firm's future and its environment to evaluate possible future developments. Another methodology they use is the *hurdle rate approach*: They seem to develop a future picture of the firm and its business environment and consider the risk that this picture will not occur to its full extend with a conservative (= high) discount rate. To assess factors

16 In order to show a clear mapping between 1st and 2nd order constructs, 2nd order constructs may be stated repeatedly in the last column of the table.

that could be used as inputs for either scenario development or hurdle rate estimation they seem to use four approaches: Assessing the *"tangibility"* or status of the running product or service development, assessing the *idea firm's management or founder team*, assessing the firm's *future business environment*. An additional approach to facilitate risk estimation is the inclusion of other *external opinions* into the valuation. To quantify risks they also seem to utilize *risk mitigation costs*.

Overall, the analysis shows that methodologies to interpret data, construct a future state and deal with risk and uncertainty, many of them qualitative in nature, seem to be more relevant compared to the application of mathematical calculation models or even quantitative tools to support data interpretation.

Information

With regard of utilized information, Table 16 sums up the empirical results including 1st and 2nd order abstractions.

Table 16. Information for the Valuation of Idea Firms

Dimensions	Collected Information	
	Empirical data (1st order construct)	Abstraction (2nd order construct)
Innovation projects	(1) Customer value	Customer value
	(2) Timing & customer's product lifecycle	Customer value
	(3) Product differentiation & properties	Differentiation potential
	(4) Patent protection	Differentiation potential
	(5) State in innovation process	Tangibility
Innovation capability	(1) Product development capabilities	Team's development execution capability
	(2) Core business process implementation capabilities	Team's firm founding
	(3) Management's track record and references	Team's firm founding
Transaction effects	(1) Brought-in network and relationships	Network synergies
	(2) Network of potential buyers at end of investment	Network synergies
	(3) Potential for management team augmentation	Augmentation of key personnel

The information used to valuate idea firms' innovation projects seem to be created *customer value, differentiation from competitors*, and *tangibility*. Valuators seem to collect information about the *value that a new product or service creates for the targeted customer group*. An interesting aspect of this information seems to be the timing of a product's or service's commercialization. Many customer groups might benefit from a certain new service or product, but not at the current time due to the shape of their industries or their current business model. Information about the *differentiation potential* from competitors' products or services seems to be collected to assess possible margins and the length that those margins can be retained.

This information could be about product properties, production processes, or patent protection. The last category is information the *tangibility* of the product or service in development. Idea firms should be majorly in the process of developing a product or service. Thus, a risk exists that the product or service cannot be developed technically and the product or service does not even reach the commercialization phase.

The information that seems to be used to assess *innovation capability* can be categorized in two categories: First, information about the team's *capability to develop a service or product*, i.e., technical skills related to research, design, and production. Second, information about the team's capability to *found a firm* around the product or service. This capability consists for example of skills to commercialize the product or service and implement the necessary business functions around the product or service. Valuators seem to collect data about the team's skills to implement and scale business processes, the team's track record as proxy for that, but also possibilities to augment the team with additional resources to support performing those business execution tasks.

With regard to *transaction effects* practitioners seem to consider information around the possibilities to include complementary resources (besides the invested money). Those complementary resources could be for example relationships to other firms to open up distribution channels, but also networks of potential buyers for the idea firm once it has left the idea stage of its lifecycle.

6.3 Valuation of Growth Firms

As stated in chapter 4.3.2 growth firms can be characterized as having it made from an idea to a firm that is able to offer a concrete product or service offering. Growth firms' major challenges lie in the areas of scaling up, defending margins, and identifying further growth potentials. For valuators the challenges lie in appraising the chances and risks associated with those major challenges.

6.3.1 Methodologies

The following section depicts the methodologies that practitioners use to appraise growth firms.

Innovation projects

(1) Valuators seem to majorly use *income approaches* to value single innovation projects as one auditor elaborating about growth firms states:

> *Welche Methoden würden Sie für ein einzelnes Projekt nehmen?* Einen wie auch immer gearteten Income-Approach. Ob man den dann als Free Cash Flow, APV oder Total Cash Flow ausgestaltet, das hängt dann von anderen Faktoren ab. (Auditing professional)

(2) They also use *hurdle rate approaches*.

> Wir rechnen das Ding durch. Also wir bilden uns eine Meinung über Top- und Bottom Line und über eine Comparables Analyse: Für wie viel Multiple würden wir es verkauft kriegen? Dann kommt ein Verkaufspreis raus und den setzen wir über eine zeitliche Beziehung in Zusammenhang mit dem Kaufpreis und bekommen einen IRR raus. Und bei dem IRR gucken wir dann: Ist der eigentlich in der Range, die wir brauchen. (Corporate venture capital professional)

(3) It seems that the common approach to appraise innovation projects is to conduct a *top-down market potential analysis* starting with a whole market's potential down to single product market potentials.

> Was Sie dann natürlich auch machen: Sie nehmen ja eine gewisse Marktentwicklung als Basis an. Die gucken wir uns an und da gehen wir wirklich top-down vor: Von der Marktentwicklung bis zum einzelnen Produkt. (Corporate venture capital professional)

(4) Professionals also check assumptions with the help of theoretical concepts such as the *experience curve*.

> Und da rein fließen ja dann noch unsere technischen Erkenntnisse wie Fehlerquote usw. rein - Ist das realistisch? Was kann ich in den vier Jahren an Erfahrungskurve tatsächlich an Lernkurve durchfahren? (Corporate venture capital professional)

(5) Comparable to idea firms, *patents seem to be assessed*, but not directly valued with a cost approach, but indirectly within the cash flows of an income approach. Thus, not the costs to produce these assets are used for valuation purposes, but the expected income (or cash flow when using the DCF approach). Associated with the valuation of patents are two other possible sources of risk that need to be considered: Will a patent protect expected high margins? Will a product, service, or technology infringe a patent owned by another firm?

Die bewerten wir aber nicht in Form von Geld. Die sind dann erst wirklich etwas wert, wenn sie ein vermarktbares Produkt hervorrufen, wenn sie zu Cash Flows werden. Wir sind keine Patentverwertungsgesellschaft, die versucht, Patente zu Geld zu machen. Was wir machen ist: Wir gucken uns diese Patente relativ genau an und gucken, ob sie halten. Also für uns ist eher das Risiko, dass das Dingel, das die gebaut haben zwar funktioniert, aber wenn jemand anders kommt und kann das auch bauen, dann ist es nicht mehr viel Wert. Das heißt, die Frage ist: Halten die Patente? Und dann eine Frage, die uns immer wieder treibt, wo man sehr viel Geld reinstecken muss, um es wirklich bewerten zu können ist: Verletzen die mit ihrem Dingel Patente von Anderen? Das ist ein Risiko, das wir nach einer einigermaßen oberflächlichen Analyse einfach auf uns nehmen müssen. Ist glücklicherweise noch nicht passiert, aber es wird früher oder später passieren. (Corporate venture capital professional)

Innovation capability

In general, valuing the innovation capability seems to be *rather unsystematic than based on a structured process* of data collection and data processing.

Das ist nicht systematisch. Das ist Bauchgefühl. (Corporate venture capital professional)

(1) Valuations seem to be conducted by using an *income approach* and taking into consideration only the *cash flows from the existing product portfolio*, i.e., the cash flows that enable the firm's current success on the market. Thus, innovation capability is included as the capability to continuously enhance and improve the products in the current portfolio in contrast to the capability to develop new products.

Bei den Firmenakquisitionen, die wir bisher durchgeführt haben, ist die Unternehmensbewertung nahezu ausschließlich aufgrund des existierenden Produktportfolios, des Marktzuganges der Firma, die letztendlich in der augenblicklichen Ertragskraft des Unternehmens münden, vorgenommen worden. Es ist also de facto nicht gemacht worden, dass man sagt: Die Firma hat die und die Produkte in der Pipeline und die bringen uns dann einen Unternehmenswert. Es ist immer sehr klassisch gerechnet worden. Wir haben heute ein Produktportfolio. Dieses Produktportfolio bringt in dem Betriebsumfeld die und die Erträge. Eine Wirtschaftsentwicklung auf die nächsten fünf Jahre in Aussicht gestellt sollte eine Ertragskraft in einem NPV von dem Unternehmen von soundso bringen plus Terminal Value. . . . Wir haben sehr wohl einen

> Wirtschaftsplan für die Unternehmen in der nächsten Zeit gemacht, aber der ist sehr stark basierend auf dem gegenwärtigen Produktportfolio. . . . . Zunächst gehen wir vom aktuellen Produktportfolio aus. (Industry business development professional)

> Ich würde sagen, die Innovationsfähigkeit, wenn sie in Leuten gebunden ist, findet sich in der Umsatzstruktur wieder. Wenn ich neue Produkte nachschieben kann, dann kann ich meinen Umsatz ausweiten. Zusätzliches Produkt bedeutet zusätzlicher Umsatz. (Corporate venture capital professional)

(2) An extension to the consideration of the current product portfolio is the consideration of *new applications for existing technologies or products*.

> Wie viel Innovationskraft steckt in der Technologie? Haben die gerade die Kernfusion erfunden? Dann könnten wir beide wahrscheinlich das ganze Flipchart an zukünftigen Anwendungsfeldern vollschreiben. Oder, um ein anderes Beispiel zu nennen: Diese komischen Gummischuhe: Croqs. Riesenumsatz mit riesiger Marge auf diese billigen Plastikschuhe. Bekommen die das noch mal hin? Ne, da können sie noch ein Riemchen links und rechts machen. Das hält sich noch ein paar Jahre und dann sind die tot. (Corporate venture capital professional)

(3) The capability to generate innovation and start new development projects seems not to be valued directly. This also means that within the used income approach a terminal value is not generated via fundamental data such as an estimated growth rate. A terminal value rather seems to be appraised via an estimated *exit multiple* projecting the estimated value to sell the firm at the end of the holding period.

> Wir bewerten das nicht direkt, aber es geht irgendwie in die Verkaufsmöglichkeiten ein. Wenn ich mit einem Unternehmen zu tun habe, das irgendwo ein Produkt und einen Markt hat, wo ich mir eine hohe Innovation auch in der Zukunft noch verspreche, dann habe ich eine relativ hohe Chance, auch wenn ich den potenziellen Käufer noch nicht so ganz abgrenzen kann. Wenn das Ding läuft, dann kriegt man das los. Irgendjemand wird Interesse haben. (Corporate venture capital professional)

(4) The quality of the collected information is evaluated by *comparing the plausibility of the business plan with respect to revenue growth and cost development with comparable firms and their cost developments or within the industry.*

> Wir gucken uns normalerweise so 3-5 Jahre an und das ist ja nun wirklich Kristallkugel bei diesen Unternehmen. Auf der anderen Seite brauche ich mal ein Gefühl dafür. Was ist eigentlich deren Zielkostenstruktur? Wie soll dieses Unternehmen eigentlich ausgestattet sein? So, und da haben Sie normalerweise das Problem, dass die das erste Jahr ausmodellieren und das auch gar nicht so schlecht und dann ziehen die die Formeln weiter. Und sie haben dann den Effekt da drin, dass ihnen ein bis zwei Kennzahlen voll durch die Decke gehen, weil man es eben nicht so machen kann. Und dann gehen wir da rein, schauen uns an, wie sieht denn jetzt ein Unternehmen aus, was 100 Millionen Umsatz hat in diesem Bereich. Da gibt es ja viele Informationen über öffentliche Quellen und Comparables. Da schauen wir an: Was haben die denn normalerweise für einen ROA, für einen ROI? Was haben die für einen Overhead? Was machen die für Gross Margins? Und passen dann die Endjahre, wo wir es hoffentlich mit einem etwas größeren Unternehmen zu tun haben, dann dementsprechend an. (Corporate venture capital professional)

> Wir hatten mal den Fall von einer Firma, die nach vier Jahren eine Milliarde Umsatz machen wollte. Das glaubt ihnen kein Mensch, wenn sie zu dem Zeitpunkt null [Milliarden] machen. Was aber realistisch ist, sind 100 bis 150 Millionen. Nur so aus dem Bauchgefühl. Wenn mir einer sagt, er macht heute null und in fünf Jahren eine Milliarde, dann winke ich sofort ab. *Wäre das dann auch ein Kriterium für die interne Perspektive [Eine Firma kann einfach nicht so viel Umsatz in fünf Jahren abbilden]?* Einerseits das, aber andererseits gibt es das auch einfach im Online- oder TK-Bereich nicht. Im Autobereich oder im Pharmabereich mag es das geben, dass ich eine Innovation oder einen Blockbuster mache. Da würde ich das glauben, dass ich damit in 5 Jahren eine Milliarde Umsatz mache, aber nicht im ITK-Umfeld. (Corporate venture capital professional)

Transaction effects

(1) Valuators seem to conduct a *standalone valuation* of the acquisition target.

> Wir machen nur eine Standalone-Bewertung, sagen aber gleichzeitig, dass wir den und den Beitrag in einer Kooperation leisten können, zum Beispiel gemeinsamer Kundenangang oder auch Kostensenkungspotenziale. Aber das rechnen wir nicht wie im klassischen M&A mit in den Case mit ein, der den Bewertungsaufschlag rechtfertigt zum Standalone. *Das heißt, Sie machen eine reine Standalone-Bewertung?* Wir

machen ja nur Minderheitsbeteiligungen. *Das bedeutet, Sie haben ja auch erst mal keine Kontrolle?* Nein, ex definitionem haben wir keine Kontrolle. . . . Dass wir Synergien durch unsere Handlungen schaffen und einen Teil dem Verkäufer geben, wie es bei z. b. bei Private Equity üblich ist, so denken wir überhaupt nicht, weil wir auch nie alleine investieren. Wir haben nur Gesellschafterrechte. (Corporate venture capital professional)

(2) For corporate venture capital, valuators also seem to indirectly and qualitatively value *synergies between the target and the corporate venture capitalist*, which originate from the network and distribution channels the corporate venture capital firm can provide to the target.

Die sagen: Du machst jetzt 5, 6, 7 Millionen Umsatz. Wenn ich jetzt 5 Millionen reingebe plus mein ganzes Corporate Netzwerk einbringe, dann sind das nicht 5, 6, 7. Dann sind das 5, 8, 15, 30. Und dann setzen wir das ganze ins Verhältnis und schauen, wie viele Anteile ich bekommen. Das kann man auch machen. Die Investoren haben ja einerseits Geld, aber dann auch ein internationales Netzwerk, das sie einbringen können. . . . das heißt, die Investorennetzwerke, gerade was das Finanzieren angeht, weitere Investoren finden oder auch bei der Personalsuche [unterstützen], sind wirklich auch was Wert, weil man eben schneller vorwärts kommt in dem ganzen Umfeld. Das richtig zu bewerten ist schwierig. Deswegen bewerten wir nur die cash flows und sagen: Das ganze Netzwerk unterscheidet uns von den anderen Investoren und wird dann eher auf der weichen Schiene als Value mit eingebracht. (Corporate venture capital professional)

Werden Synergien außer dem Investment selbst wie zum Beispiel der Marktzugang über das kaufende Unternehmen mitbewertet? Das machen wir, aber es fließt nicht wirklich in die Bewertung ein. Das ist Teil unserer strategischen Aufgabe. Deswegen sind wir ein strategischer Investor. Wir ermöglichem dem Unternehmen die Möglichkeit, mit [uns] . . . zusammen zu arbeiten. [Wir sind] . . . ja ein riesen Laden. Wir wissen, wo die Leute sitzen, wo verschiedene . . . Projekte gefahren werden, die Interesse an solch einer Technologie hätten und dann bringen wir die zusammen. Wenn die zusammen arbeiten wollen, dann müssen die einen separaten Vertrag machen. Das hat mit uns überhaupt nichts zu tun. Uns freut es, wenn sie das tun. Wenn nicht, muss man sich fragen: Warum haben wir überhaupt investiert, wenn niemand Interesse hat. Aber das tut der ganzen Sache dann keinen Abbruch. In die Bewertung mit einfließen tut es nicht, weil es zum Zeitpunkt der Investitition alles noch zu unsicher ist. (Corporate venture capital professional)

(3) A different approach used is *to estimate potential own costs to develop the product/service*. It is used to determine a comparable value for make-or-buy decisions. In comparison to the classic cost approach, the cost approach is used to estimate the costs of developing a comparable technology within the acquirer's own firm to determine an upper price limit.

> *Nutzen Sie so etwas wie den Selbsterstellungswert?* Das haben wir tatsächlich schon mal gemacht. In einem einzigen Fall. Da ging es um eine Community. Da haben wir gesagt: Wir können jetzt so eine Plattform selber entwickeln. Kostet meinetwegen 15 Millionen oder wir investieren jetzt 3 Millionen Euro in ein Unternehmen und die machen das ganz schlank und klein. Leider hat beides nicht funktioniert. Aber das kann man machen. Ist aber aufwändig. Finde ich einen interessanten Ansatz. . . . Der Punkt ist hier: Es gehört uns ja nicht, sondern zum Beispiel nur 10%. Insofern hat die Methode natürlich ihre Grenzen. (Corporate venture capital professional)

> Wir beraten ein Software-Unternehmen und da ist ganz klar: Das Entwicklungsteam, das die Software überlegt zu kaufen, sagt sich: Die Software gibt es am Markt. Wir können uns die angucken. Wir wissen, wie sie funktioniert. Wir müssen nicht mehr die Vorarbeit leisten wie die Anderen und müssen das jetzt im Prinzip nur noch kopieren von der Idee her und für uns optimieren. Das heißt, Sie können es im Prinzip noch besser umsetzen als das ursprüngliche Entwicklerteam. . . . Bei der Software würden wir den Cost Approach rechnen. Wie viel Entwicklungsaufwand ist reingeflossen? Welche Redundanzen, Schritte, Schleifen, die man gegebenenfalls nicht gebraucht hätte. Das muss im Rahmen eines Interviews mit Verantwortlichen diskutiert werden. Das ist häufig das Problem, dass die Daten nicht genug vorgehalten werden. Gab es einen Projektplan? Das ist natürlich die Idealwelt, dass man einen Projektplan hat, in Phasen und mit Zwischenzielen. Und dann entsprechend: Was für ein Zeitaufwand ist da reingeflossen? Was für Redundanzen gab es? Was für zusätzliche Hilfsmittel waren erforderlich? Das wäre so die ideale Welt, die man sich vorstellen könnte. (Auditing professional)

> Nur, wenn es de facto nicht [selbst] machbar ist, das heißt, dass es offensichtlich ist, dass eine Akquisition der günstigere Weg ist, dann beschreitet man diesen Weg. (Industry business development professional)

(4) Also, the *retention of key personnel* is a key factor that is valued either as cost factor (costs to retain critical people) and, thus, it is decreasing the valuation. Or it is considered even as a deal breaker, which would set the valuation to zero.

> *Wie gehen sie damit um, dass Schlüsselpersonen das Unternehmen nach dem Kauf verlassen können?* Das ist eine der Grundüberlegungen, die bei uns im Vordergrund steht. Was kauft man hier? In welchen Personen ruht das Know How? In welchen Personen liegt die Management-Kraft und kann man diese Leute auf Dauer binden? Sind diese Leute nicht diejenigen, die durch den Kaufpreis ausbezahlt werden und es nicht mehr notwendig haben, mit dem Unternehmen weiter zu tun und wie schaut die Ebene dahinter aus? Das schaut man sich schon sehr genau an. *Würde das dann preislich bewertet werden?* Es ist eher eine ja/nein-Entscheidung. Also die Frage, die wir uns stellen ist: Wie können wir die Fähigkeiten, die in den akquirierten Unternehmen stecken, für uns sichern? Das ist eine der Standardfragen, die natürlich gestellt werden. Welches Motiv kann ich dem bisherigen Organisator des Unternehmens bieten, dass er weiterhin für uns arbeitet? Ist das für den auch interessant? Und wenn wir diese Frage nicht mit „ja" beantworten können, dann ist eher die Tendenz bei uns, die Finger davon zu lassen. (Industry business development professional)

> *Wie sichern oder bewerten sie den potenziellen Weggang von Schlüsselpersonen?* Das, was wir schon sehr bewusst machen ist, dass wir den Kernleuten auch entsprechend große Karotten vor die Nase halten. Das, was Sie in den üblichen Finanzierungsrunden haben ist, dass die ursprünglichen Erfinder und Eigentümer, die werden so weit verbessert. Wenn da einmal schon 12 bis 15 Millionen in das Unternehmen geflossen sind, dann sind von den anfänglichen 500.000, die die da reingesteckt haben, nicht mehr viel übrig. So, und dann müssen Sie sehen, dass die auf einem, - mit Optionen können Sie das machen -, Level stehen, wo die für den Rest ihres Lebens ganz gut aufgestellt sind, wenn das Ding fliegt. Da muss man dann als Investor auch drauf achten, dass man da eine vernünftige Kompensationsstruktur hat. Das ist das Gleiche wie bei einem normalen Mitarbeiter. Wenn ich dem nicht genug zahle, dann ist der weg. (Corporate venture capital professional)

> *Aber die Leute zu halten, kostet ja auch etwas?* Ne, abgesehen davon, dass ich den Leuten ein vernünftiges Gehalt zahlen muss. Es ist ja deren Unternehmen und die wollen ihr Unternehmen zum Erfolg führen. Was wir leisten können ist, dass, wenn es ein Erfolg wird, dass es dann auch für sie persönlich ein Erfolg wird, weil sie Mit-

> eigentümer sind oder Optionen haben. Das sind normalerweise Optionsmodelle, mit denen sie so die drei bis vier Kernleute... Die müssen Sie schön mit Optionen belegen. Das können sie dann auch zeitlich staffeln, dass Sie sagen: Du hast jetzt so ein Paket von Optionen. So viel bekommst du nächstes Jahr, danach das Jahr, danach das Jahr und wenn wir den Exit machen, dann kannst du dich auf die Bahamas setzen. Die Optionen werden so bewertet, dass sie unseren Anteil am Exit natürlich reduzieren. Also wir werden verwässert. (Corporate venture capital professional)

(5) A last alternative seems to be the creation of a second *business case* considering transaction effects. Nevertheless, this business case seems to be used to adjust a valuation qualitatively after it has been calculated.

> *Die Vorteile, die sich aus dem anteilmäßigen Besitz ergeben, stellen sie dann nur qualitativ da?* Nein, auch quantitativ. Wir sagen z. B.: Durch das Produkt kann die . . . [Firma] 10 Millionen einsparen. Das ist allerdings keine belastbare Zahl und entspricht natürlich auch nicht dem Gedanken einer Synergieberechnung. Man kann nur sagen: Wenn wir da nicht investieren, kommen wir vielleicht gar nicht so einfach an die Technologie dran oder, wenn wir da nicht investieren, würden wir mit denen gar nicht kooperieren und Umsätze von XY machen. Für die Investition machen wir dann eine Standalone-Bewertung und für die Rechtfertigung gibt es dann den Business Case mit Kooperationswertbeitrag. Der steht aber isoliert daneben. Es gibt keinen Business Case, wo das dann drin ist. *Das bedeutet, er steht auf der nächsten Folie?* Genau, fände ich auch sehr grenzwertig, das anders zu machen, weil wir den Einfluss nicht haben und weil uns das Ding nicht gehört. (Corporate venture capital professional)

Risk and uncertainty

(1a) Within the DCF methodology, the *discount rate* is used to cover the risks associated with the investment in a growth firm is an important factor in valuing such an investment. This discount rate depends on different factors:

> Mit der Top Line und der Kostensicht kommen wir dann zu einem bestimmten Cash Flow und der wird diskontiert und hier geht eigentlich das implizite Risiko ein. (Corporate venture capital professional)

> Es gibt ja generell den WACC, den ich bei Seed sehr hoch ansetze und bei Later Stage etwas niedriger. Das ist ein genereller Risikofaktor. Den nutzen wir sehr intensiv. Wir haben da auch ganz genau definierte Stufen. Also wir machen keine Beta-Analyse. Wir kalkulieren jetzt den WACC nicht, wie er im Lehrbuch vorgeschrieben ist. Wir sagen halt: Seed ist 25% und Buy-out ist 15% und das passen wir über die Jahre immer mal wieder an, weil sich die Marktzinsen ja verändern. Aber das Wort „beta“ ist hier im Hause schon lange nicht mehr gefallen. (Corporate venture capital professional)

> Was wir schon mal versucht haben ist beispielsweise, dass wir gesagt haben: Wir haben einen Standard Discount Satz für verschiedene Stages und dann haben wir so ein Raster mit plus/minus. Management ist super: Ein Prozentpunkt weniger. So ein Score-Ding. Und wenn die halt überall super sind, dann brauchen wir nicht unsere 50%, sondern, da sagen wir, da können wir auch mit 40%. Wenn es da viele Fragen gibt, dann brauchen wir vielleicht mehr. Das ist so ein Ding, wo wir sehr mit der Hand am Arm kämpfen, aber ich glaube, das machen alle. (Corporate venture capital professional)

(1b) A second approach to consider risk within an income approaches such as DCF is to adjust the *number of periods*, which are estimated in detail and the number of periods, after which the terminal (going concern) value is calculated:

> Wir machen fünf Jahre detailliert, fünf Jahre weniger detailliert und dann kommt erst der Terminal Value. Wobei das auch flexibel gehandhabt wird. In den Hochzeiten der Finanzkrise haben wir auch nur drei Jahre geplant, aber bei einem stabileren Umfeld planen wir längerfristig. (Corporate venture capital professional)

> Im Wesentlichen ist die Bewertung die, dass Sie über die nächsten fünf Jahre aufgrund des Ist-Zustandes des Unternehmens einen Business Plan hochrechnen, ein paar Vorstellungen noch hineindichten, wenn ich das so sagen darf, wie sichs denn entwickeln könnte, die Ertragskraft abschätzen und dann eine NPV-Berechnung machen. Das ist sehr einfach und sehr simplizistisch. Da könnte man sicherlich mehr ins Detail gehen. (Industry business development professional)

(1c) Another used methodology is a classical *IRR hurdle rate calculation used as a feasibility check* to complement income approach. Within this approach the IRR covers the risks.

> *Richtet sich der Diskontierungssatz danach, in welchen Stages sich das Unternehmen gerade befindet?* Richtig, wobei wir von der Logik etwas anders arbeiten. Wir rechnen das Ding durch. Also wir bilden uns eine Meinung über Top- und Bottom Line und über eine Comparables Analyse: Für wie viel Multiple würden wir es verkauft kriegen? Dann kommt ein Verkaufspreis raus und den setzen wir über eine zeitliche Beziehung in Zusammenhang mit dem Kaufpreis und bekommen einen IRR raus. Und bei dem IRR gucken wir dann: Ist der eigentlich in der Range, die wir brauchen. Das heißt, das ist so eine implizite Diskontierung, die wir machen. (Corporate venture capital professional)

(2) To consider the risks associated with cash flows, valuators seem to apply *scenario probabilities* and decision trees.

> Was wir machen ist: Wir laufen so einen Investment-Tree ab, was eigentlich nichts ist als eine bedingte Wahrscheinlichkeit, ein Wahrscheinlichkeitsbaum. Den versuche ich normalerweise nicht zu kompliziert werden zu lassen. Nehmen wir beispielsweise: Also sie haben ein Ding, wo es darum geht: Die Technologie funktioniert, es geht darum, ob die jetzt vielleicht Industriestandard wird. Das ist die eine Sache. Und die andere Sache ist: Wie entwickelt sich dann der Endgerätemarkt. Das heißt, Sie haben da zwei Parameter, die können Sie ein paar Mal aufspalten, dann haben sie vier bis fünf verschiedene Szenarien. Die werden dann mit Wahrscheinlichkeiten belegt, Bauchgefühl in der Regel. Wir versuchen das natürlich mit Daten zu untermauern. Was ganz gut funktioniert, wenn es irgendwo in Richtung zu erwartende Marktgröße geht. Da können Sie sich dann an Studien entlang hangeln, GDP growth und gesundem Menschenverstand. Der Rest ist Mathematik, so dass wir dann einfach sagen: Wenn alles gut geht, es wird Industriestandard und die Geräte starten durch, dann sind wir bei dem und dem Revenue usw. Das belegt mit Wahrscheinlichkeiten, kommen Sie dann zu einem wahrscheinlichen Revenue. (Corporate venture capital professional)

> Wir haben interessanterweise ein Projekt in Schottland gemacht, naja, Realoptionen sind ja auch ein weiter Begriff, da haben wir Decision Tree Analysis angewandt, also Entscheidungsbäume. Was ja in die Richtung Real Optionen durchaus reingeht. Da haben wir sehr frühe IP [Intellectual Property] bewertet und da waren noch sehr viele Entscheidungen offen. Was macht man damit? Für welchen Markt entwickelt man das? Mit welchem Hersteller macht man es? Intern, extern, Virtual Fab? Da waren

> einfach noch so viele Stellschrauben, die halt ein bis drei Jahre in der Zukunft lagen oder wirklich signifikante Entscheidungen für den Business Plan, so dass wir dann gesagt haben: Das modellieren wir mal über so einen Entscheidungsbaum. (Corporate finance professional)

(3) Valuators also seem to conduct a *break-even analysis without considering risk and interest*.

> Die Frage, die wir uns immer stellen ist: Was muss denn so eine Company für einen Mindestumsatz machen, damit wir mit einem blauen Auge, sprich unserem Einsatz wieder herauskommen. (Corporate venture capital professional)

(4) Another methodology of dealing with risk of appraising a firm's value too high is the *adjustment of business plans* by reviewing the assumptions and correcting them to the assessment of the valuators. As it seems, in most cases these corrections change the assumptions to values, which lead to a lower valuation.

> Normalerweise gehen wir da so ran: Gib uns einen Geschäftsplan. Dann gucken wir uns die Prämissen an. Die werden dann nach unten geschraubt. Ich habs noch nie erlebt, dass die nach oben geschraubt werden. (Corporate venture capital professional)

> Ja, klar. Wir machen immer einen sogenannten . . . [eigenen Firmen]-Case. Da wird dann der Unternehmensgeschäftsplan zugrunde gelegt und dann werden die Annahmen unseren Annahmen entsprechend korrigiert. Das diskutieren wir dann auch mit denen und in der Regel ist es dann so, dass die sagen: „Um Gottes Willen. Das ist viel zu pessimistisch" usw., weil das ja auf die Bewertung geht. Aber in der Regel ist es dann so, dass wir näher an der Realität sind als die Unternehmen selber. (Corporate venture capital professional)

> *Gibt es so etwas wie einen Erfahrungswert wie man Abschläge vornimmt?* Das wäre zweifellos angebracht, aber da sind wir mit der Systematisierung bei weitem noch nicht so weit. Wenn jemand das als sein täglich Brot macht, wie eben die Investment-Halter, die hier als Berater auftreten, dann würde man das wohl tun. (Industry business development professional)

(5) If valuators use the *scenario technique*, scenarios are provided with probabilities to compute a single value.

> *Wie gehen sie mit Risiken um?* Ja, da geht man halt in die Szenarienanalyse hinein. Typischerweise haben wir da mit einer 3x3 Matrix gearbeitet, wo drei Grundszenarien genommen worden sind [best, realistic, worst case]. Das haben wir durchmodelliert und da kann man dann noch mit Wahrscheinlichkeiten spielen und dann gibt es einen kombinierten Wert. Diese Übungen haben wir schon gemacht, aber diese Übungen sind, ich würde sagen, nicht die kaufentscheidenden Übungen gewesen. Das ist ein Backup gewesen, so dass man sagt: Ok, das macht Sinn. (Industry business development professional)

(6) Another methodology to deal with risky investments is the *sensitivity analysis*. With a sensitivity analysis, the effects of minor changes in valuation assumptions on the valuation result, the firm value, are analyzed.

> *Nutzen Sie noch andere Mechanismen zur Risikobewertung?* Wir machen noch eine Sensitivitätsanalyse, dass zum Beispiel unter der Annahme, dass der Terminal Value Growth 2% ist, der Wert so ist. Also eine Kombination aus Terminal Value Growth und WACC machen wir. Und damit bekommen sie dann natürlich unterschiedliche Unternehmenswerte raus. Aber ich sage ihnen ganz ehrlich. Das treibt keine Entscheidung. (Corporate venture capital professional)

(7) Another interesting approach is the *analogy to a game of bets* regarding the value of growth firms. With this methodology the riskiness of the investment and consequently the value of a firm depends on the number of bets the valuator has to make

> Von den Unternehmen bekommen wir alles. Wir sehen alles, was wir sehen wollen. Das Problem ist halt: Man kann nicht in die Zukunft gucken. Da muss man dann halt - Es gibt normalerweise in einem Deal eine Stelle, wo ich sage: Ok, und das ist jetzt meine Wette. Ich weiß es nicht. Dafür sind wir in dem Geschäft. Dass wir Risiken eingehen. Das Risiko kann ich nicht abschätzen. Es macht alles Sinn. Aber, ob es jetzt wirklich so kommt? Ich weiß es nicht. Es gibt Deals, da haben sie drei bis fünf Stellen, wo sie anfangen zu wetten und da sage ich dann: Lass die Finger davon. Für einen Erfolg muss alles gut gehen und wenn ich 5 Stellen habe, wo ich nicht weiß, ob es gut geht, dann ist die Wahrscheinlichkeit hoch, dass es nicht gut geht. Auf der Ebene laufen die Betrachtungen meistens. (Corporate venture capital professional)

6.3.2 Information

The following sections depict, which information growth firm valuators assess to conduct their valuations.

Innovation projects

They collect information about (1) *technical feasibility* and (2) *potential customer acceptance.*

> Das ist der Vorteil daran, dass wir relativ spät ins Spiel kommen. Nämlich, wenn es schon ein Produkt gibt. Dann gibt es nämlich oft auch schon erste Kunden oder zumindest Tests. (Corporate venture capital professional)

(3) *Time-to-market information* is also a considered factor for the evaluation of an innovation project.

> Wie schnell kann das Ganze ausgerollt werden? Brauche ich da irgendwelche Standardisierungsgremien für oder weiß der Teufel was? (Corporate venture capital professional)

(4) A *firm's access to distribution channels* are considered to be very important for the commercial success of a technology or invention.

> *Man muss sich seinen eigenen Distributionskanal aufbauen?* Ja, ganz genau, der Zwischenschritt ist der Hemmschuh. Das sehen wir oft. (Corporate venture capital professional)

(5) Valuators collect information about the *applications* that an innovation project's result can have.

> Wir haben eine Firma, die stellt Funkchips her. Die sind jetzt in Fernbedienungen drin. Super, um die Company zum Starten zu bringen. . . . Wir könnten uns jetzt eine Liste runterschreiben: Wo kann ich so kleine Low-Power-Funkchips überall benutzen? Das geht von „Licht an und aus" bis Auto. Und das ist das Spiel oft. (Corporate venture capital professional)

> Oft haben diese Firmen, auch wenn es ein One-Trick-Pony ist, eine Technologie erfunden und gehen jetzt in einen Markt rein. Und dieses gleiche Ding können sie aber auch noch in zwei bis fünf Märkten, in anderen Anwendungsfeldern nehmen. Und das langt uns eigentlich, um die Firma zu verkaufen mit der Geschichte: Guck mal

> hier, das ist bewiesene Technologie. Die machen schon soundsoviel Umsatz und guck mal, wo man das noch alles brauchen kann. Das reicht ja dann erstmal für den Käufer, dass der sagt: Mensch ja, das muss ich erst mal machen und dann kümmere ich mich darum, was kommt eigentlich danach oder parallel dazu. (Corporate venture capital professional)

(6) Valuators try to understand, if the *business model* as whole has a chance to be successful.

> Ich gebe ihnen ein Beispiel: Es gibt mittlerweile Maschinen, die relativ autonom putzen können. So kleine Putzroboter. Das gibt's in einer professionellen Ausführung. Macht absolut Sinn für Flughäfen, weite Flächen, wo sie jemanden mit einem Besen rumstehen sehen oder mit einer fahrbaren Maschine. Die Dinger rechnen sich, die Dinger funktionieren. Es ist überhaupt kein Problem, das zu machen. Massenweise Firmen daran gescheitert. Warum: Der Flughafen hat einen Contract mit der Putzfirma. Diese Putzfirma tickt so, dass deren Know How ist: Wie kann ich eine Horde von 200 Leuten, die vollkommen unterbezahlt sind, hier über die Gänge scheuchen. Die denken nicht in Technologien. Und diese Firmen müsste man so ändern, dass die nicht mehr Sklavenhalter sind, sondern 10 Ingenieure beschäftigen, die einen Fuhrpark von 50 Millionen an Maschinen managen. Ganz anderes Ding. Das ist ein wichtiger Punkt. Innovation ist nicht nur Technologie. Innovation ist auch Geschäftsmodell. Wenn Sie jetzt, um bei diesem Beispiel zu bleiben, drangehen und sagen: Es reicht nicht, nur diese blöden Dinger zu bauen. Ich kaufe dazu auch noch Putzfirmen, bzw. die Contracts, und ersetze das Modell. Ich schicke jemanden mit dem Besen durch das Modell, ich schicke Technologie rein, dann kriegen sie auch Geschäft raus. Und das ist eine Geschäftsmodellinnovation und das ist nicht zu unterschätzen. Die ist mindestens genau so viel wert. (Corporate venture capital professional)

(7) They consult information about *the ability to protect a developed product or technology from being copied by competitors* and, by this, the ability to protect high margins for a certain period of time.

> Das, was für uns mindestens genau so wichtig ist wie die Innovationskraft, ist: Ist die Innovation schützbar? (Corporate venture capital professional)

Innovation capability

Valuators link innovation capability with three factors: People, technology, and market.

> *Woher kommt das Bauchgefühl außer durch die Technologie?* Es sind drei Komponenten: Es sind Leute, wobei Leute auch austauschbar sind. Wenn Sie ein Unternehmen haben, das stark wächst, müssen Sie die Leute sowieso austauschen. Es ist die Technologie: Ist das wirklich was Neues oder ist das ein kleiner evolutionärer Schritt und die bewegen sich in einer Falte des Marktes und da kann man jetzt auch gut Geld verdienen? Dann ist das aber auch irgendwann wieder durch. Und das dritte ist der Markt. Ist das jetzt ein ganz neuer Markt beispielsweise und das sind jetzt erst die ersten Anwendungen und da kann man noch viel, viel mehr machen. Nehmen Sie Internet beispielsweise. Das hat lange gedauert. Ist ja immer noch nicht ausgeschöpft, was da noch an neuen Sachen kommen kann. Das ist nicht in allen Feldern so. (Corporate venture capital professional)

(1) Valuators link innovation capability with the *team of developers and managers*.

> Also das Management-Team schauen wir uns an. (Corporate venture capital professional)

> Das, was uns besser gefällt, ist, wenn dieses Team das Potenzial hat, nicht nur diese eine Entwicklung in verschiedenen Generationen zu machen, sondern eventuell auch noch etwas Anderes. (Corporate venture capital professional)

> Das ist eine der Grundüberlegungen, die bei uns im Vordergrund steht. Was kauft man hier? In welchen Personen ruht das Know How? In welchen Personen liegt die Management-Kraft und kann man diese Leute auf Dauer binden? Sind diese Leute nicht diejenigen, die durch den Kaufpreis ausbezahlt werden und es nicht mehr notwendig haben, mit dem Unternehmen weiter zu tun. Und wie schaut die Ebene dahinter aus? Das schaut man sich schon sehr genau an. (Industry business development professional)

(2) Growth firm valuators also focus on the management team's *capability to commercialize inventions and grow a firm.*

> *Wie würden sie denn im Falle . . . [anonymized firm name] die Fähigkeiten der Firma ansehen, ihr Produkt erfolgreich in den Markt zu bringen?* Sie gucken sich natürlich das Management an. Im Idealfall ist der CEO jemand, der schon mal eine Firma aufgebaut und verkauft hat. . . . Kern ist auch immer, dass die die PS auf die Straße bringen. Die brauchen ein Vertriebsteam, das das Produkt vernünftig in den Markt

bringt. Man sollte sich da nicht auf die Entwicklungskapazitäten fokussieren. Die bekommt man hin. Oft sind Patente da, oft sind Ingenieure da, aber die Leute, die es wirklich in den Markt bringen. Die sind oft der Flaschenhals. (Corporate venture capital professional)

(3) With regard to innovation capability, valuators look at the *innovation project portfolio or pipeline*, either on product or service improvements or potential to develop completely new products or services.

Was normalerweise da ist, ist, dass die das Grundprodukt haben, das jetzt vermarktet werden soll. Und dann gibt es in der Regel schon eine Generation zwei, die so halb durchentwickelt ist und irgendwie auch eine Generation drei dieses einen Produktes. (Corporate venture capital professional)

Die haben jetzt dieses Ding hier und das verkaufen sie auch in Millionen-Stückzahlen, wunderbar, aber der Markt hat sich in zwei Jahren tot gelaufen. Was hab ich dann? Dann hab ich nichts. Das heißt, an der Stelle muss ich mehr nachweisen als nur ein gut gelaufenes Produkt. Da muss ich nachweisen, dass diese Firma eigentlich noch viel mehr wert ist, weil sie noch viel mehr im Köcher hat. (Corporate venture capital professional)

(4) They leverage own experiences regarding *learning and experience curves*.

Und da rein fließen ja dann noch unsere technischen Erkenntnisse wie Fehlerquote usw. Ist das realistisch? Was kann ich in den vier Jahren an Erfahrungskurve tatsächlich an Lernkurve durchfahren? (Corporate venture capital professional)

(5) They try to identify *comparable firms* to estimate a growth firm's value by analogical thinking.

Wie sieht denn jetzt ein Unternehmen aus, was 100 Millionen Umsatz hat in diesem Bereich. Da gibt es ja viele Informationen über öffentliche Quellen und Comparables. Da schauen wir an: Was haben die denn normalerweise für einen ROA, für einen ROI? Was haben die für einen Overhead? Was machen die für Gross Margins? Und passen dann die Endjahre, wo wir es hoffentlich mit einem etwas größeren Unternehmen zu tun haben dann dementsprechend an. . . . *Sie versuchen dann auch noch-*

mal die Kostenstrukturen an vergleichbaren Unternehmen zu plausibilisieren? Ja. (Corporate venture capital professional)

(6) For some industries, such as software, innovation capability can be related to the *scalability of technologies or products*.

> Wenn Sie jetzt Projektgeschäft machen, also zum Beispiel Software-Implementierungen: Es wird nie im Leben in SAP investiert, weil die halt von Software-Implementierung lebt und Sie das Produkt nicht beliebig skalieren können. Wenn Sie jetzt ein Internet-Bezahlsystem haben, da ist es ja egal, ob Sie eine Millionen oder 500 Millionen Kunden haben. Da müssen sie nur noch ein paar Server hinstellen, geschenkt, aber im Prinzip ist das das gleiche Produkt. Es ist wichtig, dass das Produkt skalierbar ist, Sie also eine gleichförmige Anwendung für mehrere Nutzer haben, ohne dass ich immer wieder Anpassungen machen muss. Das ist ein ganz wichtiger Faktor. (Corporate venture capital professional)

Transaction effects

Transaction effects play a substantial role in valuing growth firms.

> Es spielt durchaus eine erhebliche Rolle, dass man in der Projektion: Wie sollte das Unternehmen integriert werden? Wie schaut die gemeinsame Zukunft aus? Dass man hier bestimmte Hoffnungen hat. Die haben dort und dort gearbeitet, die haben die und die Fähigkeiten. Das könnte mit eigenen Fähigkeiten das und das ergeben. Das ist natürlich hoch spekulativ. Sie haben die zeitlichen Distanzen zwischen den Zeitzonen. Sie haben die räumlichen Distanzen, die kulturellen Unterschiede und das ist natürlich ein Riesenaufwand und ein Riesenrad, das man zu drehen hat, um über die prinzipielle Fähigkeit des Zusammenarbeitens und die prinzipiellen Synergien, die man da entdeckt, tatsächlich nutzen zu können. (Industry business development professional)

(1) Valuators seem to try to assess the *cultural fit* to evaluate future joint capabilities.

> Wenn es eine Möglichkeit gibt, das Zusammenspiel der Kulturen und der Unternehmen im Vorfeld ein klein wenig besser zu bewerten, dann würde ich das sehr begrüßen. (Industry business development professional)

(2) Information about the *network synergies* as also stated in the methodologies section seem to be regarded as relevant to assess the effects of the transaction on the innovation potential.

> Es ist selten so, dass das Unternehmen allein weiterläuft, sondern es ist der synergetische Wert, die Einbettung, ein ganz wichtiges Element. Das heißt, man hat sehr wohl Vorstellungen: Was könnte das Unternehmen in Verbindung mit unserem Unternehmen einbringen, dass dann etwas Neues geschaffen wird. Diese Vision haben wir sehr wohl hier. (Industry business development professional)

> Die Investoren haben ja einerseits Geld, aber dann auch ein internationales Netzwerk, das sie einbringen können. . . . das heißt, die Investorennetzwerke, gerade was das Finanzieren angeht, weitere Investoren finden oder auch bei der Personalsuche [unterstützen], sind wirklich auch was Wert, weil man eben schneller vorwärts kommt in dem ganzen Umfeld. (Corporate venture capital professional)

(3) Also, the *retention of key personnel* is a key factor. It even seems that the retention of key personnel is perceived as so critical that it is considered more likely as a "deal breaker" than as an influence factor of a determining firm value. Compare also the respective paragraph in the methodologies depiction (chapter 6.3.1).

> *Wie gehen sie damit um, dass Schlüsselpersonen das Unternehmen nach dem Kauf verlassen können?* Das ist eine der Grundüberlegungen, die bei uns im Vordergrund steht. Was kauft man hier? In welchen Personen ruht das Know How? In welchen Personen liegt die Management-Kraft und kann man diese Leute auf Dauer binden? Sind diese Leute nicht diejenigen, die durch den Kaufpreis ausbezahlt werden und es nicht mehr notwendig haben, mit dem Unternehmen weiter zu tun und wie schaut die Ebene dahinter aus? Das schaut man sich schon sehr genau an. *Würde das dann preislich bewertet werden?* Es ist eher eine ja/nein-Entscheidung. Also die Frage, die wir uns stellen ist: Wie können wir die Fähigkeiten, die in den akquirierten Unternehmen stecken für uns sichern? Das ist eine der Standardfragen, die natürlich gestellt werden. Welches Motiv kann ich dem bisherigen Organisator des Unternehmens bieten, dass er weiterhin für uns arbeitet? Ist das für den auch interessant? Und wenn wir diese Frage nicht mit „ja" beantworten können, dann ist eher die Tendenz bei uns, die Finger davon zu lassen. (Industry business development professional)

Data sources

The information to valuate a growth firm derives from three sources. Data given by the acquisition target's management, data gathered internally by the valuators at the buying firm, and data gathered from external sources.

(1) The information deriving from the acquisition target includes the selling management's business plan, management interviews, and information derived from due diligence processes.
(2) The valuator's information includes data from external tests of product prototypes, data from the target's existing and potential customers, from similar listed entities (for the multiples methodology), information from internal market research, and key performance indicator (KPI) comparisons with own business units in the case of CVC. The valuator's technical expertise also plays an important role for valuing the feasibility of technological product development and technological compatibility with other existing technologies and products.
(3) To check the external consistency of assumptions, professionals consult external technology experts and parties, who already evaluated the technology. These could be other parties the technology or firm is being offered to, the acquisition target's corporation partners, or institutions that funded the technology development initially, such as public research funding authorities.

6.3.3 Key Findings and Discussion

The following sections sum up the indications with regard to the valuation of growth firms derived from the empirical investigation.

Methodologies

Table 17 contains an overview of the valuation methodologies practitioners use to appraise the innovation potential of growth firms.

To appraise the value of *innovation projects*, practitioners seem to use either income approaches or hurdle rate approaches. Consequently, they tend to start a valuation process either by appraising the project's future potential with a top-down approach and, thus, the firm's future state, and discounting that value to consider risks (comparable to idea firms) or they use the project's or firm's current state as basis and appraise the firms future development based on the current state and analogies. In general, based on the investigation, one can assume that also for growth firms, the success of an individual innovation project (including commercialization) contributes a large share of its value. An important aspect seems to be the appraisal of how long product or service differentiation can be protected from competitors to protect anticipated higher margins. This is done, for example, by analyzing patent protection.

Table 17. Methodologies for the Valuation of Growth Firms

Dimensions	Valuation methodologies	
	Empirical data (1st order construct)	Abstraction (2nd order construct)
Innovation projects	(1) Income approach	*Calculation*: Start from current state
	(2) Hurdle rate approach	*Calculation*: Start from future state
	(3) Top-down market potential analysis	*Interpretation (quant.)*: Top-down market potential
	(4) Analogies with comparable product developments (experience curve)	*Interpretation (quant.)*: Product/service development analogy
	(5) Patent protection analysis	*Interpretation (qual.)*: IP protection assessment
Innovation capability	(1) Income approach with existing product portfolio	*Calculation*: Start from current state
	(2) Analysis of further applications for current product portfolio	*Interpretation (qual.)*: Assessment of further product/service applications
	(3) Exit multiple as terminal value	*Calculation*: Start from future state
	(4) Analogies with comparable firm (business case comparison)	*Interpretation (qual.)*: Firm development analogy
Transaction effects	(1) Standalone valuation	*Calculation*: Pre-transaction valuation
	(2) Network synergies	*Interpretation (qual.)*: Network synergies
	(3) Comparison with calculated/estimated own costs to develop product/service	*Interpretation (quant.)*: Own-cost comparison (cost approach)
	(4) Costs to retain key personnel	*Interpretation (quant.)*: Management retention costs
	(5) Qualitative business case	*Interpretation (qual.)*: Post-transaction valuation
Risk and uncertainty	(1a) Discount rate	*Calculation*: Discount rate
	(1b) Number of periods planned in detail	*Calculation*: Number of detailed periods
	(1c) IRR based on analogy	*Interpretation (qual.)*: Product/service development analogy
	(2) Scenario probabilities / decision trees	*Interpretation (quant.)*: Scenario probabilities
	(3) Break-even analysis	*Interpretation (quant.)*: Bottom-up/break-even analysis
	(4) Adjustment of business plan	*Interpretation (qual.)*: Overconfidence-adjustment
	(5) Scenario technique	*Interpretation (qual.)*: Scenarios
	(6) Sensitivity analysis	*Interpretation (quant.)*: Sensitivity analysis
	(7) Bet analogy, gut feeling	*Interpretation (qual.)*: Intuition

Innovation capability seems to become more relevant for growth firms than for idea firms. It seems to be assessed in two ways: The first way, is to extrapolate potentials to build future revenues on the current portfolio of products or services, e.g., by improving products in the portfolio, or by firm development analogies. The other way is, to use a firm analogy built on an anticipated future state of the firm and derive an exit multiple as terminal value for the DCF analysis. Thus, both approaches utilize an income approach such as DCF. Additionally, practitioners seem also to appraise potential for new applications for the current products or services in the portfolio.

With regard to *transaction effects*, practitioners seem to base their valuation mainly on a pre-transaction or standalone valuation. Effects of the transaction on innovation potential seem to be considered majorly qualitative by separate qualitative appraisals, e.g., of synergies deriving from the investor's business network. Two quantitative methodologies seem to be applicable, but nor majorly used: First, the quantification of costs to develop and market a similar product or service in the investing firm, and second, the quantification of costs to retain key personnel.

Risk and uncertainty seem to be majorly considered within an income approach by using the discount rate and by assessing a reasonable number of periods individually before applying a terminal value. Additionally, risks seem to be assessed either qualitatively by using different scenarios, business plan adjustments to decrease the over-confidence in provided business plans, or even gut feeling. Or they are assessed quantitatively by applying probabilities for scenarios, sensitivity analysis, break-even analyses, or simulations.

Growth firm valuators seem to possess and use a whole toolbox of methodologies. The income approach seems to be the most common calculation methodology accompanied by a mix of qualitative and quantitative interpretation methodologies to consider transaction effects and risk or uncertainty.

Information

The following table gives an overview of the relevant information to assess the innovation potential of growth firms from a practitioner's view.

Practitioners seem to consider four major factors when appraising *innovation projects* from growth firms. First, they consider the feasibility to develop the product or service. Second, they consider the value of the project for potential customers. This includes an assessment of, where the product or service can be applied and the fit of the innovative product or service in the current business models within the target industries. Third, they seem to consider the growth firms capability to commercialize the innovation (Does the firm have access to relevant markets and distribution channels? How fast can the innovation be brought to the market?). Fourth, as already stated in the methodologies section, information about the firm's ability to protect the innovation from imitation to protect higher margins seems to be regarded as relevant.

Table 18. Information for the Valuation of Growth Firms

Dimensions	Collected Information	
	Empirical data (1st order construct)	Abstraction (2nd order construct)
Innovation projects	(1) Technical feasibility	Development feasibility
	(2) Customer acceptance	Customer value
	(3) Time-to-market speed	Commercialization capability
	(4) Access to distribution channels	Commercialization capability
	(5) Applications for innovation	Current product/service portfolio
	(6) Whole business model	Business model of product/service
	(7) Protection from imitation	Protection from imitation
Innovation capability	(1) Team of developers	Team's development execution capability
	(2) Commercialization capability	Team's commercialization capability
	(3) Project portfolio or pipeline	Innovation project portfolio
	(4) Learning/experience curves	Comparable firms
	(5) Comparable firms	Comparable firms
	(6) Scalability of technology	Scalability
Transaction effects	(1) Cultural fit	Cultural fit
	(2) Network synergies	Network synergies
	(3) Retention of key personnel	Retention of key personnel

Relevant information with regard to *innovation capability* can be grouped in three categories. The first category is the founder team's capability to develop the product or service. The second one is the capability to commercialize the new product or service. And the third one is to grow the business around the commercialized products or services. With regard to the last category, practitioners seem to take a look at the innovation project portfolio and pipeline and the scalability of individual new products, services, or technology. To build analogies as depicted in the methodologies section, they also seem to use comparable firms as reference to appraise innovation capability.

With regard to *transaction effects*, practitioners seem to regard three types of information as relevant. They seem to consider the cultural fit between acquiring and acquired firm as relevant though, for them, this fit seems to be difficult to assess. Access to acquirers or investors relationships seems to be relevant. And they seem to consider the retention of key personnel as critical factor to assess the effects of a transaction and consider according information in the valuation.

6.4 Valuation of Mature Firms

In chapter 4.3.3, mature firms were characterized as having stable growth rates approaching the growth rates in the economy, stable margins, and most of their income deriving from existing assets. How do practitioners appraise those kind of firms?

6.4.1 Methodologies

The following sections depict the methodologies that are used by practitioners to appraise the innovation potential of mature firms.

Innovation projects

(1) Valuators of mature companies *do not seem to value single innovation or development projects*. Instead, they seem to consider the results of a firm's innovation activities as a whole and appraise these with a *scenario approach*. Only in the case that single innovation projects are assumed to make a major difference for the valuation, these projects are considered and valuated separately. This applies for example in the health care or pharmaceutical industry and is comparable to the valuation of idea firms.

> Wachstum ist in erster Linie Marktwachstum. . . . Wenn wir uns Unternehmen anschauen, die stark wachsen, bei denen das unter anderem durch Innovation getrieben ist, dann schauen wir uns das nicht auf Einzelobjektebene an, in der Regel, sondern das wird mal top-down- aber auch bottom-up-mäßig geplant. (Investment bank professional)

> *Sehen Sie sich einzelne Projekte an?* Das ist ganz stark industrieabhängig. Wenn ich ein produzierendes Unternehmen habe, das eine Palette von Produkten hat, dann spielen diese einzelnen kleinen neuen Produkte wahrscheinlich keine Rolle. Und auch bei Unternehmen, die in der Regel schon an der Börse gelistet sind, sind das meistens etablierte Unternehmen, die eine gewisse Reife erreicht haben, und da spielt das eigentlich keine Rolle.

> *Werden Innovationsprojekte einzeln bewertet?* Das habe ich noch nicht erlebt. Für einen Automobilzulieferer haben wir die Entwicklung einer Plattform einzeln bewertet: Was passiert, wenn sie kommt? Was passiert, wenn sie nicht kommt? Im Endef-

> fekt ist die Plattform ja nie gebaut worden. Das lag aber eher an den Umständen beim Kunden des Unternehmens. Das sind Themen, die in den Business Plan direkt einfließen, aber nicht im Sinne einer separaten Bewertung. Wir haben nicht gesagt „Das ist jetzt der Wert des Projektes", sondern das war Teil der Gesamtbewertung, aber die Faktoren sind natürlich separat eingeflossen. (Investment bank professional)

> *Werden Innovationsprojekte einzeln bewertet?* Bei Unternehmensbewertungen eher selten. Man kann das machen und das wird auch zum Teil gemacht. Einzelne Treiber [Preise, Mengen] modellieren. Ich halte nicht so viel davon, weil man den Wald vor lauter Bäumen nicht mehr sieht. Was dann passiert ist, dass das Gesamtbild aus den Einzelrechnungen keinen Sinn mehr macht. Es ist regelmäßig dann so, dass man aus der Addition dieser kleinen Summen gigantische Potenziale erhält. In der Realität gibt es Sachen, die schief gehen können, die dann nicht berücksichtigt werden. Grundsätzlich gibt es Bottom-Up und Top-Down-Ansätze. Ich halte deutlich mehr von einem Top-Down-Ansatz, um Sachen durch die Gesamtschau berücksichtigen zu können, die nicht einzeln geplant wurden und auch nicht planbar sind. Regelmäßig wird das auch von PE-Firmen so gemacht. (Investment bank professional)

> *Werden einzelne Projekte bewertet?* Ja, das gibt es. In der Branche Health Care wird das gemacht. Bei Medikamenten gibt es verschiedene Stufen. Stufen werden mit unterschiedlichen Wahrscheinlichkeiten für Cash Flows belegt. Kleinere Pharma-Unternehmen haben letztlich nur ein bis drei Produkte und da lässt sich schon sehr stark herausfiltrieren, wo die Treiber sind, und dann wird es schon so gemacht. Da wäre es dann so. Da hätte ich eigentlich eigene Produkt- GuVs und dann bewerte ich ‚Stand alone' jedes einzelne der zwei bis drei Medikamente oder Patente, die das Unternehmen hat, und rechne dann eigene DCFs und die bestimmen dann den Unternehmenswert. (Investment bank professional)

Innovation capability

(1) Valuators seem to use the *income approach* as the main approach to value mature firms and value innovation capability in the *estimated future cash flows or growth rate* implicitly.

> Die Frage ist halt: Wie definiere ich den Einfluss der Innovationsfähigkeit? Ist es so, dass eine Bewertung gemacht wird und hier habe ich Tranche 1, 2, 3, 4 und die zusammen ergeben dann die Bewertung. Dann ist es eher schwierig. . . . Das Thema Innovationsfähigkeit... Sagen wir es anders: Bei der DCF-Bewertung ist es ja so: Das

ist eine Betrachtung des Cash Flows. Meine Cash Generation in der Zukunft wird bewertet und das macht am Ende meinen Unternehmenswert aus. Insofern sich Innovationsfähigkeit in Cash niederschlägt, spielt das eine Rolle. (Investment bank professional)

Wenn ein Unternehmen innovativ ist, dann hat man aus der DCF-Perspektive am Anfang recht hohe Investitionen, was sich ja negativ auf die Cash-Flow-Betrachtung auswirken würde. Auf der anderen Seite ist es ja so, dass sich diese Innovation auf den Sales, dass neue Produkte verkauft werden bzw., wenn ich operativ innovativ bin, d. h. effizienter werde mit der Pipe, dann würde sich das auf die Margen auswirken, was dann auch wieder eine höhere Cash-Flow-Generation in der Zukunft bewirken würde, was sich dann auch auf die Bewertung auswirken würde, weil ich einfach mehr Cash habe, den ich abzinsen würde. Das ist so der Punkt. Ich weiß nicht, ob das in die richtige Richtung geht, wo Innovation bei DCF einfließen würde. Wenn ein Unternehmen überleben möchte, wenn man Innovationsfähigkeit als einen Faktor zur Sicherung des Überlebens begreift, heißt das ja, dass es profitabel ist und Cash Flow generieren muss. Dies wirkt sich dann aus in einer erhöhten Marge oder Top-Line eines erhöhten Umsatzes, die sich auch in meiner DCF-Bewertung widerspiegeln. Für Wachstum gibt es ja verschiedene Faktoren. Je stärker ein Unternehmen innovativ ist, um so stärker wird es wachsen. Es gibt natürlich auch noch andere Faktoren für Wachstum, aber das wäre dann ein Punkt, den man sich im Rahmen seiner Analyse anschauen würde. (Investment bank professional)

Oder ich habe in der DCF ein Wachstum, das über Markt liegt und bei dem mein Unternehmen Marktanteile gewinnt. So würde ich das abbilden. (Investment bank professional)

(2) Valuators seem to *extrapolate the future innovation capability from the past innovation performance*.

Wir stützen uns dann oft auf die Historie, versuchen dann eine Extrapolation der Daten hinzulegen. Weniger dann wirklich das Thema Innovation als solches, dass wir wirklich sagen: Wie wahrscheinlich ist es, dass das Unternehmen dann noch ein neues Produkt entwickelt und dann in der Lage ist, die Umsätze zu verdoppeln, beispielsweise bei einem Biotech-Unternehmen. Das kommt sehr, sehr selten vor.

> Wenn, dann greifen wir das Thema über Wachstum und dann gibt es meistens unterschiedliche Szenarien. (Investment bank professional)

> Erst mal würde man die Historie anschauen, um zu verstehen: War das Unternehmen auch in der Vergangenheit in der Lage, auch ständig auf neue Produktzyklen zu reagieren? (Investment bank professional)

(3) Another possible methodology to valuate innovation capability is to use a *market approach* and to *apply higher multiples* compared to competitors in an industry peer group, if the innovation capability is perceived higher.

> Da man die Zukunft nicht voraussehen kann, kann man entweder nur historische oder direkte Vergleichsdaten heranziehen. Letztendlich basiert ja jeder Experte, der eine hat mehr Erfahrung und Informationsquellen als der andere, seine Annahmen immer auf Vergleichen. (Investment bank professional)

> Dann würde man sich auch in der Industrie Vergleichsunternehmen anschauen: Was für Unterschiede gibt es? Das dann aber eher in der zweiten großen Methodengruppe, die eher die Marktperspektive ist. Wo man sich anschaut: Wie steht das Unternehmen im Vergleich zu Wettbewerbern da? Welche Margen haben sie? In welchen Bereichen arbeiten sie? Wie differenziert ist das Produktportfolio? (Investment bank professional)

> *Oder ich nehme eine andere Peer Group und vergleiche mit innovativen Unternehmen anderer Branchen?* Da würde ich an Ihrer Stelle eher sagen: Wir schauen uns die Multiplikatoren anderer Unternehmen und legen da noch ne Schippe drauf. (Investment bank professional)

Transaction Effects

(1) The usual methodology seems to be that valuators perform a *standalone valuation* of the target firm first. (2) Then, after the standalone valuation they perform an *extra valuation of assumed synergies* and add this value to the standalone valuation result.

> Ich habe zuerst die Standalone-Bewertung als Ausgangswert und dann gucke ich, welche Synergien habe ich und andere Sachen. Ob ich diese Zahl bereit bin zu bezahlen, ist eine andere Frage. (Investment bank professional)

> Eigentlich verstehen wir die Industrie nie besser als der Kunde. . . . Aber da hilft er uns das Synergiepotential zu bemessen und dem wird auch ein Wert beigemessen. Das ist ein Wert von X und der kann auch oft separat ermittelt werden. (Investment bank professional)

> Ist ja klar, wenn 1+1=3 ist, dann möchte ich vom Wert zwischen 2 und 3 auch was haben. Die Synergieanalyse ist eine eigene Analyse. Meist wird dann noch eine Synergie- oder Kontrollprämie bezahlt. (Investment bank professional)

> Ich sehe mir das Unternehmen an, wie es ist, und es mag den und den Wert haben. Aber, wenn ich rangehe und am Unternehmen etwas verändere, kann es sein, dass ich Potenziale freisetze. Und das würde ja Wert generieren. Dann bin ich bereit, einen höheren Preis zu zahlen, als rechnerisch der Wert ist. (Investment Bank professional)

> *Das heißt, Sie machen erst eine Standalone-Bewertung und dann berücksichtigen Sie die Auswirkungen einer Akquisition?* Ja. Ja genau. Es gibt ja operative Auswirkungen und finanzielle Auswirkungen. Wenn ich einen Sponsor berate, hat das andere Implikationen als wenn ich einen Strategen berate. Natürlich spielt der Aspekt Synergien eine riesige Rolle. Es gibt aber auch Dyssynergien eventuell, die dadurch entstehen, dass die verkaufte Einheit aus einem großen Organismus herausoperiert werden muss. Und auch das hat natürlich unheimlich viele Kosten, aber eben erstmal Dysintegrationskosten und eventuell auch HR-Implikationen. (Investment bank professional)

Regarding innovation capability in an M&A situation, valuators recommend to (3) *estimate the combined innovation capability* of both assets or firms after the acquisition and/or integration has been executed.

> *Ein Thema bei Innovationsfähigkeit könnte ja sein, dass diese dann abnimmt, wenn ein großes Unternehmen ein innovatives Unternehmen übernimmt?* Das vergessen leider viele Käufer. Und oft ist so, dass gerade in so großen Konglomeraten die Unternehmen dann an Dynamik verlieren, weil, und das ist ein guter Punkt, den Sie ansprechen, genau diese Innovationsfreudigkeit und Flexibilität der Führung verloren geht und man sich so ein bisschen der Mutter hingibt und sagt: Wir sind da eh drin und können da relativ wenig machen, weil man, sei es durch Bürokratie oder mone-

tär, nicht richtig inzentiviert ist, um genau diese Dinge zu fördern. Das gibt es oft. (Investment bank professional)

Wenn ich ein mittelständisches Unternehmen habe, das an einen Großkonzern geht, kann es schon passieren, dass die Dynamik und Flexibilität des Unternehmens eingeschränkt wird. (Investment bank professional)

Risk and uncertainty

Valuators of growth firms seem to use the following methodologies to consider risk and uncertainty in their valuations.

It seems that most valuators use the (1) *discount rate used in an income methodology,* e.g. DCF, combined with a (2) *scenario technique* to incorporate risks and uncertainties in their valuations.

Ich sehe mir erst mal an: Wie stabil ist das Unternehmen vom Set-Up? Das berücksichtige ich bei DCF durch Kapitalkosten, durch Szenarien. (Investment bank professional)

Wie gehen *sie denn mit Risiko um? Welche Methoden wenden Sie an? Wie preisen Sie das ein?* Über die vorhin genannten Cases, Upside-Cases, Szenarien und die restlichen Dinge sind in der DCF im Diskontierungsfaktor enthalten. (Investment bank professional)

Wie gehen Sie mit Risiko um? Eher mit Szenarien oder über das Diskontieren? Eher über Szenarien. (Investment bank professional)

Wird zu den Diskontierungsfaktoren auch ein Risiko-Abschlag bei den Cash-Flows genommen oder wird das über Szenarien abgedeckt? Das wird über Szenarien abgedeckt oder aufgrund der Unternehmensgröße haben wir auch, dass wir bei kleineren Unternehmen eine höhere Risikoprämie nehmen. Also nicht direkt im Beta, aber über das Market Risk. (Investment bank professional)

The alternative to consider the risks of innovation activities by using *risk adjusted cash flows* seems not to be used and superseded by the scenario technique, i.e., practitioners develop different cash flow scenarios.

> *Gibt es einen Risikoabschlag?* Der Risikoabschlag, das meine ich mit dem Wertabschlag, den es vielleicht durch fehlende Informationen gibt. Der Risikoabschlag im WACC wäre ein eigenes Thema für sich. Klar, über den WACC kann man das steuern. Auf der anderen Seite wäre der Risikoabschlag dann auch so drin, dass man einfach niedrigere Sales kalkulieren wird und, da dadurch der Cash Flow niedriger wird, wird auch die Bewertung niedriger. Ein Unternehmen, das eine höhere Unsicherheit oder Risiko hat, läuft ja dann über meine Volatilität, was dann meine Eigenkapitalkosten erhöhen würde, und da würde man das über ein höheres Beta laufen lassen. In der Regel macht man eher keinen Abschlag, sondern sucht eher eine geeignete Eigenkapitalverzinsung. (Investment bank professional)

> *Auf welcher Basis bestimmen Sie den Diskontierungsfaktor?* Da bestimmen wir den WACC über das CAPM. (Investment bank professional)

> Ich bevorzuge, aber das ist nur eine persönliche Präferenz, die predicted Barra[17] Betas, keine historischen Betas. (Investment bank professional)

It seems that in most cases *three scenarios* are created to deal with uncertain outcomes.

> Wir haben einen Management Case, einen Downside Case und einen Upside Case. . . . Man hat ja vom Unternehmen einen Business Plan vorgegeben. Dann macht man dann eine Plausibilisierung: Wenn man den genau so nehmen würde, wie es das Management vorhersagt, wenn es sich besser entwickelt oder wenn man etwas konservativer ist. (Investment bank professional)

> Ein Upside und ein Downside Case neben dem Base Case ist meistens der Standard. Mehr erhöhen meiner Ansicht nach nur die Komplexität. (Investment bank professional)

> Es gibt einen Case, den erarbeiten wir zusammen mit dem Management, und da sind sich dann alle einig: Das ist der wahrscheinlichste und dann muss man sagen: Was gibt es für Punkte, die passieren können? Da rechnet man verschiedene Szenarien, um dann eben nach unten zu sehen, was passiert, wenn diese negativen Szenarien eintreffen. Das ist aber nur für einen selber eine Absicherung: Auf welchem Floor bewege ich mich? Wie volatil ist eigentlich der Wert, den ich bekomme? Aber im

---

[17] Barra is a brand of MSCI, a provider of investment decision support tools. Barra's predicted betas are based on a predicting risk model containing 13 fundamental risk factors. Historical betas are based on regression analysis on a stock's excess returns against the market's excess returns (BARRA, 2000).

> Endeffekt ist der Base Case der Wert, den ich zusammen mit dem Management erarbeite und den ich erzielen möchte. (Investment bank professional)

> Wir haben verschiedene Szenarien gebildet: Den Downside und den Upside Case und eine Sensitivität: Was passiert, wenn es kommt, wenn es nicht kommt, wenn nur ein Teil kommt? (Investment bank professional)

> Was man im Regelfall macht, ist, dass man mit Szenarien rechnet. Grobe Keule: Umsatz mal höher mal niedriger oder: Bestimmte Produkte fliegen oder sie fliegen nicht… (Investment bank professional)

Scenario technique approaches are often accompanied by (3) *sensitivity analysis*, the simulation of cause-effect relations between small changes in business driver metrics and valuation results. One valuator even appraises the use of a sensitivity analysis as more valuable than the use of scenarios.

> Sensitivitätsanalysen sind für jemand Erfahrenen viel wichtiger, auch bei der Einbeziehung von Potenzialen. (Investment bank professional)

To support the quantification of scenarios (4), the scenarios are associated with *probabilities*.

> Ich habe das auf eine andere Art drin [als bei Realoptionen]. Ich mache ja Szenarien. Ich habe nicht nur einen Fall. Ich habe mehrere Fälle mit Downside und Upside Fällen. Dieses Verfahren [Entscheidungsbäume] hat den Vorteil, dass sie viel besser verständlich sind und sicherer in der Anwendung, weniger Fehlerquellen. (Investment bank professional)

> Man weiß es einfach nicht besser. Man kann es nicht besser greifen. Und wir bilden das dann über Wahrscheinlichkeiten und Wachstum ab. Mit einer Wahrscheinlichkeit tritt der Fall ein und mit der übrigen der andere. (Investment bank professional)

(5) *Monte Carlo simulations* are an additional methodology to simulate possible earnings of risky assets. Empirical results indicate that they are rarely used and only on customer demand.

> In ganz, ganz seltenen Fällen kommt es dann mal zu einer Monte-Carlo-Simulation. Aber das ist auch wirklich relativ selten. . . . Ich hab das selbst erst einmal gemacht. *Hat das der Kunde gefordert oder hätten Sie das auch selbst gemacht?* Jaja, der Kunde hatte das gefordert. *Hätten Sie das auch gemacht, wenn er das nicht gefordert hätte?* Es war so ne Situation, wo man nicht wusste, in welche Richtung das geht und

da war es für uns gut, das Ganze mal so zu machen, aber für die meisten Fälle ist das einfach „over engineered“. Damit gewinnt man am Ende auch nicht mehr. Wie Sie sagen: GIGO [garbage in – garbage out]. Man weiß es einfach nicht besser. Man kann es nicht besser greifen. (Investment bank professional)

(6) If market approaches are used as general valuation methodology, risks are reflected in the *multiples*. Firms with more stable business prospects seem to get higher multiples.

Bei Multiples erhält ein stabileres Geschäft eher höhere Multiplikatoren. (Investment bank professional)

Wie gehen Sie denn mit Risiko um? Welche Methoden wenden Sie an? Wie preisen Sie das ein? Über die vorhin genannten Cases, Upside-Cases, Szenarien und die restlichen Dinge sind in der DCF im Diskontierungsfaktor enthalten. Bei Multiplikatoren, da ist es dann alles indirekt in einer Zahl vermischt. (Investment bank professional)

(7) An interesting approach to appraise the quality of an intended extrapolation approach is to assess the *quality of past business planning*, e.g., planned values versus actuals. This approach can also be used to check the plausibility of a business plan provided a firm’s management.

So ein Prozess dauert ja mehrere Monate und man bekommt am Anfang diese Geschäftsplanung. Die wurde dann natürlich auch schon eine Weile vor Beginn des Prozesses erstellt. Und dann sieht man natürlich auch, wenn wir zwei, drei Monate im Prozess sind, ob wirklich die Current Trading Figures den Plan unterstützen oder nicht. *Das ist ein Indikator für die Planungsqualität?* Absolut. Natürlich werden weitere Sachen [berücksichtigt], wie: Wie hat sich der Markt entwickelt etc. oder andere Vergleichsunternehmen... Man hat ja dann ein paar Datenpunkte, an denen man sich orientieren kann. Und dann sieht man natürlich schon, wie glaubhaft die Planung ist. Ein anderer Punkt ist wichtig: Wie ist die historische Planungsqualität des Unternehmens gewesen? Man schaut sich historische Planungen, Management Accounts, an. Dann schaut man sich an: Wie akkurat war deren Planungsgenauigkeit in der Vergangenheit? Haben sie ihre Ziele eher übertroffen oder lagen sie eher darunter? (Investment bank professional)

(8) Additionally, qualitative approaches such as *trust and “gut feeling”* seem to play a role in risk estimation and should not be underestimated in final decision-making (compare chapter

6.1). Using the interviewee's definitions, "gut feeling" refers to the success or outcome of the firm's activities as a whole. Trust refers to the people that perform those activities, e.g., the management team or the R&D employees.

> Man hat irgendwie so ein „gut feeling", dass man sagt: Die schaffen das. Und wenn ich am Ende meinen Preis abgebe, dann basiere ich meinen Preis vielleicht eher auf dem Upside-Case als auf dem Base- oder dem Downside-Case. Das sind dann so versteckte Dinge, die irgendwo mein Gefühl für die ganze Sache beeinflussen. Man kennt das ja auch: Wir haben unterschiedliche Kunden beraten, die dann irgendwann gesagt haben: Ich muss das Unternehmen haben. Wir sagen dann: Hmm, das ist ein bisschen teuer. Aber die haben ein gutes Gefühl dabei und ich glaube, dann spielt das eine Rolle. (Investment bank professional)

> Da muss man halt wirklich das Vertrauen haben in die Leute, Management, Wissenschaftler, die dahinter stecken, dass die das auch so hinbekommen. (Investment bank professional)

6.4.2 Information

The following sections present the information valuators use to appraise a mature firm's innovation potential.

Innovation projects

(1) Innovation projects do not seem to be valued individually (compare methodology section above). Nevertheless, valuators seem to take a look at the *innovation project portfolio and the project pipeline* as a whole.

> Ich schaue mir an: Was gibt es in der Pipeline? Konkrete Maßnahmen. Wie weit sind diese Innovationsideen schon gediehen. Gibt es Gespräche mit Kunden? Gibt es Studien? Wie kann ich überhaupt begründen, dass das, was gerade entwickelt wird, auch vom Markt gebraucht wird? Was gibt es für Sachen, wo es die ersten Konzepte gibt? (Investment bank professional)

> Man würde versuchen zu verstehen, in welche Entwicklungen das Unternehmen investiert hat, wie die Pipeline für neue Produkte aussieht. . . . Und dann muss man in die Zukunft schauen: Was sind die Projekte, an denen gearbeitet wird? Was steht früh in der Pipeline? Wie weit sind manche Dinge schon gediehen? Gibt es irgend-

> welche Vorverträge oder Ähnliches für den Launch von weiteren Produkten? (Investment bank professional)

(2) As valuators do not seem to appraise innovation projects individually in detail, they try to appraise the *status or concreteness* and probability of success based on statistics and analogies for firms that are highly dependent on individual innovation projects such as pharmaceutical firms. With respect to the concreteness of individual projects, a methodology that valuators seem to use is to estimate success probabilities dependent on statistics, if such statistics are available.

> Was man machen kann, ist im Pharmabereich der Vergleich mit statistischen Daten. Zertifizierung durch die FDA. Es gibt da zwei bis drei Referenzstudien und man einigt sich auf eine dieser Referenzen. Das ist dann auch bekannt im Markt. Das sind dann Referenzwerte, die in der Branche gelten. (Investment bank professional)

Innovation capability

(1) The first indication from the empirical results is that valuators link innovation capability with anticipated *firm growth* that is available as information for example as part of a firm's business plan.

> An sich ist Innovation in jedem Bereich ein Thema. *Spielt es eine Rolle?* Die Frage kann ich mit ja beantworten. Es ist allerdings eher versteckt im Wachstum, das wir im Business-Plan abbilden. (Investment bank professional)

> Wenn wir uns die Sachen ansehen, ist es in der Regel so, dass wir auf Wachstum schauen. Das ist der Treiber in so einem Modell, der Ihrer Frage am nächsten kommt. (Investment bank professional)

> Für Wachstum gibt es ja verschiedene Faktoren. Je stärker ein Unternehmen innovativ ist, um so stärker wird es wachsen. Es gibt natürlich auch noch andere Faktoren für Wachstum, aber das wäre dann ein Punkt, den man sich im Rahmen seiner Analyse anschauen würde. (Investment bank professional)

> Wenn ich hierzu [Pipeline, Innovationsideen] einen Haken setzen kann, ist das für mich eine Voraussetzung, um überhaupt eine positive Entwicklung in einem Business Plan überhaupt vorherzusehen. Oder es ist eine Voraussetzung für eine stabile also nicht abfallende Entwicklung. Das Gleiche gilt, wenn ich mit Multiples arbeite.

> Ich kann kein innovationsgetriebenes Unternehmen mit einem vergleichen, das sich auf den Früchten der Vergangenheit ausruht. (Investment bank professional)

(2) Valuators regard the *management team's quality* as an important input factor for the valuation of a mature firm. If the purpose of an acquisition is to acquire intellectual capital such as patents, ideas, prototypes or products, then the management team's importance for the valuation seems to decrease.

> Das Problem ist, dass man das nicht an der Innovationsfähigkeit bemessen kann, sondern das ist eher das Gefühl für das Management. (Investment bank professional)

> *Spielt es auch eine Rolle, ob das Management als Treiber der Innovation an Bord bleibt? Kann man das bepreisen?* Leider nicht. Schwierig, einen Preis festzustellen, weil dieses Thema Innovation, das steckt in der Organisation. Das kann im Kopf vom CEO oder CFO stecken oder Technikvorstand. Es kann aber auch in der Ebene darunter stecken und das ist schwer zu beziffern. Dem kann man keinen Wert beimessen. *Würden sie versuchen Herauszufinden woran das [Innovationsfähigkeit] liegt?* Ja, natürlich. Idealerweise versuche ich als Käufer schon herauszufinden: Wer sind die treibenden Kräfte im Unternehmen und sorgen für diese Dynamik? (Investment bank professional)

Two other important categories of information are (3) *past data* and (4) *comparable firms* to use for the market approach.

> Da man die Zukunft nicht voraussehen kann, kann man entweder nur historische oder direkte Vergleichsdaten heranziehen. (Investment bank professional)

Transaction effects

(1) Valuators of mature firms use several types of information to valuate transaction effects. The first information they use is, if *cost synergies* between the buyer's and the seller's research & development department exist.

> *Welche Synergien würde man mit Innovation im Hinterkopf betrachten?* Zum einen gibt es durch Kostenreduktion Synergien. . . . Zum Beispiel kann man sich eine R&D-Abteilung sparen. (Investment bank professional)

(2) Another information they use is the *complementarity of research & development pipelines*.

> Was auch passieren kann ist, dass ein Healthcare-Unternehmen seine Pipeline mit den Produkten des gekauften Unternehmens füllen will, um seine Innovationsfähigkeit zu erhöhen. (Investment bank professional)

(3) The last information valuators seem to consider is, if *key personnel can be retained* in the acquired firm.

> Auch diese Faktoren sind natürlich wichtig: Kann ich meine Schlüsselpersonen halten? Kann ich die Forscher, die an wichtigen Projekten arbeiten, halten? Wie sind die Verträge gestaltet? Was kostet mich das, wenn jemand geht bzw. kann der einfach gehen? Welche Erfindungen hat der bereits, die ich bezahlen muss? Diese ganzen Faktoren sind natürlich Teil der Due Diligence und ein sehr wichtiger Faktor, um am Ende eine Bewertung vorzunehmen. (Investment bank professional)

> *Es spielt eine Rolle, ob ich die Treiber der Innovation habe oder nicht? Wenn ich den Gründer auszahle, was habe ich dann gekauft?* Ja, klar. Es kommt darauf an: Wie wichtig war dieser Mann? Jeder Käufer, der das ein bisschen abschätzen kann, wird ihn nie zum Golfen schicken, sondern so inzentivieren, dass er dann nach fünf Jahren golfen gehen kann, aber nicht sofort. Wenn es nur um die Patente geht, dann kann man ihn auszahlen, solange man die Dinge hat, die den Wert des Unternehmens ausmachen. (Investment bank professional)

Data sources

As for the other firm types, the information to valuate a mature firm derives from three sources. Data given by the acquisition target's management, data gathered internally by the valuators at the buying firm, and data gathered from external sources.

(1) The information provided by an acquisition target includes the selling management's business plan, management interviews, site visits, and information derived from due diligence processes.
(2) The valuator's information includes data from own experience, in-house industry experts, and information from internal industry research.

(3) To check the external consistency of assumptions professionals consult their customers (buy-side), consult external industry experts and lawyers, discuss with the sell-side advisor, and investigate comparable publically listed firms.

(4) An additional source of information in the case of a valuation service firm is its customer. Such a client of a professional valuation service provider often owns deep industry knowledge and knowledge about the object of a valuation.

> *Werden Synergien im Vorhinein bei der Bewertung berücksichtigt?* Absolut. Und da hilft uns auch immer der Kunde, der in der Regel der Industrieexperte ist. Eigentlich verstehen wir die Industrie nie besser als der Kunde. Wir sind in der Regel sein Instrument und führen das aus, was er sagt. Wir können ihn „challengen" und sind ein guter Sparringspartner. Aber da hilft er uns, das Synergiepotential zu bemessen und dem wird auch ein Wert beigemessen. . . . In der Regel kennt der Kunde die Industrie besser, wenn es ein Stratege ist. Der ist zum Glück Spezialist. Ich kann ihm die richtigen Fragen stellen und die Sachen hinterfragen, so dass er vielleicht zu einem anderen Ergebnis kommt, aber besser wissen als der Kunde tu ich das nicht. (Investment bank professional)

6.4.3 Key Findings and Discussion

The following sections sum up the indications with regard to the valuation of mature firms derived from the empirical investigation.

Methodologies

Table 19 sums up the collected empirical data and deduced abstractions.

Innovation projects do not seem to be appraised individually for mature firms except in the case that the mature firms are highly dependent on individual innovation projects, e.g., in the pharmaceutical industry.

The value of the *innovation capability* seems to be assessed majorly by income approaches such as DCF (inferring from a firm's innovation or growth history to its future prospects) or firm analogies (using a market approach and deriving a value estimation from comparable innovative firms). Though, both of these approaches are quantitative in nature, valuators also seem to adjust these valuations after the quantitative calculation with qualitative assessments based on the collected data. This process is matching the extended valuation process depicted in chapter 6.1.1.

Table 19. Methodologies for the Valuation of Mature Firms

Dimensions	Valuation methodologies	
	Empirical data (1st order construct)	Abstraction (2nd order construct)
Innovation projects	(1) No individual innovation project valuation except for firms depending highly on individual innovation projects	*No extra valuation except for firms highly dependent on individual innovation project*
Innovation capability	(1) Income approach	*Calculation*: Start from current state (income approach)
	(2) Extrapolation from past innovation performance	*Interpretation (quant.)*: Extrapolation
	(3) Market approach	*Calculation*: Start from current state (market approach)
Transaction effects	(1) Standalone valuation	*Calculation*: Pre-transaction valuation
	(2) Extra valuation of synergies	*Interpretation (qual.)*: Post-transaction valuation
	(3) Assessment of combined innovation capability	*Interpretation (qual.)*: Combined innovation capability
Risk and uncertainty	(1) Discount rate	*Calculation*: Discount rate
	(2) Scenario technique	*Interpretation (qual.)*: Scenarios
	(3) Sensitivity analysis	*Interpretation (quant.)*: Sensitivity analysis
	(4) Scenario probabilities	*Interpretation (quant.)*: Scenario probabilities
	(5) Monte-Carlo-simulation	*Interpretation (quant.)*: Simulation
	(6) Multiples	*Interpretation (qual.)*: Firm analogy
	(7) Assessment of past planning quality	*Interpretation (qual.)*: Assessment of planning quality
	(8) Trust and gut-feeling	*Interpretation*: Intuition

With regard to *transaction effects* practitioners majorly seem to only appraise the standalone or pre-transaction value of the valued firm in the case of a transaction at first an in the calculation. The standalone value is the value of the firm without considering the transaction and potential synergies that derive from the transaction. Similar to the innovation potential, synergies then adjust the calculated value in a next process step.

To assess and quantify *risks*, practitioners use multiple methodologies. The most commonly used approach seems to use an income approach such as DCF and to consider risks with a combination of creating cash flow scenarios complemented by adjusting the discount rate. Also, simulations such as sensitivity calculations and Monte-Carlo-simulations are used to appraise the risks of investments. Last but not least, even more qualitative appraisals and adjustments such as "gut feeling" are used to consider risks in a valuation.

For mature firms, generally, practitioners seem to tend more to quantitative calculation and interpretation methodologies based on past and planned financials. Qualitative assessments seem to be used to assess transaction effects and deal with risks.

Information

The following table gives an overview over the relevant information to assess innovation potential of mature firms from a practitioner's view.

Table 20. Information for the Valuation of Mature Firms

Dimensions	Collected Information	
	Empirical data (1st order construct)	Abstraction (2nd order construct)
Innovation projects	(1) Portfolio of projects	Innovation project portfolio
	(2) Status of projects in portfolio	Innovation project portfolio
Innovation capability	(1) Firm growth in business plan	General firm growth
	(2) Management team	Team's firm development capability (incl. innovation)
	(3) Past data	Past development
	(4) Comparable firms	Comparable firms
Transaction effects	(1) Cost synergies	Cost synergies
	(2) Complementarity of R&D pipelines	Portfolio synergies
	(3) Retention of key personnel	Retention of key personnel

As mentioned in the methodology section *innovation projects* seem not to be appraised individually in detail. Instead, information about the portfolio of innovation projects as a whole seems to be considered.

A firm's *innovation capability* seems not to be analyzed by its structural components such as defined innovation processes or the budget for innovation activities. The major information considered seems to be the firm's overall growth, which is assumed to reflect its innovation capability. Additionally, as further proxy for innovation capability, the management team is assessed to infer a firm's innovation capability.

Valuators use two major types of information while assessing the *transaction effects*: On the one hand synergies in the dimensions of costs and complementary innovation project portfolio and on the other hand the capability to retain qualified key personnel.

6.5 Cross-Type Comparison

The following sections give a cross-firm-type overview with regard to the valuation process and its context factors, the used methodologies to interpret data and calculate an innovation potential value, and the information perceived as relevant for the valuation of a firm's innovation potential. In the following analyses it makes sense to analyze the dimensions methodologies and information together as they are heavily interlinked and should depict relevant differences between firm types more effectively when combined.

6.5.1 Valuation Process and Context Factors

Chapter 6.1 already depicted an extended valuation process and context factors influencing this process as result of the empirical investigation. Additionally to the generic process and context factors, Table 21 depicts a cross-type comparison of context factors characteristics for each firm type.

Table 21. Cross-Type-Comparison Context Factors

Firm Type / Context factor	Idea Firms	Growth Firms	Mature Firms
Firm type:			
Existing and accessible data	(Business) idea description / business case	Mixed	Historical performance information
Valuation context:			
Purpose	Strategic investment (only minor stake)	Strategic investment / acquisition or merger (minor or major stake)	Acquisition or merger (major stake)
Risk sharing	With other investments/investors/founders	With investors/ founders/owners	No major risk sharing possible
Understanding of value	Fundamental/resource-based	←→	Market-based
Common use and comprehensibility of valuation	Minor influence	High influence	Medium influence
Market for firms	High influence on valuation	←→	Basis for valuation (market approach)
Valuator (team):			
Valuator expertise	Industry expertise (qualitative methodologies, hurdle rate approach)	Methodological expertise, (income approaches, DCF)	Firm market expertise - "Market/deal makers", less industry knowledge, (market approaches, multiples)
Role of intuition	Trust in idea	←→	Trust in management team

The *firm type* has a major influence on the accessible data and thus, on the selection of a preferred or major valuation methodology (if more than one is applied) that makes best use of this data. Major accessible data for idea firms seem to be the descriptions of their founder's ideas or the ideas' business cases. For mature firms, a wide range of historical performance information is available that could be used to assess innovation potential.

Also, the *valuation context* seems to be quite different per firm type: Idea firms seem to be regarded as strategic investments from venture capital or business angel investors. This should have two effects on the relationship between potential investor and idea firm: First, the potential investor in many cases does only have a minor stake in the idea firm, i.e., is one of few investors including the founder himself and as such does not expect to have complete control over the idea firm as result of the transaction. Second, a venture capital investor is likely to mitigate his/her risk by investing in more than one idea firm. Valuators of mature firms on the other side of the spectrum usually neither strive for minor stake investments, but for controlling the acquired firm, nor do they usually strive to mitigate risks across multiple strategic investments in firms. This difference across firm types should have an effect, how valuators deal with transaction effects or risk and uncertainty in their valuations.

> Der Punkt ist hier: Es gehört uns ja nicht, sondern zum Beispiel nur 10%. Insofern hat die Methode natürlich ihre Grenzen. (Corporate venture capital professional)

> Klar wird darüber auch das Portfolio-Risiko gehedgt. In so einem klassischen VC-Portfolio haben Sie ungefähr folgende Verteilung: Zwei bis drei aus zehn werden High-Flyer. Fünf dümpeln so rum. Da bekommen sie ihr Geld wieder. Stirbt nicht, lebt aber auch nicht, wächst langsam vor sich hin. Und dann gibt es zwei bis drei, die einfach sterben. . . . Das Portfolio muss immer noch performant sein über die Verteilung und man muss es irgendwie hin kriegen, auch die wirklichen zwei bis drei dabei zu haben in dem Portfolio. Die High-Flyer da hineinzubekommen. Mit vernünftigen Bewertungen auch noch. (Venture capital professional)

The *understanding of value* seems also to be differing between firm types. Idea firm valuators seem to investigate the intrinsic or fundamental value of the business idea or technology. Mature firm valuators seem to be more likely to focus on the market value of the valuated firm assuming that market evaluations from public stock markets are a good indicator also for innovation potential. One reason for that could be the expertise and self-understanding of respective valuators (see next paragraphs).

The *common use and comprehensibility of the valuation* is an interesting influence factor more relevant for growth and mature firms. As investors or acquirers of such firms are more likely to be corporations or institutional investors, they seem also to be more likely requiring understanding the valuation approach or applying corporate standards to valuation.

> Wenn wir dem Komitee einen Fall vorstellen, haben wir den vorher mit den Controllern diskutiert und im . . . Konzern sind die DCF- und die Multiple-Methode die Methoden der Methoden. Wenn sie da nichts haben, brauchen Sie gar nicht weiterreden.

> Das ist schlicht ein Konzern-Methoden-Thema und ich vermute mal, dass es in anderen Konzernen auch keine anderen Methoden gibt. (Corporate venture capital professional)

The *market for the valuated firm* also influences valuations differently depending on the firm type. For idea firms, their respective markets seem to be small and very reactive to market screening and investment or acquisition rumors. This is likely to have effects on the data acquisition (firms can not be officially/publicly approached to provide data) and the valuation itself, e.g., by adjusting the valuation in the direction of an anticipated market price.

> [D]as fällt - und das ist unser größtes Problem - sofort auf, dass da irgendwas los ist. Das ist in diesen kleinen Märkten so, dass wenn einer zu schnüffeln beginnt, sofort das Branchengerücht da ist und dann haben sie plötzlich das Gesetz des Handelns verloren. Es ist sofort bekannt, wenn jemand kaufen will und dann gibt es eine eigene Dynamik. (Industry business development professional)

A second aspect for idea firms is that the market is also likely to aid in assessing risk and uncertainties by offering third party opinions on idea firms and their innovation potential.

> Da sitzen fünf um den Tisch. Wenn das qualitativ hochwertige Investoren sind, von denen man weiß, sie können die Zukunft einigermaßen abschätzen, ich sags mal so, prognostizieren wäre falsch, abschätzen. Dann denkt der eine: Die Leute von 3i interessieren sich auch für das Thema. Dann interessieren sich noch weitere und dann merkt man, das ist wahrscheinlich ein Thema, wo mehrere große Organisationen herausgefunden haben, dass das zukünftig doch so kommen wird, wie wir uns das vorstellen. Es gibt ja nur 25-50 Investoren in Personen, denen man das zutraut nach vorne was einzuschätzen. Wenn sich dann ein relevanter Anteil um so einen Deal schlägt, dann denken alle: Ok, dann wird das schon hinhauen und dann wird die Eintrittswahrscheinlichkeit des Business Plans von mehr Leuten höher eingeschätzt und damit ist man dann auch bereit, einen höheren Preis zu zahlen meiner Meinung nach. (Venture capital professional)

For mature firms on the other side of the spectrum, public multiples are the basis of the valuation, if a market approach is used to value such firms. Market aspects should directly affect the calculation of such an approach.

Valuators also differ between firm types in two dimensions. First, the empirical results indicate that idea firm valuators are likely to possess high industry expertise in the industry of the idea firm they are investing in. Many seem to have been active as business managers in the respective industries and now act as business angels or venture capital investors. Growth firms are likely to be appraised majorly by corporate finance experts such as auditors or by corporate venture capital firms. Mature firms are likely to by appraised by investment bankers on their own behalf or on behalf of a strategic investor. Those different valuator characteristics are likely to influence the understanding of value and the preferred methodologies. One example is the following statement of an investment banker valuing mature firms with a clear preference for market approaches:

> Letztlich ist ein Unternehmen das wert, was der Markt oder jemand bereit ist zu bezahlen. Alles, was wir tun, ist im Prinzip eine Annäherung daran. (Investment bank professional)

Second, the role that intuition, gut feeling, or trust in an idea play are likely to be different for different firm types. Idea valuators seem to use intuition towards assessing a business idea whereas mature firm valuators at the other side of the spectrum are likely to use trust and intuition more on the evaluation of the management team as proxy for a mature firm's future access.

> I think, end of the day, it is a lot of personal intuition when you invest and then, once you invested, getting the right team and getting the right people involved. (Venture capital professional)

> Das Problem ist, dass man das nicht an der Innovationsfähigkeit bemessen kann, sondern das ist eher das Gefühl für das Management. (Investment bank professional)

Summing up the detailed discussion, one can imply that context factors do not only generally influence the valuation process and, thus, the result oft he valuation, but also that those context factors have certain different characteristics dependent on the firm type oft he firm that is appraised.

6.5.2 Methodologies and Information

The following sub-sections analyze and discuss cross-type comparisons for the sub-dimensions *innovation projects*, *innovation capability*, *transaction effects*, and *risk and uncer-*

tainty. Used methodologies and relevant information are discussed together for each sub-dimension respectively.

Innovation projects

Innovation projects seem to be individually assessed only for idea or growth firms (compare Table 22). Exceptions seem to be mature firms, which are dependent on the success of one or only a few innovation projects, such as firms from the pharmaceutical industry. A reason for the decreasing importance of individual innovation projects for the valuation of innovation potential during a firm's lifecycle can be explained by a decreasing relative contribution of such projects to a firm's future revenue streams.

> Wir gehen jetzt nicht in die Firmen und gucken, wie das Innovationspotenzial der Firma ist, sondern die hat ja schon ein innovatives Produkt im Portfolio. Und wenn ich die Firma bewerte, habe ich das Innovationspotenzial dieses Produktes bewertet und zwar völlig isoliert. *Könnte man umgekehrt sagen, dass die Firma so viel Wert ist, wie ihr Produkt?* In dem Stadium schon, ja. (Corporate venture capital professional)

> *Sehen Sie sich einzelne Projekte an?* . . . . Wenn, dann geht es um Unternehmen, die in der Start-Up-Phase sind oder die nur ein Produkt haben und dabei sind, ein zweites zu entwickeln, das dann wirklich die Umsätze verdoppeln würde. Also wo sozusagen dieser Innovationswert berücksichtigt werden muss, weil ich ansonsten den Unternehmenswert nicht richtig berücksichtigen würde. (Investment bank professional)

The major calculation *methodology* to assess idea firm innovation projects seems to be the hurdle rate approach (compare chapter 3.3.5). Valuators seem to develop a picture of an idea firm's future state, which is either heavily based on a top-down approach assessing potential market size and anticipated market share or a comparable product or even firm. For growth firms, valuators seem to use the same approach, but are also likely to use an income approach with information based on the current state of the growth firm. Starting from the current state, valuators seem to develop this current state information further based on analogies to the commercialization of already existing products and services. A good example for that approach is the analysis of patent protection for a growth firm's intellectual property. As this information is based on the current state (existing and registered patents), this fact allows valuators to assume the development of future margins (stable until the end of patent protection). A major reason for the switch from starting with a firm's future state to starting from its current state is likely to be that a growth firm's valuation depends majorly on not as risky revenue or growth based on existing assets. Thus, existing assets can be used as basis for the valuation of growth firms.

The differences between idea and growth firm valuations show also in the *information* that valuators use to assess innovation projects. For idea firms, valuators collect information about the value that an innovation project creates for a potential customer, the differentiation that it potentially offers from existing products or services on the market, and the tangibility of the current state of development of such an innovation project. This information can be brought down to two main questions: First: What is the potential market for the innovation project? Second: What are the chances that this innovation can be developed and is technical feasible? Information to assess growth firms seem to be also considering this information, but focus on two other questions: First: Is the firm able to commercialize the innovative product or service and generate revenues from it? How long will the differentiation of the developed product or service lead to reasonable high margins?

Table 22. Cross-Type-Comparison Innovation Projects

Firm Type / Dimensions	Idea Firms	Growth Firms	Mature Firms
Methodologies	*Major calculation*: Start from future state (hurdle rate approach) *Interpretation (quant.)*: Top-down market potential Product/service development analogy Bottom-up/break-even analysis *Interpretation (qual.)*: Firm analogy	*Major calculation*: Start from current state (income approach) Start from future state (hurdle rate approach) *Interpretation (quant.)*: Top-down market potential Product/service development analogy *Interpretation (qual.)*: IP protection assessment	*No extra valuation except for firms highly dependent on individual innovation project*
Information	Customer value Differentiation potential Tangibility	Development feasibility Customer value Team's commercialization capability Current product/service portfolio Business model of product/service Protection from imitation	Innovation project portfolio

Innovation capability

In general, it seems that the understanding of innovation capability differs for different firm types. For idea firms, innovation capability seems to be understood as the idea firm's capability (basically, the founder's capability) to execute an innovation project successfully and develop a technically working technology, product, or service. Growth firms' innovation capabilities, seem to be majorly understood as capabilities to commercialize products or services and grow business with further new products or services or up-scaling of the existing ones. For mature firms, innovation capability seems more associated with developing a firm further in a more general way. The management team acts as a proxy for appraising this capability. Table 23 depicts the methodologies and information utilized by practitioners in a cross-type comparison.

Table 23. Cross-Type-Comparison Innovation Capability

Firm Type / Dimensions	Idea Firms	Growth Firms	Mature Firms
Methodologies	*Interpretation (qual.)*: Team assessment	*Major calculation*: Start from current state (income approach) Start from future state (exit multiple for income approach, firm development analogy) *Interpretation (qual.)*: Firm analogy Assessment of further product/service applications	*Major calculation*: Start from current state (income approach) Start from current state (market approach) *Interpretation (quant.)*: Extrapolation *Interpretation (qual.)*: Firm analogy
Information	Team's development execution capability Team's firm founding capability	Team's development execution capability Team's commercialization capability Innovation project portfolio Comparable firms Scalability	General firm growth Team's firm development capability (incl. innovation) Past development Comparable firms

For idea firms, most aspects of innovation capability are *methodological-wise* already considered in the appraisal of the idea firm's innovation project(s) (majorly using a hurdle rate approach starting from the idea firm's future state) as the relevance of such individual projects heavily affect an idea firm's valuation (compare section above). Growth and mature firms seem to be assessed majorly starting from the current state with income approaches or market approaches.

The major *information* to assess an idea firm's innovation capability seems to be the team of founders. The quality of an idea firm's team to develop a technology, product or service and finalizing an innovation project successfully seems highly relevant. For growth firms, information about the firm's capability to commercialize its products or services seems to become more important accompanied by the capability to extend the product portfolio or find new applications for the existing technology, product, or service portfolio. Both capabilities seem to be assesses majorly by assessing the management team's skills as a proxy. To appraise the innovation capability of mature firms, valuators seem to regard the business planning's firm growth, the firm's past business development, and the management team as relevant information. For both, growth and mature firms, comparable firms are also used as references to appraise the firm's innovation capability.

Transaction effects

Based on the empirical results, the impact of a transaction can be separated in two effects. For idea and growth firms, innovation efforts can be financed and thereby innovation potential enabled. At the same time, an acquisition can also have effects deriving from integration and merging efforts after the acquisition. This seems to be more relevant for growth firms and mature firms, which are more likely to be acquired and not only funded.

Table 24. Cross-Type-Comparison Transaction Effects

Firm Type / Dimensions	Idea Firms	Growth Firms	Mature Firms
Methodologies	Major calculation: Post-transaction valuation	Major calculation: Pre-transaction valuation Interpretation (quant.): Own-cost comparison (cost approach) Management retention costs Interpretation (qual.): Post-transaction valuation Network synergies	Major calculation: Pre-transaction valuation Interpretation (qual.): Post-transaction valuation Combined innovation capability
Information	Network synergies Augmentation of key personnel	Cultural fit Network synergies Retention of key personnel	Cost synergies Portfolio synergies Retention of key personnel

From a *methodological perspective*, the basis of an idea firm's valuation seems to be post-transactional (or post-money) whereas the basis for growth and mature firms seem to be pre-transactional (or standalone). This is in accordance with the valuation methodologies used in general for those firm types, e.g., hurdle rate for idea firms and income or market approaches for growth and mature firms. For growth and mature firms, the transaction effects are appraised majorly qualitatively to adjust the calculated valuation (compare chapter 6.5.1) by assessing network synergies or a combined innovation capability. Tools to support quantifying relevant information are the calculation of management retention costs for the acquiring firm or the calculation of costs to implement necessary capabilities to develop similar technologies or products for the acquiring firm.

Relevant *information* for idea firms seems to be majorly information about the acquirer's business network and opportunities to support the idea firm with financing or augmented personnel to implement adequate organizational structures and processes. For growth firms, information about the cultural fit between acquirer and acquired firm including retention of key personnel and network synergies to commercialize the growth firm's products or services seem to be relevant. Finally, practitioners appraising the transaction effects of a mature firm acquisition tend to rely on innovation about cost synergies, innovation project portfolio synergies, and also retention of key personnel. Generally, mature firm valuators seem to assess innovation potential rather on the output level in the dimensions of costs and project portfolio than on the input or capability level as idea and growth firm valuators do.

Risk and uncertainty

Empirical results indicate that risk and uncertainty are majorly assessed by qualitative methodologies though the extent qualitative assessments influence the valuation seems to be higher for idea firms than for mature firms.

The major vehicle to cover risks methodical-wise for all firm types is the discount rate, either as hurdle rate for idea firms or as discount rate in the DCF sense. To support or accompany the estimation of this discount rate, valuators use majorly qualitative assessments such as scenario analyses. Idea firm's risks assessment is mostly qualitative assessing the "tangibility" of innovation projects, the capabilities of the development team, use external opinions from other investors investing in the same firm, and at last use their intuition or "gut feeling". Risk methodologies get more numerical with growth firms. For those firms, valuators seem to also use numerical approaches as probabilities for the developed scenarios or sensitivity analysis.

Additionally, as growth firm value seems to depend majorly on commercializing innovation projects, practitioners seem to use methodologies to assess and adjust the underlying business plans such as analogies to other firms or to other product developments they know or rules of thumb to adjust business plans for overconfidence. Finally, also for growth firms, intuition plays a role to deal with uncertainty. Mature firm's risk seems to be assessed on a firm level with an even higher influence of quantitative methodologies such as probabilities, sensitivity analysis, or even simulation approaches. For them, an additional and important approach seems to be the comparison between a firm's future prospects and its historical development (Is the firm able to perform like this (business plan), if it has performed like that in the past?). An example for that approach is the assessment of the firm's management's past planning quality to imply from that on the validity of the available business plan. As for the other firm types, intuition seems to play a role in assessing risk. For mature firms, this seems to be trust towards the credibility of the firm's management's presentations and statements.

Table 25. Cross-Type-Comparison Risk and Uncertainty

Firm Type / Dimensions	Idea Firms	Growth Firms	Mature Firms
Methodologies	*Major calculation*: Hurdle rate *Interpretation (qual.)*: Product/service tangibility assessment Scenarios Team assessment Business environment assessment External opinions Intuition	*Major calculation*: Discount rate / number of detailed periods *Interpretation (quant.)*: Bottom-up/break-even analysis Scenario probabilities Sensitivity analysis *Interpretation (qual.)* Scenarios Product/service development analogy Overconfidence-adjustment Intuition	*Major calculation*: Discount rate *Interpretation (quant.)*: Scenario probabilities Sensitivity analysis Simulation *Interpretation (qual.)*: Scenarios Firm analogy Assessment of planning quality Intuition

Overall comparison

As depicted in the previous sub-sections, *two fundamental different approaches seem to exist to appraise firms depending on their lifecycle stage*. Idea firms are valued based on the future potential that valuators expect, if those firms succeed with offering a new product or service. In contrast mature firms' valuations seem to be based majorly on their current business and business performance or on comparisons to other mature firms. Taking this reasoning further, idea firm valuations seem to be very much based on assumptions about the future whereas mature firm valuations seem to be based on the firm's history and current state. It seems that valuators switch from basing valuations on a firm's current state to future images as prospects get more risky and a firm's history is neither existent nor a good indicator for the firm's future.

The selection of this general approach also seems to depend on the perception, if the idea has matured or is developed enough technologically to commercialize it. If the idea is mature enough to commercialize it, the commercialization is planned with a classical forward-looking business case and DCF approach starting with the market potential.

> Wir wollen immer eine komplette Planung haben. Das heißt: Da ist die Bilanz drin, die GuV und die Cash Flow Rechnung. Da werden die Top-Lines, um die es ja hauptsächlich geht, unter Annahmen geplant. Das heißt: Wie viel Stück Dioden werden wann verkauft? In welchem Jahr? Dann kommt die Kostenseite. Wie viel sind die Fertigungskosten? Wie viele Leute brauche ich da dazu? Wie viel Support muss ich geben? Wie ist der zeitliche Verlauf? Und dann gibt es ja dann ein Ergebnis und das Ergebnis wird mit bestimmten Zahlungszielen versehen und kommt dann zum Cash Flow und dann kann man daraus auch die Bilanz entwickeln. (Venture capital professional)

Along with the switch from future-state-based general approach to the current-state-based one seems to occur a switch from more qualitative methodologies to more quantitative methodologies to interpret relevant data and consider it in the valuation.

Analogies to other firms and the use of multiples to appraise a firm's innovation potential seem to be generally difficult to use for idea and growth firms:

> Die größte Restriktion ist es, dass wir etwas suchen und bewerten, was einzigartig ist. Sobald Sie etwas Einzigartiges haben, haben Sie keine Vergleichbarkeit mehr mit irgendwas Existierendem. Und deswegen stochern sie schon manchmal im luftleeren Raum und versuchen krampfhaft, etwas Vergleichbares zu finden. (Corporate venture capital professional)

Valuators seem to tend more to analogies on the product/service level built into an income approach's underlying assumptions. As comparable and publicly listed firms become available (for growth and mature firms) multiples become more important as one basis of innovation potential valuation.

With regard to relevant information, valuators' *understanding of innovation potential and innovation capability seems to differ between firm types*. The significance of innovation capability seems to be more important for growth and mature firms as valuators seem to understand innovation capability rather as the capability to create new projects, broaden the product portfolio, and commercialize new products or services than the capability to successfully finish an innovation project. For idea firms, information about the innovation projects (in most cases only one) seems to be more significant than information about supporting innovation capability.

7 Implications for Existing Theory

The following section depicts the implications for existing theory based on results of the empirical investigation in the last chapter and a comparison between theory and practice (next sub-section 7.1). Subsequently, in chapter 7.2, I present hypotheses to extend existing theory derived by the means of both theoretical reasoning and empirical investigation based on those comparisons. Thus, this section takes up the procedure of comparative analysis: "The elements of theory that are generated by comparative analysis are, first, conceptual categories and their conceptual properties; and second, hypotheses or generalized relations among the categories and their properties." (Glaser & Strauss, 1967, p. 35)

7.1 Comparison Between Theory and Practice

In this section I discuss the empirical results in the light of the theoretical implications derived and depicted for each firm type in chapter 4.3. This comparison should shed light on the question "What does theory suggest and what in comparison do practitioners do?" and, thus, enable deriving hypotheses explaining differences between theory and practice.

7.1.1 Valuation Process and Context Factors

With regard to the process of valuation, valuation theory majorly focuses on the application of the suggested mathematical models. DAMODARAN (2009, pp. 3–5) suggests four steps of determining a firm's value:

(1) Determining the cash flows generated by existing assets
(2) Determining the cash flows generated by future investments and growth
(3) Determining the riskiness of cash flows and according discount rates
(4) Determining when a firm will become mature and grow at a stable rate

COPELAND ET AL. (2000, pp. 233–265) propose an iterative process of five steps to develop a view on a firm's future performance:

(1) Determine the length and level of detail for the forecast.
(2) Develop a strategic perspective on future firm performance.
(3) Translate the strategic perspective into financial forecasts: income statement, balance sheet, free cash flow, and key value drivers.
(4) Develop alternative performance scenarios to the base case developed in steps 2 and 3.

(5) Check the overall forecasts (resulting ROIC and sales and profit growth) for internal consistency and alignment with the strategic perspective.

As can be seen, those approaches majorly focus on the application of a certain methodology (e.g., determining cash flows, length of forecast period) and its calculated result. References to the availability of according information or methodologies to derive reasonable quantitative inputs with regard to a firm's future prospects are not in scope of valuation theory as also GRAHAM concludes:

> The concept of future prospects and particularly of continued growth in the future invites the application of formulas out of higher mathematics to establish the present value of the favored issue. But the combination of precise formulas with highly imprecise assumptions can be used to establish, or rather justify, practically any value one wishes, however high, for a really outstanding issue. (B. Graham, 2003, p. 564)

Two major differences seem to exist between valuation theory and practice: First, the final valuation result seems to be influenced also by qualitative adjustments and the negotiation after the calculated valuation. Thus, those process steps should be considered in theories related to valuation. Second, the process seems to be influence by context factors (for both compare chapter 6.1).

Complementing the already depicted additional process steps and context factors (compare chapter 6.1), two major differences between theory and practice are highlighted by the investigation. First, the investigation indicates that qualitative appraisals have a significant impact on the final valuation result of any firm. The major time of consideration of those qualitative appraisals seems to be after the quantitative valuation has been conducted. This behavior is slightly indicated in theory:

> It is almost a given that the value of a growth company, no matter how much we pay attention to the details and how much information we use, will be less precisely estimated than the value of a mature company. This uncertainty can lead to post-valuation angst where analysts second-guess themselves and try to reconcile differences not only between their estimates and the market price but also across different valuations (done by different analysts). (Damodaran, 2009, p. 301)

But is much more present as result of this investigation as a practitioner's statement depicts:

> Die Bewertung ist eine wichtige Nummer, aber die qualitative Bewertung ist immens wichtig. Ich muss eben beides beherrschen. Bewertung bedeutet hierbei: So würden es die Meisten bewerten. Und, wenn ich dann 20% mehr zahle, kann das immer noch ein gutes Geschäft sein. Umgekehrt kann auch die mathematische Bewertung für ein Unternehmen zu hoch sein. . . . Diese Punkte sind schlichtweg nicht in Formeln zu packen. Das ist eher ein qualitatives auch beschreibendes Wesen. Das ist das Auseinanderfallen aus dem, was die Praxis macht und der Wissenschaft. . . . Man soll es nicht übertreiben mit der Mathematik. Das entspricht einfach nicht der Wirklichkeit. Die Wissenschaft ist deutlich deterministischer, deutlich mathematischer. Die Wirklichkeit ist qualitativ und sieht auf die Spezifika der gegebenen Situation. Die Welt ist halt komplex und das ist das Spannende daran. (Investment bank professional)

Second, the extension of the valuation process to the negotiation phase allows including a new perspective of risk consideration in firm valuation. Valuators are able to transfer risk-taking partly to the selling side by using earn-out-contracts or other contracts sharing risks that derive from a firm's future prospects with the seller or borrower (compare Coff, 1999). This approach seems not to be considered in the core valuation process, but seems to be included mainly later in the adjustment and negotiation phase.

7.1.2 Methodologies and Information

Subsequent to the comparison of the valuation process, the following paragraphs and tables depict the differences between theory implications and valuation practices for innovation potential valuation.

Innovation projects

Table 26 sums up the major differences between theory and practice for the dimensions methodologies and information.

Methodology-wise major differences can be observed in the focus on quantitative and qualitative methodologies. Valuation theory suggests more or less only quantitative calculation methodologies. Practitioners majorly use quantitative and qualitative methodologies to assess innovation projects. They seem to base major parts of their valuation on interpreting available data and considering it either as assumptions for the calculation of a numerical valuation or to adjust an already calculated numerical valuation afterwards (compare previous chapter). The impact of qualitative and data interpretation methodologies seems to be higher for idea firms and lower for growth and mature firms as the major calculation methodology that practitioners seem to use is the hurdle rate approach that is highly dependent on assumptions about an innovation project's anticipated success or an idea firm's anticipated future state.

Table 26. Theory-Practice-Comparison Innovation Projects

Firm Type / Dimensions		Idea Firms	Growth Firms	Mature Firms
Methodologies	Theory	<u>*Focus on calculation*</u> DCF based on top-down or bottom-up analysis, contingent claim (real options) Private or transaction multiples	<u>*Focus on calculation*</u> DCF (differentiation between high and stable growth phase) Public multiples	*Generally not valued on individual level* <u>*Focus on calculation*</u> *Real options (for firms depending on major high-risk innovation projects)*
	Differences	Major	Medium	Minor
	Major practices	<u>*Focus on interpretation*</u> Start from future state (hurdle rate approach) Top-down market potential Product/service development analogy	<u>*Even focus (calculation and interpretation)*</u> Start from current (income approach) or from future state (hurdle rate approach) Top-down market potential Product/service development analogy IP protection assessment	*Not valued on individual level except for firms depending on major individual innovation projects*
Information	Theory	Idea / business case Team of developers/managers Observable corporate governance characteristics, e.g., incentive systems and VC participation	*Younger growth firms:* Team's industry experience Focus Lean team Utilization of advanced technologies	*Generally not valued on individual level*
	Differences	Minor	Medium	Minor
	Practice (most relevant information)	Customer value Differentiation potential Tangibility	Development feasibility Customer value Team's commercialization capability Current product/service portfolio Business model of product/service Protection from imitation	Innovation project portfolio

With regard to *information*, only minor differences seem to exist. For idea firms, practitioners do not seem to regard the idea firm's management team as highly relevant for the valuation compared to the value of the idea itself. Theory suggests the management team to be a relevant factor. Complementing theory, practitioners seem to look at two additional factors for growth firms. First, they seem to take a much closer look at the team's capabilities to commercialize an innovation project. Second they also assess more product or product portfolio specifics, such as technical feasibility, customer value, or the business model for the new product in its eco-system. Also, in practice, valuators seem to assess mature firms' innovation portfolios at a higher level.

Innovation capability

Similar to the valuation of individual innovation projects, qualitative *methodologies* to assess innovation capability seem to play a more significant role for practitioners than they do in theory for idea and growth firms. Especially for idea firms, practitioners focus on soft facts such as the evaluation of the founder team to assess innovation capability. The methodologies for mature firms suggested in theory and used in practice in contrast are basically the same.

With regard to *information*, major differences exist for the appraisal of mature firms' innovation capabilities and are also probably existent in medium peculiarity for growth firms. Theory suggests a variety of factors, which influence innovation capability in growing or mature organizations. In contrast to those factors, practitioners seem to appraise innovation capability essentially by looking at past business performance, business planning, the management team as a major factor, and comparable firms. They seem to have no applicable methodology available to assess a firm's innovation capability based on intrinsic factors:

> [D]ieses Thema Innovation, das steckt in der Organisation. Das kann im Kopf vom CEO oder CFO stecken oder Technikvorstand. Es kann aber auch in der Ebene darunter stecken und das ist schwer zu beziffern. Dem kann man keinen Wert beimessen. . . . Wenn Sie mal einen PE-Player fragen, der wird Ihnen in den meisten Fällen sagen, dass das Management mit der wichtigste Faktor bei der Transaktion ist. Ohne die richtigen Leute an Bord, weil sie wissen selbst, dass sie keine Industrieexperten sind, sondern, dass sie Leute brauchen, die das für sie umsetzen. (Investment bank professional)

Thus, it seems that innovation capability for mature firms is understood and valued more implicitly and understood as being integrated in the overall firm development expectations. The overall comparison shows that valuators rely heavily on assessing the management team to appraise innovation capability for all three firm types.

Table 27. Theory-Practice-Comparison Innovation Capability

Firm Type / Dimensions		Idea Firms	Growth Firms	Mature Firms
Methodologies	Theory	<u>*Focus on calculation*</u> Contingent claim (expand option) in addition to discounted cash flow valuation	<u>*Focus on calculation*</u> Consideration of reinvestments in DCF Public multiples	<u>*Focus on calculation*</u> Discounted cash flow / consideration of reinvestments in DCF Public multiples Assessing probability of changing management and its effects
	Differences	Major	Medium	Medium
	Major practices	<u>*Focus on interpretation*</u> Team assessment	<u>*Even focus (calculation and interpretation)*</u> Start from current state (income approach) or from future state (exit multiple for income approach, firm development analogy) Firm analogy (multiples) Assessment of further product/service applications	<u>*Focus on calculation*</u> Start from current state (income or market approach) Extrapolation Firm analogy (multiples)
Information	Theory	Team of developers/managers Relationships and network Observable corporate governance characteristics, e.g., incentive systems and VC participation	*More mature growth firms:* Team's industry experience Capabilities to broaden product portfolio Balanced team Customer relationships Observable corporate governance characteristics, e.g., incentive systems, investors, board structure	Aspects of innovation capability: Internal & external learning processes, operational and strategic coordination, firm culture supporting innovation and change Reinvestment rate and reinvestment quality
	Differences	Medium	Medium	Major
	Practice (most relevant information)	Team's development execution and firm founding capability	Team's development execution and commercialization capability Innovation project portfolio Comparable firms Scalability	General firm growth Team's firm development capability (incl. innovation) Past development Comparable firms

For idea firms, a major difference is the consideration of an idea firm's relationships and network. This factor does not seem to be considered relevant by practitioners investigating innovation capability.

Transaction effects

Major differences between theory and practice seem to exist with regard to the *methodologies* applied to assess transaction effects for growth and mature firms. Idea firms are valuated from a post-transaction view in theory and practice based on the valuation calculation. Key person discounts are quantified in theory, qualitatively considered in practice. Growth and mature firms are valued from a pre-transaction view in theory in practice with less emphasis on a combined value of target and acquiring firm. Practitioners, though, seem to qualitatively assess and interpret different aspects of the anticipated combination of target and acquiring firm, such as cultural fit or synergies with their own network, in a separate qualitative valuation. Those aspects are most likely brought into the valuation process at the adjustment step after the calculated valuation (compare Figure 3 in chapter 6.1) or even not until the negotiation with the selling party.

Regarding collected and interpreted *information* major differences seem to exist for idea and mature firms. For idea firms, theory seems to focus more on retention of key personnel whereas practitioners do not seem to consider that factor as relevant. Instead, they focus more on their own capabilities to augment the team as effect of the transaction. Also, investors seem to consider the additional relationships and network connections, they bring into the investment relationship, as relevant for the post-transaction valuation. While theory seems to be more focused on the general change capability of mature firms in a valuation, practitioners seem to only focus on synergies with regard to costs or product/service portfolio. Overall change of management and strategy seem not to be considered in large extent.

Table 28. Theory-Practice-Comparison Transaction Effects

Firm Type / Dimensions		Idea Firms	Growth Firms	Mature Firms
Methodologies	Theory	<u>*Focus on calculation*</u> Post-transaction valuation Key person discounts	*Compare idea firms for younger growth firms* *Compare mature firms for more mature growth firms*	<u>*Focus on calculation*</u> Pre-transaction valuation Appraising value of control based on value of changing management
	Differences	Minor	Major	Medium
	Major practices	<u>*Focus on calculation*</u> Post-transaction valuation	<u>*Focus on interpretation*</u> Pre-transaction valuation Own-cost comparison (cost approach) Management retention costs Post-transaction valuation (qualitative) Network synergies (qualitative)	<u>*Focus on interpretation*</u> Pre-transaction valuation Post-transaction valuation (qualitative) Combined innovation capability (qualitative)
Information	Theory	Retention of key personnel Acquirer's firm culture and organization	Retention of key personnel Acquirer's firm culture and organization Acquirer's augmentation capabilities	Probability and possible effects of changing management
	Differences	Major	Minor	Major
	Practice (most relevant information)	Network synergies Augmentation of key personnel	Cultural fit Network synergies Retention of key personnel	Cost synergies Portfolio synergies Retention of key personnel

Risk and uncertainty

The assessment of risk and uncertainty seems to differ heavily between theory and practice. Theory suggests considering risk in the calculation of the valuation, with the discount rate as vehicle to cover risks. Advanced mathematical models, simulations, or comparisons to past data or comparable firms (compare previous chapters) are supposed to support those calculations. Practitioners, in comparison, seem to use a wide range of qualitative and quantitative tools to interpret available information regarding risk and uncertainty. The tools they seem to use range from more quantitative mathematical models (simulations, probabilities or sensitivity analysis), to qualitative descriptive tools (scenarios), to highly qualitative approaches (generally adjusting for an entrepreneur's overconfidence, intuition, trust).

Table 29. Theory-Practice-Comparison Risk and Uncertainty

Firm Type / Dimensions		Idea Firms	Growth Firms	Mature Firms
Methodologies	Theory	<u>*Focus on calculation*</u> Discount rate (DCF) Advanced mathematical models or simulations for risk of non-survival	<u>*Focus on calculation*</u> Separate discount rates for high and stable growth phases (DCF) Risk of non-survival (compare idea firms) for multiple methodology Appraisal of firm network ties / other parties' appraisals	<u>*Focus on calculation*</u> Discount rate (DCF)
	Differences	Major	Major	Major
	Major practices	<u>*Focus on interpretation*</u> Hurdle rate Product/service tangibility assessment Scenarios Team assessment Business environment assessment External opinions Intuition	<u>*Focus on interpretation*</u> Discount rate / number of detailed periods Bottom-up/break-even analysis Scenario probabilities Sensitivity analysis Scenarios Product/service development analogy Overconfidence-adjustment Intuition	<u>*Focus on interpretation*</u> Discount rate Scenario probabilities Sensitivity analysis Simulation Scenarios Firm analogy Assessment of planning quality Intuition

Quantitative methodologies seem to focus on downside risks. Quantitative approaches to value upside risks (chances) except assigning probabilities to scenarios seem not to be used by practitioners. The valuation of upside risk seems to be postponed to the adjustment step or the even to the negotiation in the valuation process (compare chapter 6.1).

Overall comparison

In practice, *methodologies to assess innovation potential, transaction effects and associated risks qualitatively* are much more represented than in existing valuation literature and suggestions. In contrast, *highly sophisticated theory-suggested mathematical methodologies seem to be avoided.* Though, real option methodology for example is recommended to appraise risky projects and firms (Bowman & Moskowitz, 2001; Fredberg, 2007) or to link strategy with corporate finance (Reuer & Tong, 2007), it is not used. Valuation context factors are likely to explain this difference (compare corresponding hypothesis in next chapter).

With regard to the considered *information* for the valuation, availability, access, and interpretation approaches do not seem to be available to practitioners to the cost-benefit ratio that major relevant factors suggested by innovation theory can be considered thoroughly. Innovation potential, thus, seems to be considered majorly either by a closer assessment of individual innovation projects or by the use of higher-level proxies.

7.2 Implications for Existing Theory

As stated in the introduction and the research objectives, the objective of this dissertation is the creation of hypotheses to extend existing theory. The derived hypotheses take into account what theory suggests (chapters 3 and 4), what the empirical investigation of valuation practices indicates (chapter 6), and what the difference between existing theory and the empirical investigation suggests (chapter 7.1). Table 30 contains an overview of derived hypotheses, the subsequent sections present and discuss those hypotheses with regard to the respective theories depicted in chapter 3.

The following section contains hypotheses in the areas of valuation theory, but also in the areas of innovation and underlying theories. The latter hypotheses are either based on existing theory with new relationships inspired by the empirical investigation results or based on the interviewees' expertise in and perception of theoretical constructs such as innovation potential, sources of growth, or boundaries of firms to imply from their perception of those constructs to characteristics of the nature of those constructs.

The order of theories follows abstraction logic, as implications for more abstract theories are majorly build upon implications for less abstract theories. Thus, first, implications for valuation theory are presented and thereafter implications for innovation and underlying theories. The focus is on explaining the "why" and "how" of the implications, or the "arrows" instead of the "boxes" as THOMAS ET AL. (2011) state.

Table 30. Contribution to Existing Theory – Hypotheses

Theory	Hypotheses
Valuation theory	Hypothesis 1: The innovation potential as defined in this dissertation is considered in the valuation of a firm.
	Hypothesis 2: Innovation potential is appraised and understood differently depending on the firm type of the appraised firm.
	Hypothesis 2a: Valuators' understanding of innovation capability and expectations regarding innovation are different depending on the firm type of the appraised firm.
	Hypothesis 2b: Individual innovation projects become less important and innovation capability more important for the valuation of firms over their lifecycle.
	Hypothesis 3: Identifying relevant qualitative information, interpreting it, and translating it into numerical data has more influence on the result of innovation potential valuation than the selection and application of the best-suited valuation methodology.
	Hypothesis 4: Practitioners make only limited use of available data and information to assess innovation capability and instead rely on proxies.
	Hypothesis 4a: Structural and procedural components of valuation capability are not considered in reasonable extent for the valuation of a firm's innovation potential.
	Hypothesis 4b: The basis of the valuation changes through the lifecycle of the target firm from a future state based on a business case to a current state based on backward-looking financials.
	Hypothesis 4c: The management team's significance as proxy for innovation potential increases during the development from idea to growth firm and decreases again during the development from growth to mature firm.
	Hypothesis 4d: The significance of a team's preparedness in a presentation to valuators switches to passion during the lifecycle of the appraised firm.
	Hypothesis 4e: Prototypes are significant for the valuation of idea firm, patents for the valuation of growth firms.
	Hypothesis 4f: The valuation of a target firm's network embeddedness is less reflected in valuation theory and valuation methodologies.
	Hypothesis 4g: Signaling is a highly relevant theory to investigate innovation potential valuation.
	Hypothesis 5: The anticipation of transaction effects for innovation potential differs significantly across firm types.
	Hypothesis 6: Valuators prefer qualitative methodologies in situations with incomplete information, risk, and uncertainty compared to sophisticated theory-suggested quantitative methodologies.

Table 30. Contribution to Existing Theory – Hypotheses (continued)

Theory	Hypotheses
Valuation theory	Hypothesis 7: Valuation context and human behavioral aspects influence the valuation process and the valuation result significantly.
	Hypothesis 7a: Budget, perceived benefit-cost-ratio, and comprehensibility of the methodology influence and constrain the selection of valuation methodology and collected data.
	Hypothesis 7b: Valuators significantly influence and constrain the selection of the valuation methodology and collected data.
	Hypothesis 7c: Market for potential target firms influences valuation results.
	Hypothesis 7d: Innovation potential valuations are prone to different biases dependent on the target firm's lifecycle stage.
	Hypothesis 7e: The framing of the anticipated negotiation influences the valuation process and the valuation result.
Innovation and underlying theories	Hypothesis 8: Innovation capability is a dynamic capability that changes a firm's configuration of innovation-related capabilities according to the firm's position in its lifecycle and is in its core common to all firms.
	Hypothesis 9: Signaling is an element of innovation capability. Firm managements need to send different signals based on firm type to promote their innovation potential to investors or acquirers.
	Hypothesis 10: In the context of innovation potential valuation, information asymmetry exists between buyer and seller in both ways.
	Hypothesis 11: Valuation practices constrain the thorough valuation of transaction effects with regard to innovation potential and, therefore, contribute to explain low M&A performance.

7.2.1 Valuation Theory

The following hypotheses are derived directly from the empirical results in chapter 6 and the comparison to theory in chapter 7.1.

Hypothesis 1: The innovation potential as defined in this dissertation is considered in the valuation of a firm.

This hypothesis might be obvious having in mind the research objectives of this dissertation. The findings of the empirical investigation support the hypothesis that a firm's innovation potential is considered in its valuation. Innovation potential is regarded as a main driver for growth or even only further existence of a firm and, thus, regarded as important to assess during a valuation. Innovation potential seems also to be considered for all firm types. Differences between firm types seem to rather exist in the understanding of innovation potential than in the importance.

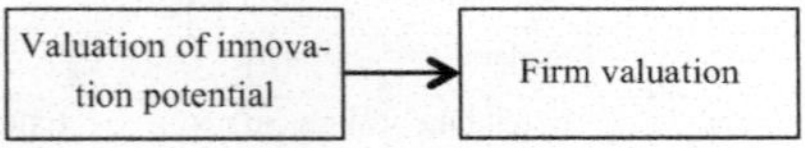

Figure 4. Influence of Innovation Potential on Firm Valuation

Hypothesis 2: Innovation potential is appraised and understood differently depending on the firm type of the appraised firm.

The empirical investigation implies that significant differences exist to appraise innovation potential dependent on the target firm type. The differences occur in both dimensions methodologies and relevant information and in all sub-dimensions (compare chapter 6).

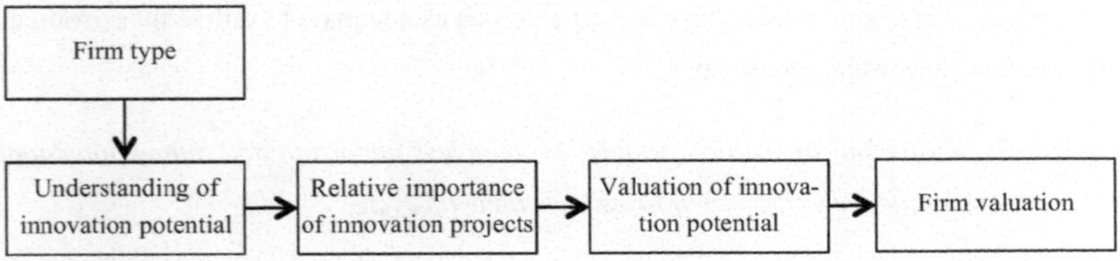

Figure 5. Understanding and Valuation of Innovation Potential

The reasons for those differences seem to be valuators' different expectations towards innovation capability and the relevance of individual innovation projects on the valuation of firms as stated in more detail by the following hypotheses.

Hypothesis 2a: Valuators' understanding of innovation capability and expectations regarding innovation are different depending on the firm type of the appraised firm.

As indicated for the previous hypothesis, valuators seem to understand innovation capability differently depending on the firm type of the appraised firm. The results of the theory-driven and empirical investigations suggest the following understandings of innovation capability and expectations towards innovation depending on the appraised firm's type (compare Table 31).

Table 31. Understanding of Innovation Capability

Firm Type / Hypothesis	Idea Firms	Growth Firms	Mature Firms
Understanding of innovation capability	Team's development execution capability Team's firm founding capability	Team's development execution capability Team's commercialization capability Innovation project portfolio Scalability	General firm growth Team's firm development capability (incl. innovation)
Expected major value creation potential	New differentiating product or service	Extending business in new markets and with new product variants	Extending business or increasing efficiency
Expected major type of innovation	Revolutionary / niche	Regular	Architectural / business model innovation

The reasons for the differences in the understanding of innovation capability most likely lie in the different types of innovation and different sources of value that valuators expect from certain firm types. Thus, capabilities have to be perceived as adequate to utilize those sources of value and create according innovations.

Hypothesis 2b: Individual innovation projects become less important and innovation capability more important for the valuation of firms over their lifecycle.

Subsequent to the first hypothesis, the empirical investigation suggests that assessing individual innovation projects as part of a valuation is the core activity for idea firms and becomes less important for mature firms. An explanation for this is the relevance of individual innovation projects on a firm's future prospects. For idea firms, almost the complete commercial prospects are based on such a project whereas for mature firms, most they tend to be less relevant and commercial prospects are based on existing revenue streams. This view is compatible to DAMODARAN'S general approach on valuation to separate revenues from existing assets and from new assets or investments (Damodaran, 2009, pp. 24–33). Valuators also seem to associate an innovation project more with the idea and its business potential than with the team and its capability to execute the project. A symptom for this understanding is that risks are covered mostly by a simple hurdle rate calculation with pre-defined hurdle rates based on experience. One reason for that is that valuators do not seem to have adequate tools to effectively assess a founder team's capabilities. The other is that some investors anticipate the possibility of augmenting the original team as risk mitigation. Thus, it seems, the team's innovation capability is not regarded as highly relevant. Innovation capability seems to be more associated with growth and mature firms and understood as the capability to start new innovation projects to develop new products or services or improve existing ones.

Hypothesis 3: Identifying relevant qualitative information, interpreting it and translating it into numerical data has more influence on the result of innovation potential valuation than the selection and application of the best-suited valuation methodology.

The empirical investigation indicates that the selection of relevant qualitative proxy data, the translation of this data into meaningful qualitative information, and the quantification of the information as input data for the methodologies has significant more influence of the valuation result than the application of any methodology itself has.

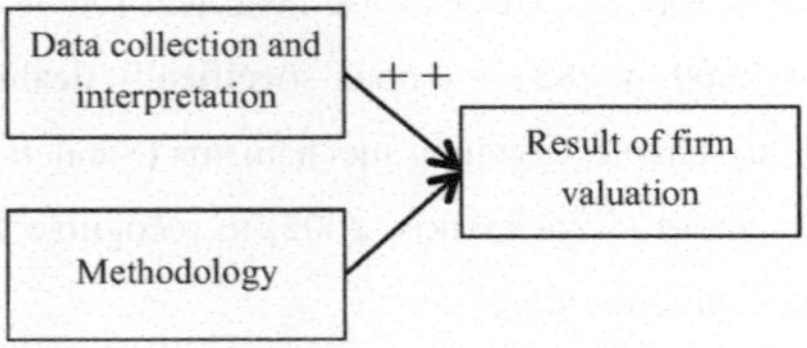

Figure 6. Relevance of Methodology and Information on Valuation Result

The difference magnitudes of influence show also clearly in the results of the empirical investigation. Practitioners, when asked about their valuation practices with regard to innovation potential, elaborated more about the data interpretation than the application of any methodology itself (compare chapter 6.5). Also, the investigation of the valuation process (chapter 6.1) indicates that the result of a calculated valuation is not only heavily influenced by the creation of assumptions, it is likely to be adjusted qualitatively after its calculation and before its use as decision criteria.

The reasons should lie in the strong dependence of the valuation results on assumptions about a firm's future prospects or the success of innovation projects. Those assumptions seem to rely on either incomplete information to assess the investigation topic or unclear significance of available and collected data for the investigation topic. Nevertheless, most of the major standard literature aimed at practitioners has a clear focus on valuation methodology or financial statement analysis (Brealey & Myers, 2003; Copeland & Antikarov, 2001; Damodaran, 2002; Koller et al., 2005; Penman, 2006a). The following practitioner statement is exemplary for this indicated theory/practice disconnect.

> Das ist auch eine wichtige Message. Man macht Multiples, und neun mal EBITDA ist der Wert. DCF kann auch jeder nach dem Praktikum. Im Endeffekt sind die Methoden nicht so schwierig. Die aber richtig anzuwenden und umfassend aufs Unternehmen anzuwenden, das ist die eigentlich Aufgabe. *Eigentlich muss man ja auch eher Branchenexperte sein, weil die Methode ja davon lebt, welche Daten man da reinsteckt?* Das ist genau der Punkt. (Investment bank professional).

Innovation potential as part of a firm's fundamental or intrinsic source of value creation has not been identified as critical input factor in valuation research. The input side of valuation seems to be often neglected in valuation standard literature or focused on analysis of financials or even only backward-looking financial statements. For example, even DAMODARAN recommends to investigate historical data or to use historical sector data for the valuation of growth firms (Damodaran, 2009, p. 283) in a book specifically dealing with idea and growth firms. Thus, investigating reasonable screening mechanisms (Sanders & Boivie, 2004; Weiss, 1995) or decision aids (Shepherd & Zacharakis, 2002) to recognize the quality of innovation potential promises to support practitioners.

Hypothesis 4: Practitioners make only limited use of available data and information to assess innovation capability and instead rely on proxies.

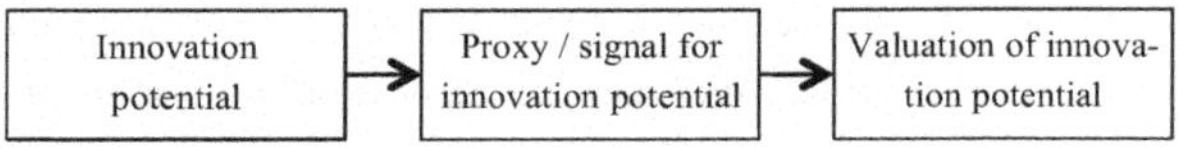

Figure 7. Use of Proxies for the Valuation of Innovation Potential

The empirical research indicates that valuators do not investigate innovation-theory-suggested information in large extent to assess a firm's innovation potential. One main reason for this behavior seems to be that the valuation process is limited and influenced by context factors (compare hypothesis 7) and, thus, efforts for data collection seem to be limited by external factors. This restrictions lead to the relevance of information asymmetry with regard to a firm's innovation potential as one of its qualities (Akerlof, 1970) and the relevance of signaling (Riley, 1989; Sanders & Boivie, 2004; Spence, 1973, 1974) (compare chapter 3.4.2).

Hypothesis 4a: Structural and procedural components of valuation capability are not considered in reasonable extent for the valuation of a firm's innovation potential.

The empirical results indicate that especially for growth and mature firms with a grown base of structures and processes that this base is not considered accordingly in a valuation. Figure 8 shows the indicated gap between innovation theory and valuation theory and practice.

Innovation theory suggests that as firms get larger and more mature, they develop innovation processes, processes of strategic and operational coordination, learning processes, or the development of supporting organization and firm culture (compare chapters 3.2.1 and 3.2.2).

Firm Type / Characteristics	Idea Firms	Growth Firms	Mature Firms
Impact of Structure and Processes on Innovation Capability	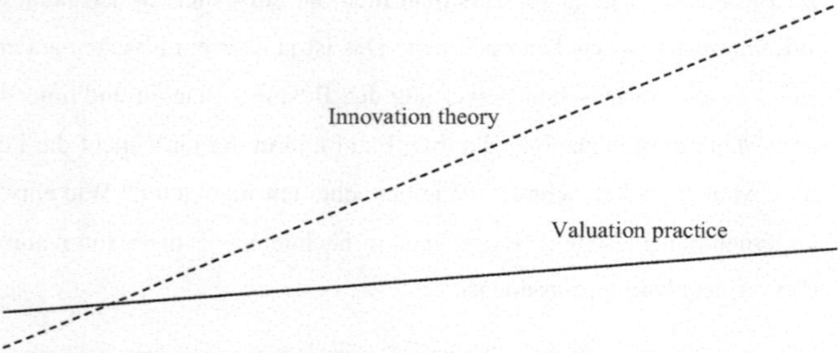		
Theory	Depending on inventor or management team to develop product or service	Depending on management team, structures, and procedures to commercialize innovation and broaden product/service portfolio	Depending on organizational routines and processes and top management to change firm overall

Figure 8. Innovation Capability and Organizational Structures & Procedures

Valuation practitioners, however, restricted by the context factors mentioned above, seem to neglect to investigate the quality of those processes and supporting structures and use proxy information instead. Even more practice-focused innovation capability assessment methodologies or criteria lists (compare for example Buchmann & Kissel, 2010; Chiesa, Frattini, Lazzarotti, & Manzini, 2009; C. M. Christensen, 2001; Cooper, Edgett, & Kleinschmidt, 2004; Gerybadze, 2005; Scholich, Gleich, & Grobusch, 2006) seem not to be utilized. Even less used seem to be assessments of firm culture or work environment (Amabile, Conti, Coon, Lazenby, & Herron, 1996; Hofstede, Neuijen, Ohayv, & Sanders, 1990) or assessments of a firm's governance characteristics (Sanders & Boivie, 2004).

The following statements underline that practitioners neither use assessments to appraise structural or procedural aspects nor do they seem to have a structural approach or a common understanding to do so:

> Es ist allgemein nicht so in der Betrachtungsweise, dass man da einzelne Faktoren rausbricht. Es ist eher alles miteinander verlinkt, man versucht halt die verschiedenen Prozesse: Wie spielt was mit rein? Wie spielen verschiedene Faktoren zusammen? Aber dass sich dann ein Faktor so herauskristallisieren lässt, ist teilweise schwierig. In der praktischen Betrachtung gibt es so viele Punkte, die ineinander verschmelzen, dass es da schwierig ist einzelne wie Innovation in der Bewertung auch konkret anzuwenden, weil sie indirekt auftauchen. Und da muss man dann halt auch versuchen, einzelne Faktoren wieder herauszubrechen. (Investment bank professional)

> Im Endeffekt ist es ja so, dass man nicht an ein Unternehmen herangeht und fragt: Wie innovativ ist das Unternehmen? Das ist ja eher ein bisschen anders. Man schaut sich aus der intrinsischen Bewertung den Business Plan an und untersucht den Business Plan auf die einzelnen Treiber. Es gibt ja in der GuV nicht die Position Innovation. Man muss halt schauen: Wie betrachte ich Innovation? Wie entwickelt sich das Unternehmen in seiner Gesamtheit, je nachdem wie dann Innovation definiert ist. (Investment bank professional)

> Innovation kann ja in vielerlei Hinsicht stattfinden: Am Produkt, an den Prozessen, an der Distribution, wie ich mein Geschäft betreibe. (Investment bank professional)

> Das Gesamtbild besteht natürlich aus einzelnen Sachen, da muss ich konkret verstehen. Aber ich kann nicht mit einer Checkliste vergleichen. Ich muss diese zehn Punkte haben, dann ist das Unternehmen innovativ, weil das immer unterschiedlich sein kann. Zum Beispiel weil sie schlanke Strukturen haben und schnell zu Entscheidungen kommen oder es kann sein, dass sie gute Leute haben. (Investment bank professional)

The reasons for this gap are most likely the constraints caused by context factors and the expertise of the valuation practitioners dealing with growth and mature firms (compare Table 21).

The minor availability of information about innovation potential in comparison to easily accessible data such as published financials or risk reports is likely to explain the effect that more information about a target firm seems to negatively bias firm valuations (Puranam, Powell, & Singh, 2006).

As described in hypothesis 4, valuators seem to assess innovation potential through proxies. Two relevant proxies seem to be financials on the one hand and the management team on the other.

Hypothesis 4b: The basis of the valuation changes through the lifecycle of the target firm from a future state based on a business case to a current state based on backward-looking financials.

The empirical investigation indicates that practitioners use two fundamentally different approaches to appraise idea firms on one side of the spectrum and mature firms on the other. Idea firm valuations seem to start with envisioning a firm's future state whereas mature firm valuations seem to begin with taking the firm's current state and extrapolating from this state. Thus, idea firm valuations seem to be based on a business case and mature firms on backward-looking financials. The reason for this switch can be found in the different sources of future revenues. For idea firms, the complete future revenues derive from the success of an innovation project, whereas for mature firms, a major share of revenues is assumed to derive from existing products or services. This general approach can be reflected with DAMODARAN'S income approach methodology that differentiates between revenue or growth based on existing and on future assets (Damodaran, 2009, pp. 24–33). The future-state approach that requires a solid and achievable depiction of that future state gives a good explanation, why even for idea firms, financials in the shape of business planning and management targets are a relevant indicator as suggested by WIKLUND ET AL. (2010).

A consequence of those two different approaches is that valuators are prone to significantly different biases with those approaches (compare hypothesis 7c). Table 32 depicts the relationship between firm types and financial proxy data.

Table 32. Financial Data as Proxy

Firm Type / Hypothesis	Idea Firms	Growth Firms	Mature Firms
Valuation basis	Future state	Future state / current state	Current state
Financial proxy data	Business case / Top-down estimation	Business planning / Bottom-up estimation	Backward-looking financials

Hypothesis 4c: The management team's significance as proxy for innovation potential increases during the development from idea to growth firm and decreases again during the development from growth to mature firm.

The second relevant proxy seems to be the management team. The empirical results indicate that the significance of the management team on innovation potential valuation develops in an inverted U-shape along the lifecycle of the target firm. The development can be explained by the perceived role of the management with regard to innovation potential or the overall development of the firm (compare Table 33). For idea firms, the idea seems to be the major source of value. Management teams are perceived to be substitutable or augmentable. Growth firms, having already successfully developed first products or services, face the challenge to grow and develop not only business, but also the firm and its structures. For those types of firm, the management team seems to by highly relevant as the following statement exemplary shows:

> *Spielt die Unternehmensgröße bei der Abhängigkeit von Personen eine Rolle?* Vollkommen richtig. Wir sind nicht in einer Liga, wo wir sehr gut organisierte Unternehmen kaufen. Selbst ein Unternehmen mit 60 Millionen Dollar [Umsatz] ist noch ein absolut mittelständisches Unternehmen, das zumindest in unserer Branche nur teilweise in Prozessen organisiert ist, was sehr stark von den Persönlichkeiten abhängt. (Industry business development professional)

Though mature firms' management teams seem to be perceived as having only limited possibilities to change mature firms (at least short- to mid-term), they seem to represent the firm's capability to drive change and innovation. Thus, the management team acts as relevant proxy for the valuation of innovation potential. Additionally, valuators are restricted in their information collection and, thus, have to take the management team, its presentation and forward-looking statements as significant input to appraise innovation potential.

Table 33. Significance of Team as Proxy

Firm Type / Hypothesis	Idea Firms	Growth Firms	Mature Firms
Relevance of founder / management team as proxy	Minor	Major	Medium
Value depending on	Idea / business case	Management team's capability to grow business	Management team's overall management and change capabilities restricted by governance and existing structures

Hypothesis 4d: The significance of a team's preparedness in a presentation to valuators switches to passion during the lifecycle of the appraised firm.

The last hypothesis could also give causal explanations to theory about a management team's role in firm valuation. Theory suggests that an idea firm's management team's preparedness is more relevant to investors than its passion (X.-P. Chen et al., 2009). An explanation based on the current research is that valuators seem to focus more on an idea firm's idea and the according well-prepared business case and less on the team's personal characteristics, such as passion for the idea, as the team is perceived to be substitutable or augmentable, if needed. Venture capitalists' staff augmentation of idea firms could also be one reason to explain an increased likelihood of team changes and the performance of ventures (Boeker & Wiltbank, 2005).

Table 34. Significance of a Team's Preparedness and Passion

Firm Type / Hypothesis	Idea Firms	Growth Firms	Mature Firms
Value depending on	Idea / business case	Management team's capability to grow business	Management team's overall management and change capabilities restricted by governance and existing structures
Team should be	Prepared	Passionate and prepared	Passionate

The investigation also allows deriving implications for the other firm types with regard to preparedness and passion (Cardon, Gregoire, Stevens, & Patel, 2013; Mitteness, Sudek, & Cardon, 2012) in the context of innovation potential valuation. Passion should get more relevant during the lifecycle of a firm because more financial data and history gets available for growth and mature firms and valuators are able to prepare financial analyses themselves.

Thus, the management team's contribution is to convince valuators that commercialization plans are realized and rigid organizations can be changed, e.g. a team's perceived energy level (Baron, Hmieleski, & Henry, 2012) might be an indicator for the innovation potential of growth and mature firms too.

Hypothesis 4e: Prototypes are significant for the valuation of idea firm, patents for the valuation of growth firms.

Continuing research on the impacts of prototypes and patents on the valuation of idea and growth firms (Audretsch, Bönte, & Mahagaonkar, 2012), the investigation allows a more differentiated view on the phenomenon. AUDRETSCH ET AL. suggest that prototypes as signals of feasibility are more significant than patents as signals of appropriability, but that both signals together support their effects reciprocative. The empirical results support the hypothesis that investors screen and value prototypes or other signals of an innovation project's tangibility. They do not seem to interpret patents as signs of appropriability, but as significant signs of margin protection to enable profiting from the developed new product or service when idea firms develop into growth firms.

Hypothesis 4f: The valuation of a target firm's network embeddedness is less reflected in valuation theory and valuation methodologies.

Theory suggests the significance of network relationships and alliances especially for the business success of idea and growth firms (Gulati & Higgins, 2003; Haeussler, Patzelt, & Zahra, 2012; Teece, 1992; Tzabbar, Aharonson, & Amburgey, 2013; Zheng et al., 2010). Practitioners, in contrast, do not seem to take information about alliances and relationships as important input for their valuations, except the relationship they themselves bring into an investment or acquisition. Two reasons seem to be the cause for that theory-practice gap. First, valuators tend to regard a "firm" as object of their valuations based on the approaches suggested in standard literature neglecting firm-external relationships. Second, they do not seem to exist practicable methodologies to value networks and alliances. Thus, if those relationships are valued at all, they seem to be integrated via a post-calculation adjustment.

Hypothesis 4g: Signaling is a highly relevant theory to investigate innovation potential valuation.

A further implication of the complete previously stated hypotheses is that innovation potential valuation occurs under either known (information can not be collected due to context factor restrictions) or even unknown (the extent of relevance of the information can not be judged) information asymmetry. Therefore, signaling theory (Akerlof, 1970; Leland & Pyle, 1977; Spence, 1973) should be a highly relevant theory to further investigate innovation potential valuation on a detail level.

Hypothesis 5: The anticipation of transaction effects for innovation potential differs significantly across firm types.

Similar to hypothesis 4, anticipated transaction effects do not seem to be appraised to an extent that mirrors their theoretical significance. The anticipation in the valuation seems to decrease through the target firm's lifecycle. Except for an idea-firm's post-money valuation, which considers the anticipated funding in the mathematical model, appraisals of transaction effects seems to be performed majorly qualitatively. Valuators seem to majorly use standalone DCF valuations or public multiples, which do not allow to integrate transaction effects. The qualitative appraisals are than majorly used to influence the valuation after a valuation model has been calculated. That leaves the valuation open to behavioral biases or even the negotiation step in the M&A process.

The following two statements show two examples for that approach:

> Ich habe zuerst die Standalone-Bewertung als Ausgangswert und dann gucke ich, welche Synergien habe ich und andere Sachen. Ob ich diese Zahl bereit bin zu bezahlen, ist eine andere Frage. (Investment bank professional)

> Ich sehe mir das Unternehmen an, wie es ist. Und es mag den und den Wert haben. Aber, wenn ich rangehe und am Unternehmen etwas verändere, kann es sein, dass ich Potenziale freisetze. Und das würde ja Wert generieren. Dann bin ich bereit einen höheren Preis zu zahlen als rechnerisch der Wert ist. (Investment bank professional)

Besides the funding aspect, a transaction can have two major effects: First, an effect on the innovation potential of the acquired firm and, second, an effect of the acquiring firm or the combined firm (for both compare theoretical implications in chapter 4.1.2). The first aspect seems to be considered qualitatively mainly by appraising management retention or the value of the acquirer's or investors network for the target firm.

The second aspect is closely related to investigating a potential new use and the capabilities to absorb and re-combine the acquired firm's resources (Cohen & Levinthal, 1990; Zahra &

George, 2002). This factor does not seem to be appraised thoroughly with the exception of current project portfolio synergies.

The qualitative appraisal of transaction effects does not only leave a significant impact on firm value open to biased adjustments or negotiation, but also depicts a rather significant gap between resource-based view requirements (compare chapter 4.1.2) and valuation practice.

Hypothesis 6: Valuators prefer qualitative methodologies in situations with incomplete information, risk, and uncertainty compared to sophisticated theory-suggested quantitative methodologies.

An important hypothesis with regard to valuation methodologies relates to the diffusion of sophisticated mathematical methodologies to appraise the value of risky enterprises. Valuators seem to prefer qualitative methodologies compared to mathematical models in situations of risk and uncertainty such as valuating innovation potential as the following statements demonstrate:

> Wir kalkulieren jetzt den WACC nicht, wie er im Lehrbuch vorgeschrieben ist. Wir sagen halt: Seed ist 25% und Buy-out ist 15% und das passen wir über die Jahre immer mal wieder an, weil sich die Marktzinsen ja verändern. Aber das Wort „beta" ist hier im Hause schon lange nicht mehr gefallen. (Corporate venture capital professional)

> Diese Punkte sind schlichtweg nicht in Formeln zu packen. Das ist eher ein qualitatives auch beschreibendes Wesen. Das ist das Auseinanderfallen aus dem, was die Praxis macht und der Wissenschaft. . . . Man soll es nicht übertreiben mit der Mathematik. Das entspricht einfach nicht der Wirklichkeit. Die Wissenschaft ist deutlich deterministischer, deutlich mathematischer. Die Wirklichkeit ist qualitativ und sieht auf die Spezifika der gegebenen Situation. Die Welt ist halt komplex und das ist das Spannende daran. (Investment bank professional)

> Ich versuche so viele Anhaltspunkte wie möglich zu erfassen. Tatsächlich ist das Verständnis für die großen Treiber wichtig. Es ist qualitativ, ja es ist so. Das muss ich dann versuchen zu quantifizieren. . . . Es ist ein komplexes Bild. (Investment bank professional)

The reason for that preference is for idea firms and other risky or uncertain enterprises most likely rooted in the general approach to assess the firm's or the idea's anticipated future-state, which complicates mathematical models and fits to qualitative approaches such as scenario technique. For all firm types, but specifically for mature firms with many external relationships and internal dependencies, the perceived complexity of the firm and its environment seems too complex to consider in a mathematical model.

Existing research has already investigated the adequateness of DCF analysis and qualitative (non-financial) appraisals (for example S. Chen, 2008). The results of this investigation suggest that for idea firms the risk and uncertainty of their prospects and for mature firms the complexity of their structure and environment restrict the perceived usefulness of sophisticated mathematical models.

Hypothesis 7: Valuation context and human behavioral aspects influence the valuation process and the valuation result significantly.

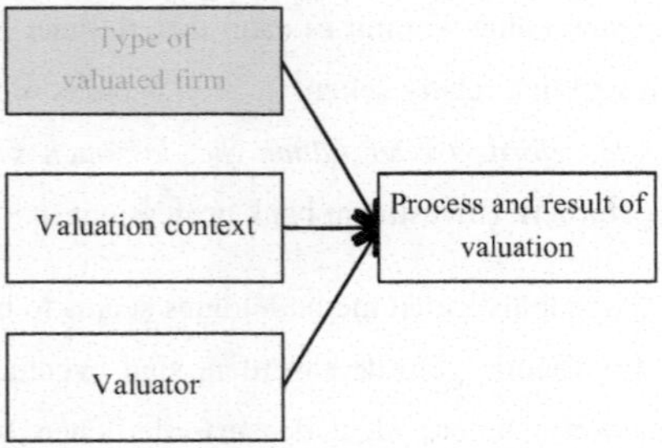

Figure 9. Significant Context Factors

As already depicted in detail in chapter 6.1, the empirical results indicate that the context of the valuation as well as the valuator or team of valuators influence the process and the result of the valuation.

Two major hypotheses with regard to theory can be derived from the current investigation:

Hypothesis 7a: Budget, perceived benefit-cost-ratio, and comprehensibility of the methodology significantly influence and constrain the selection of valuation methodology and collected data.

"The concept of future prospects and particularly of continued growth in the future invites the application of formulas out of higher mathematics", as GRAHAM (2003, p. 564) states; but why are very sophisticated and well-developed methods derived from theory not used in practice in context of innovation potential valuation as the empirical results indicate (compare hypothesis 6)? Reasons for this phenomenon can be found in the context factors derived by the current research.

Time and budget driven by customer requirements and the purpose of the valuation seem to be one factor influencing the selection of methodologies as two professional service firm experts openly state:

> Die Quintessenz ist, dass vieles von dem, was wir tun, vom Zweck des Projektes und dann auch, - ganz offenes Visier -, von der Zahlungsbereitschaft des Mandanten abhängt. Natürlich kann es manchmal sinnvoll sein, Realoptionen zu rechnen. Wenn der Kunde aber nur 30.000 € bezahlt, werde ich das nicht tun. (Auditing professional)

> In ganz, ganz seltenen Fällen kommt es dann mal zu einer Monte-Carlo-Simulation. Aber das ist auch wirklich relativ selten. . . . Ich hab das selbst erst einmal gemacht. *Hat das der Kunde gefordert oder hätten Sie das auch selbst gemacht?* Jaja, der Kunde hatte das gefordert. (Investment bank professional)

Also, the benefit-cost-ratio of sophisticated methodologies seems to be doubted by practitioners: "Die Punkte, die in der Theorie gefordert werden, sind eventuell in der Praxis einfach nicht verfügbar beziehungsweise liefern nicht den erforderlichen Mehrwert für geleisteten Aufwand." (Investment bank professional)

The last surprising important influencing context factor seems to be the comprehensibility and common use of the methodology. It seems that valuators, their customers, and their negotiation partners demand to understand the reasoning of the valuation, which is only possible by the use of methodologies they understand and know. Two practitioners for example elaborate about the use of real options:

> Real Optionen? Hab ich nie verstanden. Ich glaube, wenn ich hier im Hause rumfrage, wird jeder sagen: Ja die Methode gibt's, aber die ist ja kaum praktikabel. Ich weiß auch gar nicht, wie die Methode in die Theorie gekommen ist. (Corporate venture capital professional)

> Dieses Verfahren [Entscheidungsbäume] hat den Vorteil, dass sie viel besser verständlich sind und sicherer in der Anwendung, weniger Fehlerquellen. (Investment bank professional)

All of the above mentioned context factors also influence the diffusion of real options negatively. COPELAND AND ANTIKAROV stated more than ten years ago: "In ten years, real options will replace NPV as the central paradigm for investment decisions." (Copeland & Antikarov, 2001, p. vi). The empirical investigation shows no evidence of such a development.

The valuation context factors as depicted above should extend the on the use and diffusion of valuation methodologies by adding reasoning to the mostly quantitative studies (Arnold & Hatzopoulos, 2000; S. Chen, 2008; Imam et al., 2008; R. H. Pike, 1988; R. Pike, 1996).

Hypothesis 7b: Valuators significantly influence and constrain the selection of the valuation methodology and collected data.

The selection of the applied valuation methodology seems not only to depend on the valuation context described above, but also on the valuator's experience, education, personal preferences and professional environment. A practitioner states about his personal preference and the influence of his professional environment:

> Real Optionen habe ich seit meiner Unizeit nie wieder angeschaut. Wirklich. Das war auch eine Sache, die mich überrascht hat. Ich hatte da ein Faible für und dann kam ich in die Bank und habe gemerkt, dass die das überhaupt nicht interessiert. Und auch bei DCF… Ja gut, da kommt es darauf an. Aber das, wo die erfahrenen Banker drauf geschaut haben, waren die Multiplikatoren. (Investment bank professional)

Based on the personal characteristics of the interviews experts and their mapping of to firm types based on their stated valuation experience, one hypothesize the following mapping of preferred valuation methodologies and firm types.

Table 35. Valuators' Expertise per Firm Type

Firm Type / Hypothesis	Idea Firms	Growth Firms	Mature Firms
Valuator expertise	Industry expertise (qualitative methodologies, hurdle rate approach)	Methodological expertise, (income approaches, DCF)	Firm market expertise - "Market/deal makers", less industry knowledge, (market approaches, multiples)

Hypothesis 7c: Market for potential target firms influences valuation results.

The current research also indicates that the market for potential target firms influences the valuation result. Calculated fundamental valuations seem to be crosschecked with market-based multiples or the expectations of the market. Thus, one can reasonably assume that the market environment does not only affect the negotiation, but also the influences and possibly guides the whole process of valuation and, thus, influences the result of the valuation:

> Was muss ich eigentlich bezahlen, um an die Firma heranzukommen? Das ist ja eine Frage von Wettbewerb. (Investment bank professional)
>
> Am Ende des Tages geht Bewertung auch darum herauszufinden: Was machen die Bewerter, die in den anderen Türmen sitzen? (Investment bank professional)
>
> Das [der Wettbewerb der Bieter] hat auf jeden Fall einen relevanten Einfluss auf die Preisbildung. Nicht auf die Bewertung an sich, sondern auf die Risikofreudigkeit der Investoren. Da gibt es so ein Bild: Alle Sharks schwimmen im Becken. Einer beißt rein. Kaum beißt der eine rein, gibt es ein riesen Gewimmel. Das ist bei den VCs manchmal ein bisserl das Gleiche. (Venture capital investor)

Hypothesis 7d: Innovation potential valuations are prone to different biases dependent on the target firm's lifecycle stage.

Taking into account the relevance of qualitative assessments in the valuation process, caused by risk, uncertainty, and information asymmetry, one can imply that valuations are likely to be biased according to those factors. The following table shows a mapping of relevant biases per firm type (for definitions compare chapter 3.4).

Table 36. Relevant Biases per Firm Type

Firm Type / Hypothesis	Idea Firms	Growth Firms	Mature Firms
Valuation basis	Future state	Future state / current state	Current state
Role of intuition	Trust in idea	Trust in management team	Trust in management team
Biases	Overconfidence	Representativeness Anchoring Overconfidence Certainty (risk aversity)	Anchoring Certainty (risk aversity) Representativeness

As the valuation of innovation potential seems to depend on rare information about future developments (majorly idea firms), complex organizational processes and structures (majorly mature firms), or both, one can hypothesize that the availability bias is affecting all three firm types.

Idea firm valuations should additionally be majorly affected by the overconfidence bias. Current research implies that valuators create a mental representation of an idea's or firm's future state that represents a successful implementation of an innovation project. This approach is likely to be prone to the overconfidence bias. A practitioner states for example:

> Im Augenblick der Investition muss ich ja dran glauben. Wenn es dann nicht so kommt, ok. (Corporate venture capital professional)

Existing theory suggests that more available information about a venture leads to perceived "better informed decisions" and, thus, to overconfidence (Zacharakis & Shepherd, 2001). The idea of the future-state's mental representation allows to extent that theory with the assumption that a consistent mental presentation of the future leads to the same bias.

Mature firm valuations of innovation potential on the other end of the firm type spectrum should be prone majorly to the anchoring bias as valuators seem to start their valuations from the firm's current state and then extrapolating the firm's future development based on that state. They are also prone to the certainty bias and the bias of representativeness, which shows in the preference of the chosen methodologies. The use of income approaches with discount factors and neither the inclusion of innovation potential nor the inclusion of transaction effects for the acquiring firm in the calculated valuation fits the certainty bias. The use of multiples gives an indication of the representativeness bias.

The current investigation indicates that growth firm innovation potential valuations might be influenced majorly by the representativeness bias. The major innovation potential challenge of growth firms is the commercialization of developed products or services. This challenge seems likely to be comparable to other growth firms that have scaled up their businesses. Otherwise, growth firms should be affected by the same biases as idea or mature firms depending on their proximity to the other two firm-types within the growth stage. Overconfidence and certainty effects are likely to be balanced.

From the current research one can even imply that different biases are also significant for different types of innovation. The development of a future state picture and the implication for the applicability of biases can be related to revolutionary or radical innovation, the current-state evaluation approach to regular or incremental innovation.

Hypothesis 7e: The framing of the anticipated negotiation influences the valuation process and the valuation result.

Valuations seem to be implicitly influenced by the objective to achieve the highest price for the selling party or the lowest price for the buyer. This influence most probably does not only influence the negotiation after an "objective" valuation, but also the valuation process as a whole and, thus, the calculated result. A practitioner explains the effect as follows:

> Man ist davon nicht frei, dass man da eine positive Brille aufsetzt. Und letztlich muss man das für den Kunden auch, denn man wird dafür bezahlt, dass man Gewinnmaximierung betreibt und die positiven Aspekte hervorhebt ohne natürlich das Negative unter den Tisch zu kehren. (Investment bank professional)

7.2.2 Innovation and Underlying Theories

The empirical implications for valuation theory should also allow the theoretical investigation and creation of hypotheses with regard to innovation theory and further underlying theories based on the assumption of the interpretivist approach: What experts perceive innovation capability to be can indicate what its characteristics are. The following hypotheses are either based on existing theory with new relationships inspired by the empirical investigation results or based on the interviewees' expertise in and perception of theoretical constructs such as innovation potential, sources of growth, or boundaries of firms to imply from their perception of those constructs to characteristics of the nature of those constructs.

Hypothesis 8: Innovation capability is a dynamic capability that changes a firm's configuration of innovation-related capabilities according to the firm's position in its lifecycle and is in its core common to all firms.

The stated hypothesis builds on two aspects of dynamic capabilities in existing theory. First, EISENHARD AND MARTIN suggest that commonalities across firms exist for dynamic capabilities:

> Although dynamic capabilities are idiosyncratic in their details and path dependent in their emergence, they have significant commonalities across firms (popularly termed 'best practice'). This suggests that they are more homogeneous, fungible, equifinal, and substitutable than is usually assumed. (Eisenhardt & Martin, 2000, p. 1105)

Second, in the same context, they point out that resource configurations and not dynamic capabilities, which they define as well-known learning mechanisms, lead to competitive advantage: "More broadly, we conclude that long-term competitive advantage lies in resource configurations, not dynamic capabilities." (Eisenhardt & Martin, 2000, p. 1118) ZAHRA ET AL. also apply that reasoning to innovation:

> Yet, to date, research has not provided a compelling explanation for the ability of some new and established companies to continuously create, define, discover and exploit entrepreneurial opportunities. We propose that one source of these differences lies in these firms' developing and applying different dynamic capabilities, which we define as *the abilities to reconfigure a firm's resources and routines in the manner envisioned and deemed appropriate by its principal decision-maker(s).* (Zahra, Sapienza, & Davidsson, 2006, pp. 917–918)

One can conclude, combining those two theory arguments, that common paths of resource or capability configurations should exist across firms. The current investigation based on a lifecycle typology with types specified by theory and practice research (compare hypothesis 2a) offers a specification of such a path of capability configurations (Table 37).

Table 37. Innovation Capability's Path of Capability Configurations

Firm Type / Hypothesis	Idea Firms	Growth Firms	Mature Firms
Innovation capability configuration path	Technical development capability Project management capability Firm founding capability	Commercialization capability Portfolio management capability	Portfolio management capability Capability to overcome rigidities
Major value creation potential	New differentiating product or service	Extending business in new markets and with new product variants	Extending business or increasing efficiency
Major type of innovation	Revolutionary / niche	Regular	Architectural

As can be seen, the capability configurations per firm type specify a development path for innovation capability. Innovation capability can thereafter be specified as the capability that enables to move through this path.

Therefore, the path allows also implying on more specific dynamic sub-capabilities of innovation capability:

(1) The first dynamic sub-capability is the capability to *augment or change personnel* dynamically to adjust to the requirements of the according capability configurations. Venture capitalists for example support this capability by augmenting a founder team of technology experts with business experts to establish or grow the business.
(2) Complementing the change of personnel firms need the capability to *adjust their processes and structures* from small and medium local enterprises (example for idea firms) to international corporations (example for mature firms). Especially mature firms need the capability to overcome structural rigidities to change their business behavior or reinvent themselves.
(3) The last sub-capability is the *capability to adapt firm networks and communication* to the requirements of the according configuration. Idea firms for example need capabilities to get in touch with venture capital investors and present their idea using adequate signals. Growth firms need access to customer, distribution-channels, and suppliers. Mature firms might need investor relations to address the public stock market or private equity.

Hypothesis 9: Signaling is an element of innovation capability. Firm managements need to send different signals based on firm type to promote their innovation potential to investors or acquirers.

Acquiring funding for idea firms should be regarded as a core element of innovation capability. But also for growth and mature firms seeking equity or appraised in an M&A valuation process signaling valuation potential can be significant. The signals depicted in Table 38 seem to be regarded as relevant by valuators based on the empirical investigation of their practices.

Table 38. Signals to Indicate Innovation Potential

Firm Type / Signals	Idea Firms	Growth Firms	Mature Firms
Financial	Business case / Top-down estimation	Business planning / Bottom-up estimation	Backward-looking financials
Non-financial	Prototypes	Patents	Innovation performance reports Patents
Team	Not as relevant	Management team's capability to grow business Passion	Management team's overall management and change capabilities Passion

Signaling innovation capability (in contrast to a potential success of an innovation project) seems to start becoming important for firms entering their growth phase understood as the capability to grow business by commercializing innovation projects or broaden the product portfolio. For mature firms, innovation capability seems to be screened by assessing the mature firm's past performance.

As already depicted in the previous sections, valuators do rather understand the value and feasibility of the business idea than the team as relevant indicator for innovation potential. In accordance with the significance of innovation capability, the management team starts to become relevant once a firm enters the its growth phase.

Hypothesis 10: In the context of innovation potential valuation, information asymmetry exists between buyer and seller in both ways.

The investigation also sheds an interesting light on the argumentation about information asymmetry. According to the resource-based view, information asymmetry should exist between the potential buyer of a resource or firms and the seller of such a resource. The RBV argues that the potential buyer should have more information on the asset and its potential uses than the seller or the market to gain economic profit from such a transaction (Barney, 1988).

Information asymmetry literature based on the seminal work of AKERLOF (1970) on the other hand proposes that the seller has more information about the asset he is selling. As both a theoretical deduction and the empirical results show, each side owns more information than the other side in a different aspect. The seller knows more about "the quality" of his resource than the buyer. The buyer knows a new use or new combination for the potentially acquired resource that is unknown to the seller.

Empirical results indicate the following relationships:

Table 39. Information Asymmetry Between Buyer and Seller

Firm Type / Hypothesis	Idea Firms	Growth Firms	Mature Firms
Information asymmetry	Seller knows slightly more than investor about idea or market	Seller knows more about technology, idea implementation Buyer knows more about market	Seller knows more about firm and market

This theoretical deduction supported by empirical evidence sheds an interesting light on corporate finance-focused valuation literature and also valuation practices. In valuation literature and valuation practices transaction effects with regard to the new use or absorption of new knowledge seems to be underrepresented compared to the efforts to shed light into assessing the target's "quality", e.g., by due diligence or similar approaches.

Hypothesis 11: Valuation practices constrain the thorough valuation of transaction effects with regard to innovation potential and, therefore, contribute to explain low M&A performance.

A study of HITT ET AL. state that "inadequate target evaluation was a factor in 11 of the 12 acquisitions with low performance." (M. Hitt et al., 1998). Taking additionally hypothesis 5 (neglected consideration of innovation potential transaction effects) into consideration, it is likely that the neglected valuation of transaction effects with regard to innovation potential significantly affect M&A performance for mature and growth firms.

8 Conclusion

8.1 Summary

The main result of the research at hand is the depiction and structural analysis of a highly complex phenomenon. The valuation of firms' innovation potentials is affected by a combination factors rooted in different theoretical foundations such as corporate finance theory, innovation theory, and behavioral decision-theories.

The contributions of this dissertation can be grouped in five categories: (1) A theoretically-guided general understanding of a firm's innovation potential, (2) a dynamic perspective on the understanding and valuation of a firm's innovation potential by utilizing a typology approach based on a firm's lifecycle, (3) an empirical descriptive and analytic investigation of practices to appraise a firm's innovation potential, (4) an analytical comparison between theory and practice, and (5) an extension of existing theory based on the conducted comparisons between firm types and theory and practice.

General understanding of innovation potential

An innovation potential construct that separates delimitable innovation projects and innovation capability has been developed. This construct has been proven useful to investigate on the one hand the valuation of innovation potential and on the other hand to facilitate the investigation of innovation capability by researching how valuators perceive this innovation capability.

Dynamic perspective on innovation potential

To facilitate the investigation of the research objectives three firm types have been specified based on a firm's lifecycle: Idea firms, growth firms, and mature firms. Adding this *dynamic perspective* to the theoretical and empirical investigation did not only enabled a contingent investigation of valuation practices with regard to a firm's innovation potential, but also a contingent investigation of the understanding of innovation capability.

Results of the qualitative empirical analysis

The design of the empirical investigation to research valuation practices was guided by the assumption that "[h]igher levels of direct contact with practitioners should improve the quality of academic research" (Rynes et al., 2001, p. 349) and therefore conducted by expert interviews with experts selected by theoretical sampling.

Valuation *practices seem to differ significantly contingent on the defined firm types*. Two fundamental different approaches seem to exist to appraise firms depending on their lifecycle stage. Idea firms seem to be valued based on the future potential that valuators expect, if those firms succeed with offering a new product or service. In contrast mature firms' valuations seem to be based majorly on their current business and business performance or on comparisons to other mature firms. Thus, idea firm valuations seem to be very much based on assumptions about the future whereas mature firm valuations seem to be based on the firm's history and current state. Along with the switch from future-state-based general approach to the current-state-based one seems to occur a switch from more qualitative methodologies to more quantitative methodologies to interpret relevant data and consider it in the valuation.

Also, valuators' *understanding of innovation potential and innovation capability seem to differ between firm types*. The significance of innovation capability seems to be more important for growth and mature firms as valuators seem to understand innovation capability rather as the capability to create new projects, broaden the product portfolio, and commercialize new products or services than the capability to successfully finish an innovation project. For idea firms, information about the innovation projects (in most cases only one) seems to be more significant than information about supporting innovation capability.

The *validity and reliability of the qualitative empirical investigation* should be at a reasonable level. On the one hand, the large majority of interviewees either work for professional service firms or equity investors that should be involved in the majority of relevant firm valuations and conduct valuations as their profession (validity). On the other, the interviewees are equipped with an average experience of about seven years in their valuation jobs and should have participated in a significant number of valuations (reliability).

Comparison between theory and practice

The *comparison between theory and practice* depicted a major gap between methodologies and relevant information suggested by valuation literature and innovation theory on the one hand and the approaches and challenges of valuation practitioners on the other. The investigation did not only enable insights into the special aspect of innovation potential valuation, but also in the valuation practices and the valuation process in particular in a more general way.

The reason for this is that it was not possible to investigate the valuation practices to appraise a firm's innovation potential without investigating the valuation practices for complete firms.

With regard to the *valuation process*, two major differences seem to exist between valuation theory and practice: First, the final valuation result seems to be significantly influenced by qualitative adjustment after the calculated valuation. Thus, according process steps should be considered in theories that are related to valuation. Second, the complete valuation process seems to be influence by context factors (for both compare chapter 6.1).

In practice, *methodologies* to assess innovation potential, transaction effects and associated risks qualitatively are much more represented than in existing valuation literature and suggestions. In contrast, highly sophisticated theory-suggested mathematical methodologies seem to be avoided.

With regard to the considered *information* for the valuation, availability, access, and interpretation approaches do not seem to be available to practitioners to the cost-benefit ratio that major relevant factors suggested by innovation theory can be considered thoroughly. Innovation potential, thus, seems to be considered majorly either by a closer assessment of individual innovation projects or by the use of higher-level proxies.

Hence, the empirical investigation and comparison led to an extension of the valuation process depicted in common valuation literature and the identification of relevant context factors influencing the process as a whole and process steps such as methodology selection and information collection. A restriction affecting the diffusion of real options and other more sophisticated mathematical models seem for example to be corporate or customer requirements to comprehend the methodology.

Extensions of existing theory

I derived hypotheses on the basis of the conducted empirical cross-type analysis, the comparison between theory and practice, and the causal relationships indicated by those two comparisons. The hypotheses are grouped into two groups: Hypotheses extending valuation theory and hypotheses extending innovation and further underlying theories on the basis of the investigation of valuation practices. The major hypotheses for both groups are:

Valuation theory

(1) Innovation potential as defined in the dissertation seems to be considered in the valuation of firms.
(2) Innovation potential seems to be appraised and understood differently depending on the firm type of the appraised firm.
(3) Identifying relevant qualitative information, interpreting it, and translating it into numerical data seems to have more influence on the result of innovation potential valuation than the selection and application of the best-suited valuation methodology.
(4) Practitioners seem to make only limited use of available data and information to assess innovation capability and instead rely on proxies.
(5) The anticipation of transaction effects for innovation potential seems to differ significantly across firm types.
(6) Valuators seem to prefer qualitative methodologies in situations with incomplete information, risk, and uncertainty compared to sophisticated theory-suggested quantitative methodologies.
(7) Valuation context and behavioral aspects seem to influence the valuation process and the valuation result significantly.

Innovation and underlying theories

(1) Innovation capability seems to be a dynamic capability that changes a firm's configuration of innovation-related capabilities according to the firm's position in its lifecycle and is in its core common to all firms.
(2) Signaling seems to be an element of innovation capability. Firm managements need to send different signals based on firm type to promote their innovation potential to investors or acquirers.
(3) In the context of innovation potential valuation, information asymmetry seems to exist between buyer and seller in both ways.
(4) Valuation practices seem to constrain the thorough valuation of transaction effects with regard to innovation potential and, therefore, contribute to explain low M&A performance.

8.2 Implications for Future Research

As this research is theory-guided and based on a qualitative empirical investigation, all generated hypotheses are only a first step to explain and confirm described constructs and relationships. Some of the hypotheses should be considered as invitation to confirmatory research others highlight a more general relationship between two theoretical constructs and invite to a closer investigation of qualitative causal relationships.

The implications for future research can be grouped in analogy to the derived hypotheses (compare last chapter):

Valuation theory

Five areas of further research with regard to valuation are recommended based on this investigation's findings:

(1) The first starting point for future research should be *confirmatory research* based on the derived hypotheses.
(2) Further investigations of the approaches that valuators take to *interpret qualitative data and create assumptions* should be valuable to further extent non-mathematical valuation theory. The application of screening and signaling theories on valuation in general and on valuation of innovation potential could be a valid theoretical underlying for such investigations.
(3) Further *conceptual research in decision aids* (Shepherd & Zacharakis, 2002) or in valuator's learning mechanisms (Shepherd, Zacharakis, & Baron, 2003; Yang, Narayanan, & Zahra, 2009) should benefit not only researchers, but also aid practitioners.
(4) As the investigation points out, the *appraisal of a transaction's effects* on the future development potential of either or both firms seems to be a significant area of improvement to valuation practice. Therefore conceptual research should be highly welcome by researchers and practitioners alike.
(5) In the current research, a first model of an extended *valuation process and according context factors* was derived and presented. Further investigations of process and context factors should yield more insights into the complex practices of valuation.
(6) An important result of this investigation is the relevance of qualitative methodologies to assess and appraise innovation potential. Further investigations of the *applicability of behavioral theories* to valuation theory on the level of individual valuations should complement not only the current research, but lead valuation literature also into a new direction.

(7) A last, but very ambitious field of research would be investigating approaches to *measure the quality of valuation methodologies and practices* as this gap constrains confirmatory research.

Innovation and underlying theories

Additionally to the implications for future valuation research, two areas of innovation and M&A research seem to promise further elaboration of theory:

(1) The current research presents an *innovation capability concept* based on the lifecycle of firms. Fellow researchers are strongly invited to further specify the concept and also to conduct confirmatory research.
(2) A second stream of suggested research is to investigate the *relationship between valuation and M&A success*. Though this investigation indicates that valuation has high impact on M&A access, only very sparse research exists (M. Hitt et al., 1998).

In general, qualitative investigations into practice researching complex decision problems seem to offer great potential for theory building and are highly recommended.

8.3 Implications for Managerial Practice

Though the investigation is not confirmatory in nature, the derived hypotheses (compare chapter 7.2) are able to give a certain level of guidance to practitioners and managerial practice because of the data samples validity and reliability (compare chapter 5.5).

The implications for managerial practice address two groups of practitioners: First, *valuation practitioners* and, second, *firm founders and owners* that want to collect funding for their innovation endeavors or sell their firm.

Implications for valuation practitioners

The investigation of what valuation practitioners do to appraise innovation potential was the core part of this dissertation. Comparing those practices with theory, practitioners are likely to improve their valuation practices the following ways:

The investigation has indicated the usefulness of the *separation between delimitable innovation projects and innovation capability* bound in people and organizational structures. Thus, practitioners should try to identify relevant innovation projects and utilize a similar separation. This way, also, it is likely that innovation capability receives more emphasize in valuation practice.

The use of more relevant innovation capability data to substitute high-level proxies should also aid valuators in assessing firms' innovation potentials. The results of this investigation with regard to relevant information (chapters 4.3 and 7.1.1) could aid as guideline to such relevant information per firm type.

A particular area of improvement seems to be the *thorough investigation and valuation of the new use the acquired firm* (or resource) is brought to by the transaction. Especially for growth and mature firms, this aspect tends to be left to qualitative adjustments or even the negotiation. Numerical valuations majorly seem to be conducted to determine the target's standalone value.

An implication for practitioners and researchers alike is to refocus further development of valuation theory or methodology from numerical valuation models to *methodologies to screen, interpret, or translate qualitative information into numerical valuation inputs in an effective way*, e.g., by developing effective assessments, checklists, or scoring models.

Finally, *promotion and education of sophisticated valuation methodologies* in practitioners and customers communities seems to be necessary as preliminary condition for their further diffusion. Researchers and practitioners have to increase the understanding, transparency, and benefit-cost-ratio of such methodologies for end-customers of valuation services and colleagues.

Implications for firm founders and owners

A key result of this investigation is that valuators seem to screen for proxies to evaluate firms' innovation potentials as they are constrained in time and budget and are not able to conduct a thorough analysis of relevant innovation potential information. Thus, firm founders or owners are likely to be able to influence valuations by sending signals to valuators indicating the value of innovation potential within their idea or firm.

Idea firm founders or owners looking for funding should emphasize the future value of their idea or innovation project. They should support potential investors envisioning the realized idea, potential customers, market shares, and how their idea is going to affect the targeted industry. With regard to innovation capability, they should emphasize the team's capability to develop the promised product or service and have indications of tangibility or feasibility, e.g.

prototypes, of the product or service available. The other aspect of innovation capability that should be emphasized is the capability to found a working firm including working core business processes and realize the presented business plan. This capability, though, seems not to be as important for investors as they can augment this capability, if needed.

Growth firm owners should emphasize their personal or the firm's capabilities to commercialize innovations and grow their firm. With regard to the potentials of innovation projects, they should either depict the potential deriving from the overall project portfolio or the scalability of major innovative products or services. Additionally, they should present mechanisms to protect the erosion of margins, e.g., patent protection.

Owners of *mature firms* should focus on depicting past achievements based on quantitative data as valuators' perception of innovation value seems to be based on history and extrapolation of this data. Thus, better reporting and presentation of information regarding past innovation achievements and measures to support innovation activities seem to be a reasonable way to aid valuators restricted by time and budget requirements. Additionally, the management team itself seems to be an important proxy for innovation potential specifically with regard to business model innovation or reinvention including conducting the necessary changes within the mature organization. Thus, management teams should try to emphasize their strengths with regard to those characteristics to valuators.

Finally, one of the main results of the empirical investigation with regard to *valuation process and context factors* is that innovation potential is valued rather qualitatively or implicitly than quantitatively for all firm types. Owners and management teams should try to get as much information covered as possible in the mathematical valuation by aiding valuators with reasonable quantifications or, as an alternative approach, reasonable analogies to other products or firms. Otherwise the value of innovation potential might be left to valuators qualitative and possibly biased adjustments to either assumptions or the calculation results or it could even be left for discussion in a negotiation context. The same is true for the value of the combined innovation potential of acquiring and acquired firm.

Reference List

Abernathy, W. J., & Clark, K. B. (1985). Innovation: Mapping the winds of creative destruction. *Research Policy*, *14*(1), 3–22. doi:10.1016/0048-7333(85)90021-6

Agrawal, A., Jaffe, J. F., & Mandelker, G. N. (1992). The post-merger performance of acquiring firms: A re-examination of an anomaly. *Journal of Finance*, *47*(4), 1605–1621.

Ahuja, G., & Katila, R. (2001). Technological acquisitions and the innovation performance of acquiring firms: A longitudinal study. *Strategic Management Journal*, *22*(3), 197–220.

Akerlof, G. A. (1970). The market for "lemons": Quality uncertainty and the market mechanism. *Quarterly Journal of Economics*, *84*(3), 488–500.

Alkaraan, F., & Northcott, D. (2006). Strategic capital investment decision-making: A role for emergent analysis tools?: A study of practice in large UK manufacturing companies. *The British Accounting Review*, *38*(2), 149–173. doi:10.1016/j.bar.2005.10.003

Amabile, T. M., Conti, R., Coon, H., Lazenby, J., & Herron, M. (1996). Assessing the work environment for creativity. *Academy of Management Journal*, *39*(5), 1154–1184.

Amit, R., & Schoemaker, P. J. H. (1993). Strategic assets and organizational rent. *Strategic Management Journal*, *14*(1), 33–46.

Andersen, K. V. (2013). The problem of embeddedness revisited: Collaboration and market types. *Research Policy*, *42*(1), 139–148. doi:10.1016/j.respol.2012.05.005

Angwin, D. (2007). Motive archetypes in mergers and acquisitions (M&A): The implications of a configurational approach to performance. In C. L. Cooper & S. Finkelstein (Eds.), *Advances in Mergers and Acquisitions* (Vol. 6, pp. 77–105). JAI.

Antoniou, A., Petmezas, D., & Zhao, H. (2007). Bidder gains and losses of firms involved in many acquisitions. *Journal of Business Finance & Accounting*, *34*(7/8), 1221–1244.

Arnold, G. C., & Hatzopoulos, P. D. (2000). The theory-practice gap in capital budgeting: Evidence from the United Kingdom. *Journal of Business Finance & Accounting*, *27*(5/6), 603–626.

Audretsch, D. B., Bönte, W., & Mahagaonkar, P. (2012). Financial signaling by innovative nascent ventures: The relevance of patents and prototypes. *Research Policy*, *41*(8), 1407–1421. doi:10.1016/j.respol.2012.02.003

Balogun, J., Huff, A. S., & Johnson, P. (2003). Three responses to the methodological challenges of studying strategizing. *Journal of Management Studies*, *40*(1), 197–224.

Barney, J. B. (1986). Strategic factor markets: Expectations, luck, and business strategy. *Management Science*, *32*(10), 1231–1241.

Barney, J. B. (1988). Returns to bidding firms in mergers and acquisitions: Reconsidering the relatedness hypothesis. *Strategic Management Journal*, *9*, 71–78. doi:10.2307/2486213

Barney, J. B. (1991). Firm resources and sustained competitive advantage. *Journal of Management*, *17*(1), 99–120.

Barney, J. B. (1996). The resource-based theory of the firm. *Organization Science*, *7*(5), 469.

Barney, J. B. (1999). How a firm's capabilities affect boundary decisions. *Sloan Management Review*, *40*(3), 137–145.

Baron, R. A., Hmieleski, K. M., & Henry, R. A. (2012). Entrepreneurs' dispositional positive affect: The potential benefits – and potential costs – of being "up." *Journal of Business Venturing*, *27*(3), 310–324. doi:10.1016/j.jbusvent.2011.04.002

BARRA. (2000). *Predicted Beta*. Retrieved from http://www.barra.com/support/library/PredictedBeta.pdf

Benkler, Y. (2002). Coase's penguin, or, linux and the nature of the firm. *Yale Law Journal*, *112*(3), 369–411.

Bennett, A., & Elman, C. (2006). Qualitative research: Recent developments in case study methods. *Annual Review of Political Science*, *9*(1), 455–476. doi:10.1146/annurev.polisci.8.082103.104918

Benninga, S., & Sarig, O. (1997). *Corporate finance. A valuation approach.* New York, NY: McGraw-Hill.

Birkinshaw, J., Hamel, G., & Mol, M. J. (2008). Management innovation. *Academy of Management Review*, *33*(4), 825–845.

Block, S. B. (1999). A study of financial analysts: Practice and theory. *Financial Analysts Journal*, *55*(4), 86–95.

Bodie, Z., Kane, A., & Marcus, A. J. (2008). *Investments* (7th Edition. International Edition.). New York, NY: McGraw-Hill/Irwin.

Boeker, W., & Wiltbank, R. (2005). New venture evolution and managerial capabilities. *Organization Science*, *16*(2), 123–133. doi:10.2307/25145955

Bowman, E. H., & Moskowitz, G. T. (2001). Real options analysis and strategic decision making. *Organization Science*, *12*(6), 772–777.

Bradley, M., Desai, A., & Kim, E. H. (1988). Synergistic gains from corporate acquisitions and their division between the stockholders of target and acquiring firms. *Journal of Financial Economics*, *21*(1), 3–40.

Bradshaw, M. T. (2002). The use of target prices to justify sell-side analysts' stock recommendations. *Accounting Horizons*, *16*(1), 27–41.

Bradshaw, M. T. (2004). How do analysts use their earnings forecasts in generating stock recommendations? *Accounting Review*, *79*(1), 25–50.

Brandão, L. E., Dyer, J. S., & Hahn, W. J. (2005). Using binomial decision trees to solve real-option valuation problems. *Decision Analysis*, *2*(2), 69–88. doi:10.1287/deca.1050.0040

Brealey, R. A., & Myers, S. C. (2003). *Principles of corporate finance* (7th ed.). McGraw-Hill Inc.,US.

Brown, S. L., & Eisenhardt, K. M. (1995). Product development: Past research, present findings, and future directions. *Academy of Management Review*, *20*(2), 343–378.

Brown, S. L., & Eisenhardt, K. M. (1998). *Competing on the edge: Strategy as structured chaos*. Boston, MA: Harvard Business School Press. Retrieved from http://search.ebscohost.com/login.aspx?direct=true&scope=site&db=nlebk&db=nlabk&AN=35049

Brush, T. H., & Artz, K. W. (1999). Toward a contingent resource-based theory: The impact of information asymmetry on the value of capabilities in veterinary medicine. *Strategic Management Journal*, *20*(3), 223–250.

Bryman, A. (2004). *Social research methods* (2nd ed.). Oxford: Oxford University Press.

Buchmann, J., & Kissel, F. (2010). Innovation capability due diligence: Investigating the innovation capability of companies. In R. Gleich, G. Kierans, & T. Hasselbach (Eds.), *Value in due diligence. Contemporary strategies for merger and acquisition success.* (pp. 81–100). Farnham, UK: Gower Publishing, Ltd.

Buganza, T., & Verganti, R. (2006). Life-cycle flexibility: How to measure and improve the innovative capability in turbulent environments. *Journal of Product Innovation Management, 23*(5), 393–407. doi:10.1111/j.1540-5885.2006.00212.x

Butler, R., Davies, L., Pike, R., & Sharp, J. (1993). *Strategic investment decisions. Theory, practice & process.* London: Routledge.

Capron, L., & Pistre, N. (2002). When do acquirers earn abnormal returns? *Strategic Management Journal, 23*(9), 781–794.

Capron, L., & Shen, J.-C. (2007). Acquisitions of private vs. public firms: Private information, target selection, and acquirer returns. *Strategic Management Journal, 28*(9), 891–911.

Cardon, M. S., Gregoire, D. A., Stevens, C. E., & Patel, P. C. (2013). Measuring entrepreneurial passion: Conceptual foundations and scale validation. *Journal of Business Venturing, 28*(3), 373–396. doi:10.1016/j.jbusvent.2012.03.003

Cassiman, B., Colombo, M. G., Garrone, P., & Veugelers, R. (2005). The impact of M&A on the R&D process: An empirical analysis of the role of technological- and market-relatedness. *Research Policy, 34*(2), 195–220. doi:10.1016/j.respol.2005.01.002

Cassimon, D., De Backer, M., Engelen, P. J., Van Wouwe, M., & Yordanov, V. (2011). Incorporating technical risk in compound real option models to value a pharmaceutical R&D licensing opportunity. *Research Policy, 40*(9), 1200–1216. doi:10.1016/j.respol.2011.05.020

Chandy, R. K., & Tellis, G. J. (1998). Organizing for radical product innovation: The overlooked role of willingness to cannibalize. *Journal of Marketing Research (JMR), 35*(4), 474–487.

Chandy, R. K., & Tellis, G. J. (2000). The incumbent's curse? Incumbency, size, and radical product innovation. *Journal of Marketing, 64*(3), 1–17.

Chen, S. (2008). DCF techniques and nonfinancial measures in capital budgeting: A contingency approach analysis. *Behavioral Research in Accounting*, *20*(1), 13–29.

Chen, X.-P., Yao, X., & Kotha, S. (2009). Entrepreneur passion and preparedness in business plan presentations: A persuasion analysis of venture capitalists' funding decisions. *Academy of Management Journal*, *52*(1), 199–214.

Chesbrough, H. W. (2005). *Open innovation: The new imperative for creating and profiting from technology.* (First Trade Paper Edition.). Boston, MA: Harvard Business Press.

Chiara Di Guardo, M., & Valentini, G. (2007). Explaining the effect of M&A on technological performance. In C. L. Cooper & S. Finkelstein (Eds.), *Advances in Mergers and Acquisitions* (Vol. 6, pp. 107–125). JAI.

Chiesa, V., Frattini, F., Lazzarotti, V., & Manzini, R. (2009). Performance measurement of research and development activities. *European Journal of Innovation Management*, *12*(1), 25–61.

Christensen, C. M. (1997). *The innovator's dilemma: When new technologies cause great firms to fail.* Boston, MA: Harvard Business School Press.

Christensen, C. M. (2001). Assessing your organization's innovation capabilities. *Leader to Leader*, *2001*(21), 27–37.

Christensen, C. M., & Raynor, M. E. (2003). *The innovator's solution: Creating and sustaining successful growth.* Boston, MA: Harvard Business School Press.

Christensen, K. S. (2006). Losing innovativeness: The challenge of being acquired. *Management Decision*, *49*(9), 1161–1182.

Cloodt, M., Hagedoorn, J., & Van Kranenburg, H. (2006). Mergers and acquisitions: Their effect on the innovative performance of companies in high-tech industries. *Research Policy*, *35*(5), 642–654. doi:10.1016/j.respol.2006.02.007

Coase, R. H. (1937). The nature of the firm. *Economica*, *4*(16), 386–405.

Coff, R. W. (1999). How buyers cope with uncertainty when acquiring firms in knowledge-intensive industries: Caveat emptor. *Organization Science*, *10*(2), 144–161.

Cohen, W. M., & Levinthal, D. A. (1990). Absorptive capacity: A new perspective on learning and innovation. *Administrative Science Quarterly*, *35*(1), 128–152.

Cooper, R. G. (1990). Stage-gate systems: A new tool for managing new products. *Business Horizons*, *33*(3), 44–54.

Cooper, R. G., Edgett, S. J., & Kleinschmidt, E. J. (1999). New product portfolio management: practices and performance. *Journal of Product Innovation Management*, *16*(4), 333–350.

Cooper, R. G., Edgett, S. J., & Kleinschmidt, E. J. (2004). Benchmarking best NPD practices - I. *Research Technology Management*, *47*(1), 31–43.

Copeland, T. (2001). The real-options approach to capital allocation. *Strategic Finance*, *83*(4), 33–37.

Copeland, T., & Antikarov, V. (2001). *Real options: A practitioner's guide*. Texere.

Copeland, T., Koller, T., & Murrin, J. (2000). *Valuation. Measuring and managing the value of companies* (3rd ed.). New York, NY: Wiley.

Corbin, J. M., & Strauss, A. L. (1990). Grounded theory research: Procedures, canons, and evaluative criteria. *Qualitative Sociology*, *13*(1), 3–21. doi:10.1007/BF00988593

Cornelius, P., Van de Putte, A., & Romani, M. (2005). Three decades of scenario planning in shell. *California Management Review*, *48*(1), 92–109.

Corvello, V., Iazzolino, G., & Ritrovato, V. (2013). Evaluating technological innovations: A method based on comparable transactions. *European Journal of Economics, Finance & Administrative Sciences*, (56), 37–50.

Criscuolo, P., Nicolaou, N., & Salter, A. (2008). The elixir (or burden) of youth? Exploring differences in innovation between start-ups and established firms. *Academy of Management Proceedings*, 1–6.

Damodaran, A. (2002). *Investment valuation: Tools and techniques for determining the value of any asset.* (0002 ed.). New York, NY: Wiley & Sons.

Damodaran, A. (2009). *The dark side of valuation: Valuing young, distressed, and complex businesses.* (2nd ed.). Upper Saddle River, NJ: FT Press.

Das, T. K., & Teng, B.-S. (2000). A resource-based theory of strategic alliances. *Journal of Management*, *26*(1), 31–62.

Datta, D. K., Pinches, G. E., & Narayanan, V. K. (1992). Factors influencing wealth creation from mergers and acquisitions: A meta-analysis. *Strategic Management Journal*, *13*(1), 67–84.

Demirakos, E. G., Strong, N. C., & Walker, M. (2004). What valuation models do analysts use? *Accounting Horizons*, *18*(4), 221–240.

Denrell, J., Fang, C., & Winter, S. G. (2003). The economics of strategic opportunity. *Strategic Management Journal*, *24*(10), 977–990.

Desyllas, P., & Hughes, A. (2008). Sourcing technological knowledge through corporate acquisition: Evidence from an international sample of high technology firms. *The Journal of High Technology Management Research*, *18*(2), 157–172. doi:10.1016/j.hitech.2007.12.003

Dierickx, I., & Cool, K. (1989). Asset stock accumulation and sustainability of competitive advantage. *Management Science*, *35*(12), 1504–1511.

Dosi, G. (1982). Technological paradigms and technological trajectories: A suggested interpretation of the determinants and directions of technical change. *Research Policy*, *11*(3), 147–162. doi:10.1016/0048-7333(82)90016-6

Drucker, P. F. (1985). *Innovation and entrepreneurship: Practice and principles.* (1st ed.). New York, NY: Harper & Row.

Dushnitsky, G., & Shapira, Z. (2010). Entrepreneurial finance meets organizational reality: Comparing investment practices and performance of corporate and independent venture capitalists. *Strategic Management Journal*, *Forthcoming*.

Dyer, J. H., & Singh, H. (1998). The relational view: Cooperative strategy and sources of interorganizational competitive advantage. *Academy of Management Review*, *23*(4), 660–679.

Ebbers, J. J., & Wijnberg, N. M. (2012). Nascent ventures competing for start-up capital: Matching reputations and investors. *Journal of Business Venturing*, *27*(3), 372–384. doi:10.1016/j.jbusvent.2011.02.001

Eisenhardt, K. M. (1989). Building theories from case study research. *Academy of Management Review*, *14*(4), 532–550.

Eisenhardt, K. M. (1999). Strategy as strategic decision making. *Sloan Management Review, 40*(3), 65–72.

Eisenhardt, K. M., & Brown, S. L. (1999). Patching. *Harvard Business Review, 77*(3), 72–82.

Eisenhardt, K. M., & Graebner, M. E. (2007). Theory building from cases: Opportunities and challenges. *Academy of Management Journal, 50*(1), 25–32.

Eisenhardt, K. M., & Martin, J. A. (2000). Dynamic capabilities: What are they? *Strategic Management Journal, 21*(10/11), 1105–1121.

Ernst, H., & Vitt, J. (2000). The influence of corporate acquisitions on the behavior of key inventors. *R&D Management, 30*(2), 105–119.

Farjoun, M. (2010). Beyond dualism: Stability and change as a duality. *Academy of Management Review, 35*(2), 202–225.

Farragher, E. J., & Kleiman, R. T. (1999). Current capital investment practices. *Engineering Economist, 44*(2), 137–150.

Franke, N., Gruber, M., Harhoff, D., & Henkel, J. (2008). Venture capitalists' evaluations of start-up teams: Trade-offs, knock-out criteria, and the impact of VC experience. *Entrepreneurship Theory and Practice, 32*, 459–483. doi:10.1111/j.1540-6520.2008.00236.x

Fredberg, T. (2007). Real options for innovation management. *International Journal of Technology Management, 39*(1/2), 72–85.

Froehle, C. M., & Roth, A. V. (2007). A resource-process framework of new service development. *Production & Operations Management, 16*(2), 169–188.

Garcia, R., & Calantone, R. J. (2002). A critical look at technological innovation typology and innovativeness terminology: A literature review. *Journal of Product Innovation Management, 19*(2), 110–132. doi:10.1016/S0737-6782(01)00132-1

George, A. L., & Bennett, A. (2005). *Case studies and theory development in the social sciences*. Cambridge Mass.: MIT Press.

Gephart, R. P. (2004). Qualitative research and the Academy of Management Journal. *Academy of Management Journal, 47*(4), 454–462.

Gerybadze, A. (2005). Innovationskompetenz bewerten. Innovation Audit als Standortbestimmung. *Management und Qualität*, *7*(7-8), 6–11.

Gilsing, V., Nooteboom, B., Vanhaverbeke, W., Duysters, G., & Oord, A. van den. (2008). Network embeddedness and the exploration of novel technologies: Technological distance, betweenness centrality and density. *Research Policy*, *37*(10), 1717–1731. doi:DOI: 10.1016/j.respol.2008.08.010

Girotra, K., Terwiesch, C., & Ulrich, K. T. (2007). Valuing R&D projects in a portfolio: Evidence from the pharmaceutical industry. *Management Science*, *53*(9), 1452–1466.

Glaser, B. G., & Strauss, A. L. (1967). *The discovery of grounded theory: Strategies for qualitative research*. New York, NY: Aldine.

Gompers, P. A., & Lerner, J. (2004). *The venture capital cycle* (2nd ed.). Cambridge, MA: MIT Press.

Gorman, M., & Sahlman, W. A. (1989). What do venture capitalists do? *Journal of Business Venturing*, *4*(4), 231–248. doi:10.1016/0883-9026(89)90014-1

Graebner, M. E. (2004). Momentum and serendipity: How acquired leaders create value in the integration of technology firms. *Strategic Management Journal*, *25*(8/9), 751–777. doi:10.1002/smj.419

Graham, B. (2003). *The intelligent investor* (rev. ed.). New York, NY: HarperCollins.

Graham, J. R., & Harvey, C. R. (2001). The theory and practice of corporate finance: Evidence from the field. *Journal of Financial Economics*, *60*(2-3), 187–243.

Granig, P. (2007). *Innovationsbewertung : Potentialprognose und -steuerung durch Ertrags- und Risikosimulation* (1. Aufl.). Wiesbaden: Dt. Univ.-Verl.

Grant, R. M. (1991). The resource-based theory of competitive advantage: Implications for strategy formulation. *California Management Review*, *33*(3), 114–135.

Grant, R. M. (1996). Toward a knowledge-based theory of the firm. *Strategic Management Journal*, *17*(Winter Special Issue), 109–122.

Gulati, R., & Higgins, M. C. (2003). Which ties matter when? The contingent effects of interorganizational partnerships on IPO success. *Strategic Management Journal*, *24*(2), 127–144. doi:10.1002/smj.287

Gulati, R., Nohria, N., & Zaheer, A. (2000). Strategic networks. *Strategic Management Journal*, *21*(3), 203–215.

Haeussler, C., Patzelt, H., & Zahra, S. A. (2012). Strategic alliances and product development in high technology new firms: The moderating effect of technological capabilities. *Journal of Business Venturing*, *27*(2), 217–233. doi:10.1016/j.jbusvent.2010.10.002

Hagedoorn, J., & Cloodt, M. (2003). Measuring innovative performance: Is there an advantage in using multiple indicators? *Research Policy*, *32*(8), 1365–1379. doi:10.1016/S0048-7333(02)00137-3

Hagedoorn, J., & Duysters, G. (2002). External sources of innovative capabilities: The preference for strategic alliances or mergers and acquisitions. *Journal of Management Studies*, *39*(2), 167–188.

Hall, J., & Hofer, C. W. (1993). Venture capitalists' decision criteria in new venture evaluation. *Journal of Business Venturing*, *8*(1), 25–42. doi:10.1016/0883-9026(93)90009-T

Hall, R. (1992). The strategic analysis of intangible resources. *Strategic Management Journal*, *13*(2), 135–144.

Harmancioglu, N., Dröge, C., & Calantone, R. J. (2009). Theoretical lenses and domain definitions in innovation research. *European Journal of Marketing*, *43*(1/2), 229–263. doi:10.1108/03090560910923319

Harrison, J. S., Hitt, M. A., Hoskisson, R. E., & Ireland, R. D. (1991). Synergies and post-acquisition performance: Differences versus similarities in resource allocations. *Journal of Management*, *17*(1), 173–190.

Harrison, J. S., Hitt, M. A., Hoskisson, R. E., & Ireland, R. D. (2001). Resource complementarity in business combinations: Extending the logic to organizational alliances. *Journal of Management*, *27*(6), 679–690.

Hartmann, M., & Hassan, A. (2006). Application of real options analysis for pharmaceutical R&D project valuation - empirical results from a survey. *Research Policy*, *35*(3), 343–354. doi:10.1016/j.respol.2005.12.005

Haunschild, P. R. (1994). How much is that company worth? Interorganizational relationships, uncertainty, and acquisition premiums. *Administrative Science Quarterly*, *39*(3), 391–411.

Healy, P. M., Palepu, K. G., & Ruback, R. S. (1992). Does corporate performance improve after mergers? *Journal of Financial Economics*, *31*(2), 135–175.

Healy, P. M., Palepu, K. G., & Ruback, R. S. (1997). Which takeovers are profitable? Strategic or financial? *Sloan Management Review*, *38*(4), 45–57.

Helfat, C. E. (2007). Stylized facts, empirical research and theory development in management. *Strategic Organization*, *5*(2), 185–192. doi:10.1177/1476127007077559

Helfat, C. E., & Peteraf, M. A. (2003). The dynamic resource-based view: Capability lifecycles. *Strategic Management Journal*, *24*(10), 997–1010.

Henderson, A. D. (1999). Firm strategy and age dependence: A contingent view of the liabilities of newness, adolescence, and obsolescence. *Administrative Science Quarterly*, *44*(2), 281–314.

Henderson, R. M., & Clark, K. B. (1990). Architectural innovation: The reconfiguration of existing product technologies and the failure of established firms. *Administrative Science Quarterly*, *35*(1), 9–30.

Henschke, S. (2009). *Towards a more accurate equity valuation: An empirical analysis* (1st ed.). Wiesbaden, Germany: Gabler.

Hertzel, M., & Smith, R. L. (1993). Market discounts and shareholder gains for placing equity privately. *The Journal of Finance*, *48*(2), 459–485. doi:10.2307/2328908

Hitt, M. A., Hoskisson, R. E., Johnson, R. A., & Moesel, D. D. (1996). The market for corporate control and firm innovation. *Academy of Management Journal*, *39*(5), 1084–1119.

Hitt, M. A., Ireland, R. D., Harrison, J. S., & Hoskisson, R. E. (1991). Effects of acquisitions on R&D inputs and outputs. *Academy of Management Journal*, *34*(3), 693–706.

Hitt, M., Harrison, J., Ireland, R. D., & Best, A. (1998). Attributes of successful and unsuccessful acquisitions of US firms. *British Journal of Management*, *9*(2), 91–114.

Hofstede, G., Neuijen, B., Ohayv, D. D., & Sanders, G. (1990). Measuring organizational cultures: A qualitative and quantitative study across twenty cases. *Administrative Science Quarterly*, *35*(2), 286–316.

Holt, C. C. (1962). The influence of growth duration on share prices. *The Journal of Finance*, *17*(3), 465–475. doi:10.2307/2977053

Hunt, J. W. (1990). Changing pattern of acquisition behaviour in takeovers and the consequences for acquisition processes. *Strategic Management Journal*, *11*(1), 69–77.

Imam, S., Barker, R., & Clubb, C. (2008). The use of valuation models by UK investment analysts. *European Accounting Review*, *17*(3), 503–535. doi:10.1080/09638180802016650

Ingham, H., Kran, I., & Lovestam, A. (1992). Mergers and profitability: A managerial success story? *Journal of Management Studies*, *29*(2), 195–208.

Jarzabkowski, P., & Kaplan, S. (2008). Using strategy tools in practice: An exploration of "technologies of rationality" in use. *Academy of Management Proceedings*, 1–6.

Jemison, D. B., & Sitkin, S. B. (1986). Corporate acquisitions: A process perspective. *Academy of Management Review*, *11*(1), 145–163.

Jensen, M. C., & Ruback, R. S. (1983). The market for corporate control: The scientific evidence. *Journal of Financial Economics*, *11*(1-4), 5–50. doi:10.1016/0304-405X(83)90004-1

Johne, F. A., & Snelson, P. A. (1988). Success factors in product innovation: A selective review of the literature. *Journal of Product Innovation Management*, *5*(2), 114–128. doi:10.1016/0737-6782(88)90003-3

Kahneman, D., & Tversky, A. (1979). Prospect theory: An analysis of decision under risk. *Econometrica*, *47*(2), 263–291.

Kaplan, S. (2008). Framing contests: Strategy making under uncertainty. *Organization Science*, *19*(5), 729–752.

Kaplan, S. N., & Ruback, R. S. (1995). The valuation of cash flow forecasts: An empirical analysis. *Journal of Finance*, *50*(4), 1059–1093.

Kaplan, S. N., & Weisbach, M. S. (1992). The success of acquisitions: Evidence from divestitures. *Journal of Finance*, *47*(1), 107–138.

Kim, W. C., & Mauborgne, R. (2005). *Blue ocean strategy: How to create uncontested market space and make the competition irrelevant.* Boston, MA: Harvard Business School Press.

King, D. R., Dalton, D. R., Daily, C. M., & Covin, J. G. (2004). Meta-analyses of post-acquisition performance: Indications of unidentified moderators. *Strategic Management Journal*, *25*(2), 187–200.

Koller, T., Goedhart, M., & Wessels, D. (2005). *Valuation. Measuring and managing the value of companies* (4th ed.). Hoboken, NJ: Wiley.

Lawson, B., & Samson, D. (2001). Developing innovation capability in organisations: a dynamic capabilities approach. *International Journal of Innovation Management*, *5*(3), 377–400.

Lee, C., Lee, K., & Pennings, J. M. (2001). Internal Capabilities, External Networks, and Performance: A Study on Technology-Based Ventures. *Strategic Management Journal*, *22*(6/7), 615. doi:10.1002/smj.181

Leland, H. E., & Pyle, D. H. (1977). Informational asymmetries, financial structure, and financial intermediation. *Journal of Finance*, *32*(2), 371–387.

Lengnick-Hall, C. A. (1992). Innovation and competitive advantage: What we know and what we need to learn. *Journal of Management*, *18*(2), 399–429.

Leonard-Barton, D. (1992). Core capabilities and core rigidities: A paradox in managing new product development. *Strategic Management Journal*, *13*(S1), 111–125.

Lichtenthaler, U. (2009). Absorptive capacity, environmental turbulence, and the complementarity of organizational learning processes. *Academy of Management Journal*, *52*(4), 822–846.

Lintner, J. (1965). The valuation of risk assets and the selection of risky investments in stock portfolios and capital budgets. *The Review of Economics and Statistics*, *47*(1), 13–37.

Lippman, S. A., & Rumelt, R. P. (2003). A bargaining perspective on resource advantage. *Strategic Management Journal*, *24*(11), 1069–1086.

Lubatkin, M. (1983). Mergers and the performance of the acquiring firm. *Academy of Management Review*, *8*(2), 218–225.

MacCormack, A., Baldwin, C., & Rusnak, J. (2012). Exploring the duality between product and organizational architectures: A test of the "mirroring" hypothesis. *Research Policy*, *41*(8), 1309–1324. doi:10.1016/j.respol.2012.04.011

MacMillan, I. C., Siegel, R., & Narasimha, P. N. S. (1985). Criteria used by venture capitalists to evaluate new venture proposals. *Journal of Business Venturing*, *1*(1), 119–128. doi:10.1016/0883-9026(85)90011-4

March, J. G. (1991). Exploration and exploitation in organizational learning. *Organization Science*, *2*(1), 71–87.

March, J. G., & Simon, H. A. (1958). *Organizations*. New York, NY: Wiley & Sons.

Martin, J. A., & Eisenhardt, K. M. (2004). Coping with decline in dynamic markets: Corporate entrepreneurship and the recombinative organizational form. In J. A. C. Baum & A. M. McGahan (Eds.), *Business Strategy over the Industry Lifecycle* (Vol. 21, pp. 357–382). No longer published by Elsevier. Retrieved from http://www.sciencedirect.com.library.myebs.de/science/article/B75FG-4DK5XKS-H/2/8ea0b8d5fb48d0b9a7c12993a2c90b6f

Martin, P. Y., & Turner, B. A. (1986). Grounded theory and organizational research. *Journal of Applied Behavioral Science*, *22*(2), 141–157. doi:10.1177/002188638602200207

Mason, C., & Stark, M. (2004). What do investors look for in a business plan? A comparison of the investment criteria of bankers, venture capitalists and business angels. *International Small Business Journal*, *22*(3), 227–248. doi:10.1177/0266242604042377

McGrath, R. G., & Nerkar, A. (2004). Real options reasoning and a new look at the R&D investment strategies of pharmaceutical firms. *Strategic Management Journal*, *25*(1), 1–21.

Melone, N. P. (1994). Reasoning in the executive suit: The influence of role/experience-based expertise on decision processes of corporate executives. *Organization Science*, *5*(3), 438–455.

Miller, M. H., & Modigliani, F. (1961). Dividend policy, growth, and the valuation of shares. *The Journal of Business*, *34*(4), 411–433.

Mitteness, C., Sudek, R., & Cardon, M. S. (2012). Angel investor characteristics that determine whether perceived passion leads to higher evaluations of funding potential. *Journal of Business Venturing*, *27*(5), 592–606. doi:10.1016/j.jbusvent.2011.11.003

Morgan, G., & Smircich, L. (1980). The case for qualitative research. *Academy of Management Review*, *5*(4), 491–500.

Myers, S. C. (1977). Determinants of corporate borrowing. *Journal of Financial Economics*, *5*(2), 147–175. doi:10.1016/0304-405X(77)90015-0

Myers, S. C. (1984). Finance theory and financial strategy. *Interfaces*, *14*(1), 126–137.

Myers, S. C., & Majluf, N. S. (1984). Corporate financing and investment decisions when firms have information that investors do not have. *Journal of Financial Economics*, *13*(2), 187–221. doi:10.1016/0304-405X(84)90023-0

Nelson, R., & Winter, S. G. (1982). *An evolutionary theory of economic change*. Cambridge, MA: Harvard University Press.

Nooteboom, B., Haverbeke, W. V., Duysters, G., Gilsing, V., & Oord, A. van den. (2007). Optimal cognitive distance and absorptive capacity. *Research Policy*, *36*(7), 1016–1034. doi:DOI: 10.1016/j.respol.2007.04.003

O'Reilly III, C. A., & Tushman, M. L. (2004). The ambidextrous organization. *Harvard Business Review*, *82*(4), 74–81.

O'Reilly III, C. A., & Tushman, M. L. (2008). Ambidexterity as a dynamic capability: Resolving the innovator's dilemma. *Research in Organizational Behavior*, *28*, 185–206. doi:10.1016/j.riob.2008.06.002

OECD. (1991). *The nature of innovation and the evolution of the productive system, technology and productivity. The challenge for economic policy.* Paris.

Pablo, A. L., Sitkin, S. B., & Jemison, D. B. (1996). Acquisition decision-making processes: The central role of risk. *Journal of Management*, *22*(5), 723–746.

Paruchuri, S., Nerkar, A., & Hambrick, D. C. (2006). Acquisition integration and productivity losses in the technical core: Disruption of inventors in acquired companies. *Organization Science*, *17*(5), 545–562.

Penman, S. H. (2006a). *Financial statement analysis and security valuation* (3rd ed.). Mcgraw-Hill Higher Education.

Penman, S. H. (2006b). Handling valuation models. *Journal of Applied Corporate Finance, 18*(2), 48–55. doi:10.1111/j.1745-6622.2006.00087.x

Penman, S. H., & Sougiannis, T. (1998). A comparison of dividend, cash flow, and earnings approaches to equity valuation. *Contemporary Accounting Research, 15*(3), 343–383.

Penrose, E. (1959). *The theory of the growth of the firm*. Oxford: Basil Blackwell.

Peteraf, M. A. (1993). The cornerstones of competitive advantage: A resource-based view. *Strategic Management Journal, 14*(3), 179–191.

Pike, R. (1996). A longitudinal survey on capital budgeting practices. *Journal of Business Finance & Accounting, 23*(1), 79–92.

Pike, R. H. (1988). An empirical study of the adoption of sophisticated capital budgeting practices and decision-making effectiveness. *Accounting & Business Research, 18*(72), 341–351.

Pike, R., Meerjanssen, J., & Chadwick, L. (1993). The appraisal of ordinary shares by investment analysts in the UK and Germany. *Accounting & Business Research, 23*(92), 489–499.

Popper, K. (2002). *The Logic of Scientific Discovery*. London: Routledge.

Porter, M. E. (1998). *Competitive strategy: Techniques for analyzing industries and competitors* (1st ed.). Free Press.

Prabhu, J. C., Chandy, R. K., & Ellis, M. E. (2005). The impact of acquisitions on innovation: Poison pill, placebo, or tonic? *Journal of Marketing, 69*(1), 114–130.

Prahalad, C. K., & Hamel, G. (1990). The core competence of the corporation. *Harvard Business Review, 68*(3), 79–91.

Pratt, M. G. (2009). For the lack of a boilerplate: Tips on writing up (and reviewing) qualitative research. *Academy of Management Journal, 52*(5), 856–862.

Priem, R. L., & Butler, J. E. (2001a). Is the Resource-Based "View" a Useful Perspective for Strategic Management Research? *Academy of Management Review, 26*(1), 22–40.

Priem, R. L., & Butler, J. E. (2001b). Tautology in the resource-based view and the implications of externally determined resource value: Further comments. *Academy of Management Review*, *26*(1), 57–66.

Puranam, P., Powell, B. C., & Singh, H. (2006). Due diligence failure as a signal detection problem. *Strategic Organization*, *4*(4), 319–348. doi:10.1177/1476127006069426

Puranam, P., & Srikanth, K. (2007). What they know vs. what they do: How acquirers leverage technology acquisitions. *Strategic Management Journal*, *28*(8), 805–825.

Rappaport, A. (1979). Strategic analysis for more profitable acquisitions. *Harvard Business Review*, *57*(4), 99–110.

Rappaport, A., & Mauboussin, M. J. (2002). Valuation matters. *Harvard Business Review*, *80*(3), 24–25.

Reilly, R. F., & Schweihs, R. P. (2000). *Handbook of advanced business valuation*. New York, NY: McGraw-Hill.

Reuer, J. J., & Tong, T. W. (2007). How do real options matter? Empirical research on strategic investments and firm performance. In J. J. Reuer & T. W. Tong (Eds.), *Real Options Theory* (Vol. 24, pp. 145–173). No longer published by Elsevier.

Riley, J. G. (1989). Signaling. In J. Eatwell, M. Milgate, & P. Newman (Eds.), *Allocation, information, and markets* (pp. 287–194). New York, NY: Norton.

Robins, J. A. (1992). Organizational considerations in the evaluation of capital assets: Toward a resource-based view of strategic investment by firms. *Organization Science*, *3*(4), 522–536.

Rogers, E. M. (1976). New product adoption and diffusion. *Journal of Consumer Research*, *2*(4), 290–301.

Ruback, R. S. (2002). Capital cash flows: A simple approach to valuing risky cash flows. *Financial Management (Blackwell Publishing Limited)*, *31*(2), 85–103.

Rumelt, R. P. (1984). Towards a strategic theory of the firm. In *Competitive Strategic Management* (pp. 556–570). Englewood Cliffs, NJ: Prentice Hall.

Rynes, S. L., Bartunek, J. M., & Daft, R. L. (2001). Across the great divide: Knowledge creation and transfer between practitioners and academics. *Academy of Management Journal*, *44*(2), 340–355.

Sammerl, N. (2006). *Innovationsfähigkeit und nachhaltiger Wettbewerbsvorteil. Messung - Determinanten - Wirkungen*. Wiesbaden, Germany: DUV.

Sanders, W. G., & Boivie, S. (2004). Sorting things out: Valuation of new firms in uncertain markets. *Strategic Management Journal*, *25*(2), 167–186. doi:10.1002/smj .370

Sangster, A. (1993). Capital investment appraisal techniques: A survey of current usage. *Journal of Business Finance & Accounting*, *20*(3), 307–332.

Schall, L., Sundem, G. L., & Geijsbeek Jr., W. R. (1978). Survey and analysis of capital budgeting methods. *Journal of Finance*, *33*(1), 281–287.

Scholich, M., Gleich, R., & Grobusch, H. (Eds.). (2006). Innovation Performance. Das Erfolgsgeheimnis innovativer Dienstleister.

Schreiner, A. (2007). *Equity valuation using multiples: An empirical investigation* (1st ed.). Wiesbaden, Germany: Gabler.

Schumpeter, J. A. (1997). *Theorie der wirtschaftlichen Entwicklung - Eine Untersuchung über Unternehmergewinn, Kapital, Kredit, Zins und den Konjunkturzyklus* (9th ed.). Berlin: Duncker und Humblot.

Schwartz, E. S., & Moon, M. (2000). Rational pricing of internet companies. *Financial Analysts Journal*, *56*(3), 62–75.

Sharpe, W. F. (1964). Capital asset prices: A theory of market equilibrium under conditions of risk. *The Journal of Finance*, *19*(3), 425–442.

Shepherd, D. A. (1999). Venture capitalists' assessment of new venture survival. *Management Science*, *45*(5), 621–632.

Shepherd, D. A., Ettenson, R., & Crouch, A. (2000). New venture strategy and profitability: A venture capitalist's assessment. *Journal of Business Venturing*, *15*(5-6), 449–467. doi:10.1016/S0883-9026(98)00007-X

Shepherd, D. A., & Zacharakis, A. L. (2002). Venture capitalists' expertise: A call for research into decision aids and cognitive feedback. *Journal of Business Venturing*, *17*(1), 1–20. doi:10.1016/S0883-9026(00)00051-3

Shepherd, D. A., Zacharakis, A. L., & Baron, R. A. (2003). VCs' decision processes: Evidence suggesting more experience may not always be better. *Journal of Business Venturing*, *18*(3), 381–401. doi:10.1016/S0883-9026(02)00099-X

Siegel, R., Siegel, E., & MacMillan, I. C. (1993). Characteristics distinguishing high-growth ventures. *Journal of Business Venturing*, *8*(2), 169–180. doi:10.1016/0883-9026(93)90018-Z

Sirmon, D. G., Hitt, M. A., & Ireland, R. D. (2007). Managing firm resources in dynamic environments to create value: Looking inside the black box. *Academy of Management Review*, *32*(1), 273–292.

Sitkin, S. B., & Pablo, A. L. (1992). Reconceptualizing the determinants of risk behavior. *Academy of Management Review*, *17*(1), 9–38.

Sitkin, S. B., & Weingart, L. R. (1995). Determinants of risky decision-making behavior: A test of the mediating role of risk perceptions and propensity. *Academy of Management Journal*, *38*(6), 1573–1592.

Song, M., Podoynitsyna, K., van der Bij, H., & Halman, J. I. M. (2008). Success factors in new ventures: A meta-analysis. *Journal of Product Innovation Management*, *25*(1), 7–27. doi:10.1111/j.1540-5885.2007.00280.x

Song, X. M., & Montoya-Weiss, M. M. (1998). Critical development activities for really new versus incremental products. *Journal of Product Innovation Management*, *15*(2), 124–135.

Sørensen, M., Strömberg, P., & Lerner, J. (2008). Private equity and long-run investment: The case of innovation. *SSRN eLibrary*. Retrieved from http://papers.ssrn.com/sol3/papers.cfm?abstract_id=1088543

Spee, A. P., & Jarzabkowski, P. (2009). Strategy tools as boundary objects. *Strategic Organization*, *7*(2), 223–232. doi:10.1177/1476127009102674

Spence, M. (1973). Job market signaling. *The Quarterly Journal of Economics*, *87*(3), 355–374. doi:10.2307/1882010

Spence, M. (1974). *Market signaling: Informational transfer in hiring and related screening processes*. Cambridge, MA: Harvard University Press.

Stewart, G. B. (1991). *The quest for value: A guide for senior managers*. New York, NY: HarperCollins Publishers.

Stiglitz, J. E. (1985). Information and economic analysis: A perspective. *The Economic Journal*, *95*, 21–41. doi:10.2307/2232867

Straub, T. (2007). *Reasons for frequent failure in mergers and acquisitions. A comprehensive analysis*. Wiesbaden, Germany: DUV.

Suddaby, R. (2006). What grounded theory is not. *Academy of Management Journal*, *49*(4), 633–642.

Teece, D. J. (1986). Profiting from technological innovation: Implications for integration, collaboration, licensing and public policy. *Research Policy*, *15*(6), 285–305. doi:10.1016/0048-7333(86)90027-2

Teece, D. J. (1992). Competition, cooperation, and innovation: Organizational arrangements for regimes of rapid technological progress. *Journal of Economic Behavior & Organization*, *18*(1), 1–25. doi:10.1016/0167-2681(92)90050-L

Teece, D. J., Pisano, G., & Shuen, A. (1997). Dynamic capabilities and strategic management. *Strategic Management Journal*, *18*(7), 509–533.

Thomas, D. C., Cuervo-Cazurra, A., & Brannen, M. Y. (2011). From the editors: Explaining theoretical relationships in international business research: focusing on the arrows, not the boxes. *Journal of International Business Studies*, *42*(9), 1073–1078. doi:10.1057/jibs.2011.44

Tsai, K.-H., & Wang, J.-C. (2008). External technology acquisition and firm performance: A longitudinal study. *Journal of Business Venturing*, *23*(1), 91–112.

Tushman, M. L., & O'Reilly III, C. A. (1996). Ambidextrous organizations: Managing evolutionary and revolutionary change. *California Management Review*, *38*(4), 8–30.

Tversky, A., & Kahneman, D. (1974). Judgment under uncertainty: Heuristics and biases. *Science*, *185*(4157), 1124–1131. doi:10.1126/science.185.4157.1124

Tversky, A., & Kahneman, D. (1981). The framing of decisions and the psychology of choice. *Science*, *211*(4481), 453–458. doi:10.1126/science.7455683

Tversky, A., & Kahneman, D. (1986). Rational choice and the framing of decisions. *Journal of Business*, *59*(4), S251–S278.

Tversky, A., & Kahneman, D. (1992). Advances in prospect theory: Cumulative representation of uncertainty. *Journal of Risk & Uncertainty*, *5*(4), 297–323.

Tzabbar, D., Aharonson, B. S., & Amburgey, T. L. (2013). When does tapping external sources of knowledge result in knowledge integration? *Research Policy*, *42*(2), 481–494. doi:10.1016/j.respol.2012.07.007

Von Hippel, E. (1988). *The sources of innovation*. New York, NY: Oxford University Press.

Von Hippel, E. (2005). *Democratizing innovation*. Cambridge Mass.: MIT Press.

Weber, Y., Reichel, A., & Tarba, S. Y. (2006). International mergers and acquisitions performance: Acquirer nationality and integration approaches. *Academy of Management Proceedings*, R1–R5.

Weiss, A. (1995). Human capital vs. signalling explanations of wages. *Journal of Economic Perspectives*, *9*(4), 133–154.

Wernerfelt, B. (1984). A resource-based view of the firm. *Strategic Management Journal*, *5*(2), 171–180.

Wernerfelt, B. (1995). The resource-based view of the firm: Ten years after. *Strategic Management Journal*, *16*(3), 171–174.

Wernerfelt, B. (2005). Product development resources and the scope of the firm. *Journal of Marketing*, *69*(2), 15–23.

Whittington, R. (1996). Strategy as practice. *Long Range Planning*, *29*(5), 731–735.

Whittington, R. (2003). The work of strategizing and organizing: For a practice perspective. (pp. 117–125).

Whittington, R., Jarzabkowski, P., Mayer, M., Mounoud, E., Nahapiet, J., & Rouleau, L. (2003). Taking strategy seriously: Responsibility and reform for an important social practice. *Journal of Management Inquiry*, *12*(4), 396–409.

Whittington, R., Molloy, E., Mayer, M., & Smith, A. (2006). Practices of strategising/organising: Broadening strategy work and skills. *Long Range Planning, 39*(6), 615–629.

Wiklund, J., Baker, T., & Shepherd, D. (2010). The age-effect of financial indicators as buffers against the liability of newness. *Journal of Business Venturing, 25*(4), 423–437. doi:10.1016/j.jbusvent.2008.10.011

Williamson, O. E. (1975). *Markets and hierarchies: Analysis and antitrust implications: A study in the economics of internal organization.* New York, NY: Free Press.

Williamson, O. E. (1981). The economics of organization: The transaction cost approach. *The American Journal of Sociology, 87*(3), 548–577.

Williamson, O. E. (2010). Transaction cost economics: The natural progression. *American Economic Review, 100*(3), 673–690. doi:10.1257/aer.100.3.673

Yang, Y., Narayanan, V. K., & Zahra, S. (2009). Developing the selection and valuation capabilities through learning: The case of corporate venture capital. *Journal of Business Venturing, 24*(3), 261–273. doi:10.1016/j.jbusvent.2008.05.001

Yin, R. K. (2003). *Case study research. Design and methods* (3rd ed.). Thousand Oaks, CA: Sage Publications.

Zacharakis, A. L., & Shepherd, D. A. (2001). The nature of information and overconfidence on venture capitalists' decision making. *Journal of Business Venturing, 16*(4), 311–332. doi:10.1016/S0883-9026(99)00052-X

Zahra, S. A., Filatotchev, I., & Wright, M. (2009). How do threshold firms sustain corporate entrepreneurship? The role of boards and absorptive capacity. *Journal of Business Venturing, 24*(3), 248–260. doi:10.1016/j.jbusvent.2008.09.001

Zahra, S. A., & George, G. (2002). Absorptive capacity: A review, reconceptualization, and extension. *Academy of Management Review, 27*(2), 185–203.

Zahra, S. A., Sapienza, H. J., & Davidsson, P. (2006). Entrepreneurship and dynamic capabilities: A review, model and research agenda. *Journal of Management Studies, 43*(4), 917–955. doi:10.1111/j.1467-6486.2006.00616.x

Zheng, Y., Liu, J., & George, G. (2010). The dynamic impact of innovative capability and inter-firm network on firm valuation: A longitudinal study of biotechnology start-ups. *Journal of Business Venturing*, *25*(6), 593–609. doi:10.1016/j.jbusvent.2009.02.001

Zingales, L. (2000). In search of new foundations. *Journal of Finance*, *55*(4), 1623–1653.

Zollo, M., & Meier, D. (2008). What is M&A performance? *Academy of Management Perspectives*, *22*(3), 55–77.

Appendixes

Appendix A: Interview Partners

I conducted interviews with the following interview partners (the career positions are the ones at the times of the interviews):

Managing Partner
Munich, Germany
Personal Background: N/A
Experience: 15 years
Company Business: Venture Capital

Director and Head of Business Development/M&A
Istanbul, Turkey / Berlin, Germany
Personal Background: 12 years consulting, 5 years business development / M&A
Experience: 5 years
Company Business: E-Commerce

Managing Partner
Munich, Germany
Personal Background: Finance, corporate finance
Experience: More than 10 years
Company Business: Valuation Services, corporate finance advisory

Senior Manager
Frankfurt am Main, Germany
Personal Background: Bachelor in Finance, corporate Finance
Experience: 10 years
Company Business: Corporate finance advisory, valuation services

Associate
Vienna, Austria
Personal Background: Diploma in business & administration
Experience: More than 3 years
Company Business: Investment banking

Associate

Frankfurt am Main, Germany

Personal Background: Bachelor in finance and accounting, investment banking

Experience: 4 years

Company Business: Investment banking

Director / Prokurist

Frankfurt am Main, Germany

Personal Background: Studies in business administration, concentration on auditing and accounting

Experience: 5 years

Company Business: Corporate finance advisory, valuation services

Managing Director

Berlin, Germany

Personal Background: Finance, CFO/CEO internet startup, investment banking

Experience: more than 10 years

Company Business: Investment banking

Managing Partner

Munich, Germany

Personal Background: Degree in business administration, funding of 10 projects, majorly in e-commerce area

Experience: 5 years

Company Business: Business angel

Managing Director

Munich, Germany

Personal Background: Degree in business administration and engineering, Oracle, Technologieholding, 3i

Experience: 11 years

Company Business: Venture capital

Director
Frankfurt am Main, Germany
Personal Background: Finance diploma, investment banking
Experience: More than 5 years
Company Business: Investment banking

Lawyer
Frankfurt am Main, Germany
Personal Background: Lawyer; patent, brand, and intangible specialist
Experience: More than 25 years
Company Business: Legal

Investment Banking Germany & Austria
Frankfurt am Main, Germany
Personal Background: Lawyer, MBA, investment banking
Experience: More than 3 years (Investment banking, before that: M&A legal)
Company Business: Investment banking

Managing Director
Munich, Germany
Personal Background: N/A
Experience: 20 years
Company Business: Corporate finance advisory

Assistant Manager
Frankfurt am Main, Germany
Personal Background: Finance studies, corporate finance
Experience: 4 years
Company Business: Corporate finance advisory

Head of Finance & Controlling
Bonn, Germany
Personal Background: N/A
Experience: 10 years
Company Business: Corporate venture capital

Senior Associate
San Francisco, California
Personal Background: Career at Intel, 1.5 years at CMEA Capital
Experience: 11 years (building companies, 1.5 years venture capital)
Company Business: Venture capital

Vice President
Frankfurt am Main, Germany
Personal Background: Diploma in finance, investment banking
Experience: More than 10
Company Business: Investment banking

Head of Business Development & Innovation Head of Engine Solutions
Vienna, Austria
Personal Background: Engineering degree, business development, innovation manager Experience: 3 years (dealing with firm acquisitions)
Company Business: Industry/mechanical engineering

Investment Principal
Frankfurt am Main, Germany
Personal Background: Studies in business administration & engineering, Work experience in business consulting, strategy development with automotive supplier in Asia
Experience: 1 year (venture capital), several years strategic acquisitions at automotive supplier
Company Business: Corporate venture capital

One interviewee/company preferred to stay completely anonymous:

Investment Professional
Leading global private equity company
Frankfurt am Main, Germany
Personal Background: N/A
Experience: N/A
Company Business: Private equity investments

Appendix B: Interview Guideline

I used the following interview guideline to conduct the explorative investigation:

Table 40. Interview Guideline

Structure	Interview parts/questions
Introduction	Introduction of research project Introduction of and discussion about relevant terminology and how it is used in this research, e.g. innovation projects, innovation capability Clarification of data use (anonymous use, open use)
Descriptive data	*What firm types does/did interview partner valuate?* *How many years of experience?* *Data about interview partner's firm and his/her role in the firm*
Valuation of running innovation projects	*Which data and data collection approaches do you use for your valuations?* *Which methods do you use for your valuations?* *How do you define and estimate risk for such projects?* *How do you determine or estimate the probability of success of an innovation project?* *How do you determine or estimate the value contribution of an innovation project?*
Valuation of innovation capability	*Which data do you use for your valuations to appraise innovation capability?* *- Capability to start new projects?* *- Capability to successfully conduct innovation projects?* *Which data collection approaches do you use for your valuations?* *Which methods do you use for your valuations?* *How do you consider intangible assets such as patents or similar?*
Valuation of transaction effects, acquisitions, and synergies	*How do you valuate control over an innovation asset?* *How do you valuate intellectual property / intangible assets?* *How do you valuate the opportunities that arise for a firm by investing in it or integrating it?* *How do you valuate the effects of firm cultures merging or being integrated on innovation capability and future value?* *How do you valuate the similarity or differences of (innovation) processes in two merging firms or the integration of one firm into another?* *Which methods do you use for your valuations?*
Contextual factors	*Which barriers or problems do you face while valuating innovation potential?* *- Data collection?* *- Use of methodologies?* *Which firm-internal or –external entities do you incorporate or consult during your valuation?*
Success variable / dependent variable / improvement potential	*How do you appraise the quality of your approach?* *Would you recommend your approach to other practitioners or theory?* *What would you improve in your approach?* *- Which data that you usually do not have access to would improve the valuation most?* *- Which data is missing in many cases and is covered by assumptions, scenarios, or sensitivity analyses in your valuations?*
Closure	*Which further interview partners would you suggest?* *Do you have relevant materials that I can use for my research (notes, presentations, ...)?* Explanation of the next steps and usage of collected data

Appendix C: Interview Database and Interview Analysis

The following tables depict the qualitative research process. First, I transcribed all interviews into a spreadsheet table (sample table Table 41, column "data") filled by more than 1,200 statements and assigned them to their corresponding investigation area of the interview guideline (columns "code1" and "code2"). Depending on the firm type the interviewee works for, I also assigned a firm type of the developed typology (column "typology_type"). Afterwards, I also assigned a code depending on, if the statement contains information about the used valuation methodology, data, or process (column "code3"). At last, I made a first classification of interview results in the column "code4".

To enable a type-specific analysis of the statements, I created three new sheets, one for each firm type (sample table Table 42 (for growth firms)), and identified a firm-specific aggregated second-level classification (column "idea"). Each item of these classifications contains references to according statements in the column "statement". The information of these spreadsheets is the basis for the investigation results in chapter 6.

Since empirical data is difficult and expensive to gather, the database is available upon request (janbuchmann@yahoo.de) to fellow researchers in the case they want to conduct their own research on this data set. It is available in an anonymized way such as presented in the samples below to protect the anonymity of the interview partners' statements.

Table 41. Interview Analysis Sample – Coding of Statements

comp_ code2	comp_ type	typology_type	code1	code2	code3	code4	data
aud1	aud	growth, mature	20 - projects		methods	market	order-backlog (Auftragseingang) mit Wahrscheinlichkeiten gewichtet fortgeschrieben (für bestehende Produkte)
aud1	aud	growth, mature	20 - projects		data	market, network	Wie viele Kontakte gibt es zu den Kunden? Wie ist das Netzwerk?
aud1	aud	growth, mature	20 - projects		data	history	Umsatzströme aus realisierten Projekten
aud1	aud	growth, mature	10 - general		methods, data	dcf	Wachstum, das wir jetzt haben und das zukünftige greifbar zu machen, indem wir es auf Umsätze herunterbrechen und darauf eine Marge für die Kosten zu rechnen, um daraus die Free Cash Flows abzinsen zu können
aud1	aud	growth, mature	20 - projects		data	history	Wir sehen uns an, wie präzise das Planungsmanagement in der Vergangenheit war.
aud1	aud	growth, mature	10 - general		data	business plan	Planung der nächsten zwei Jahre wird versucht abzubilden, danach wird versucht, fortzuschreiben
aud1	aud	growth, mature	10 - general		data		Nach zwei Jahren hat man ja gar keine Informationen mehr.
aud1	aud	growth, mature	10 - general		data	history	Wir sehen uns an, wie erfolgreich das Unternehmen in der Vergangenheit war, um daraus Rückschlüsse auf die nahe Zukunft und das weiter entfernte nehmen zu können.
aud1	aud	growth, mature	10 - general		methods	dcf	In einem Beispiel haben wir 4-5 Jahre eine Detailplanung gemacht, haben diese dann zwei weitere Jahre versucht fortzuschreiben und sind dann in die Terminal Value-Berechnung gegangen.
aud1	aud	growth, mature	10 - general		methods	market view, dcf	Länger als 4-5 Jahre macht es keinen Sinn, weil ich dann schätzen muss, wie sich der Markt entwickelt und dann kann ich gleich in den Terminal Value gehen.
aud1	aud	growth, mature	30 - capability		methods	rule of thumb, dcf	Wachstumsrate im Terminal Value? Das ist eine gute Frage. Es gibt immer die Aussagen, dass dies maximal 2% sein kann, weil man sonst schneller wächst als der Markt.
aud1	aud	growth, mature	30 - capability		methods, data	dcf	Wachstumsrate ist bei klassischen Unternehmen (Energieunternehmen) 0,5 bis 0,7% und bei einem Wachstumsunternehmen würde ich so 1-1,5%, 2 max. nehmen.
aud1	aud	growth, mature	30 - capability		data	market view, industry	Hängt diese Wachstumsrate vom Markt ab (JA) oder auch vom Unternehmen? Wir würden unterscheiden zwischen klassischen Unternehmen (Wert niedriger) und Wachstumsunternehmen (Wert

						höher) und nicht mehr differenzieren, ob z. B. das Management da jetzt gut ist oder nicht.
aud1	aud	growth, mature	30 - capability		data	history, industry	Ob es ein Wachstumsunternehmen ist oder nicht, bestimmen wir aus der Branche.
aud1	aud	growth, mature	30 - capability	10 - general	methods, data	rule of thumb	Der Wert im Terminal Value ist mehr so eine Bauchentscheidung.
aud1	aud	growth, mature	30 - capability		methods	negotiation, sensitivity	Wir richten uns auch nach dem Verhandlungsspielraum und machen eine Sensitivitätsanalyse über die Wachstumsrate.
aud1	aud	growth, mature	30 - capability		methods		Wir geben eine Spanne an.
aud1	aud	growth, mature	70 - risk	10 - general	methods	scenarios	Wie geht ihr mit Risiko und Unsicherheit um? Es gibt immer verschiedene Szenarien. Wir adjustieren die Management-planung nach unserer Einschätzung. Wir nehmen meistens drei Cases. Wenn man mehr Cases macht, verliert man den Überblick und den Blick auf die Stellschrauben.
aud1	aud	growth, mature	70 - risk	30 - capability	methods	band width	Wir nehmen die Wertbandbreiten der verschiedenen Methoden und kommen dann darauf, dass im Durchschnitt eine gewisse Spanne herauskommen wird. Wir nehmen den Fall mit den meisten Überlappungen.
aud1	aud	growth, mature	10 - general		methods	price	Wir einigen uns beim Kaufpreis auf einen Umsatz- oder EBIT-Multiplikator, lassen evtl. den EBIT von einer Wirtschaftsprüfungsgesellschaft bestätigen und das ist dann der Kaufpreis.
aud1	aud	growth, mature	70 - risk	30 - capability	methods, data	risk transfer	Wenn sehr großes Risiko enthalten ist, dann wird über einen earn out diskutiert, ein gewisser Teil des Kaufpreises (z. B. 20%) wird an die zukünftige Gewinnerwartung gekoppelt. Ähnlich ist vendor loan, der Verkäufer gibt ein Darlehen, dessen Rückzahlung ebenfalls an den Eintritt der zukünftigen Gewinnerwartung gekoppelt ist.
aud1	aud	growth, mature	70 - risk	30 - capability	data	management	Einschätzung des Risikos. Man sieht an earn out oder vendor loan sehr gut, wie fest das Management an seine zukünftige Gewinnerwartung glaubt.
aud1	aud	growth, mature	20 - projects		data	market view, internal view	wie ist die Technik
aud1	aud	growth, mature	20 - projects		data	market view	wie entwickelt sich der Markt
aud1	aud	growth, mature	20 - projects		data, process	3rd party	Es werden Spezialisten wie das Fraunhofer Institut befragt, um Technik/Markt-Kombinationen einzuschätzen. Ergebnis sind Gut-

						achten, aus denen wir versuchen, Schlüsse zu ziehen.
aud1	aud	growth, mature	30 - capab-ility	data		Es gibt auch noch, dass man schaut, wie das Unternehmen in-tern aufgestellt ist. Operational due diligence (Produktion aufrecht erhalten, das Wachstum abzubil-den, Produktionskapazität auszu-bauen, wie ist das Management?)
aud1	aud	growth, mature	30 - capab-ility	data	history	Wie wurde das Wachstum in den letzten Jahren bewältigt?
aud1	aud	growth, mature	30 - capab-ility	data	manage-nage-ment	Management wird im Detail ange-sehen. Woher kommen die, was können die, wie gut sind die, wo kann man sie unterstützen? Um abschätzen zu können, ob sie das projizierte zukünftige Wachstum bewältigen können.
aud1	aud	growth, mature	30 - capab-ility	data		Wie werden Daten über die bishe-rigen Fähigkeiten erhoben? Inter-views. Wie ist zum Beispiel der Fertigungsprozess aufgestellt?

Table 42. Interview Analysis Sample – Growth Firms

dimension	sub-dimension	item	statement
10 - general	1 - data	business model	1008
10 - general	1 - data	challenge: data availability	934,1146
10 - general	1 - data	data sources: business plan	920
10 - general	1 - data	data sources: due diligence comparison of numbers with internal businesses (cvc)	969
10 - general	1 - data	data sources: external information: tests	1016,1017
10 - general	1 - data	data sources: information from existing customer-supplier-relationship	1178
10 - general	1 - data	data sources: internal market information	921
10 - general	1 - data	data sources: listed entities for multiples	922
10 - general	1 - data	data sources: technical expertise	1019
10 - general	1 - data	difficult to check assumptions. Data sources: external experts, network, other potential buyers	1015,1018
10 - general	1 - data	due diligence: data through interviews (explanation of product pipeline and single projects)	1065
10 - general	1 - data	due diligence: market, operations (incl. Innovation mgmt.), hr, legal, financial, it, systems & processes	1064
10 - general	1 - data	external valuation conditions for vc: preferred shares…	1199
10 - general	1 - data	IRR > 25% or multiple 2,5, but not decision relevant	925
10 - general	1 - data	looking for business model innovations not only technology innovations	1266
10 - general	1 - data	market intransparency is challenge (have to be insider), challenge: building market models for product groups (sales & revenue planning, competitors strengths & weaknesses)	1058-1063
10 - general	1 - data	methods result is heavily dependent on data quality, gigo	1164,935
10 - general	1 - data	motive for cvcs is interest in complementary technologies	904
10 - general	1 - data	top-line at high-time of firm	1186
10 - general	2 - methods	capm: not suitable for vc-investments, investments not diversified, time longer than 1 year, but vc also market dependent	1244
10 - general	2 - methods	discussion of assumptions	935
10 - general	2 - methods	financial investment and strategic component on top	995,996
10 - general	2 - methods	inner logic consistent, but not checkable vs. Real world, preparation for negotiation	1012-1014
10 - general	2 - methods	method knowledge (3rd party) vs. Industry knowledge. Best: combine both worlds	1009,1010, 1011
10 - general	2 - methods	methods: dcf	919,1143,1 196,1008
10 - general	2 - methods	methods: dcf weaknesses are known (static)	1022
10 - general	2 - methods	methods: multiples	1128,923,9 22,1139
10 - general	2 - methods	methods: multiples used by seller to determine expected price (EV/EBITDA)	1049
10 - general	2 - methods	methods: standalone value via dcf	1048

Appendix D: Literature Database

During the course of this research I collected, analyzed and sorted a comprehensive library of existing scientific research on the topics resource-based view, innovation theory, valuation & corporate finance theory as well as decision theory. The library contains around 1,000 categorized and sorted entries and is available upon request from the author (e-mail: janbuchmann@yahoo.de) via the Zotero (www.zotero.org) or Mendeley (www.mendeley.com) research networks.

The manufacturer's authorised representative in the EU is Springer Nature Customer Service Centre GmbH, Europaplatz 3, 69115 Heidelberg, Germany. If you have any concerns regarding our products, please contact ProductSafety@springernature.com

Printed and bound by CPI Group (UK) Ltd, Croydon, CR0 4YY
30/09/2026
02225597-0002